The
Unsung Heart
of
Black America

The Unsung Heart

University of Missouri Press

COLUMBIA AND LONDON

# of Black America

A Middle-Class Church at Midcentury

Dona L. Irvin

5 4 3 2 1   96 95 94 93 92

Liberty of Congress Cataloging-in-Publication Data

Irvin, Dona L., 1917–
    The unsung heart of Black America : a middle-class church at
midcentury / Dona L. Irvin.
        p.   cm.
    ISBN 0–8262–0841–X (alk. paper)
    1. Downs Memorial United Methodist Church (Oakland, Calif.)—
History.   2. Oakland (Calif.)—Church history.   3. Sociology,
Christian—California—Oakland.   4. Afro-American Methodists—
California—Oakland—Biography.   5. Oakland (Calif.)—Biography.
I. Title.
BX8481.O3I78   1992
287′.679466—dc20   92-5209
                                                                                    CIP

∞™ This paper meets the requirements of the
American National Standard for Permanence of Paper
for Printed Library Materials, Z39.48, 1984.

Designer: Elizabeth Fett
Typesetter: Connell-Zeko Type & Graphics
Printer and Binder: Thomson-Shore, Inc.
Typeface: ITC Century Book

Frontispiece picture is of the procession at the dedication of Downs
Memorial Methodist Church, November 5, 1948. *Left to right:* Rev. Dillon
Throckmorton, District Superintendent, Sacramento District; Rev. Rector
Johnson, District Superintendent, Bayview District; James McGriffin,
Youth Director, Northern California-Nevada Annual Conference; Rev.
Charles Warren, pastor, Taylor Memorial Methodist Church, Oakland; Rev.
Frank Toothacker, pastor, First Methodist Church, Oakland; Rev. R. Mar-
vin Stuart, pastor, First Methodist Church, Palo Alto; Rev. Warren Bonner,
Superintendent, Central District; Rev. H. T. S. Johnson, retired minister;
Rev. Hamilton Boswell, pastor, Jones Memorial Methodist Church, San
Francisco; Bishop Donald Harvey Tippett, Northern California-Nevada
Annual Conference; Rev. John Doggett, Jr., pastor, Downs Memorial Meth-
odist Church, Oakland.

All photographs of reunion by Jonathan Eubanks.

For **FRANK EDWARD IRVIN, Sr.**

Without his love, cheering, and understanding,
The Unsung Heart of Black America would not be.

Contents

Acknowledgments

This book became a reality with the help of many people. I am indebted to the librarians of the Oakland Public Library for their willingness to respond to my frequent inquiries. I am pleased to thank the late Alden Whitman, Nellie McKay, and Randall Kenan for their advice to a neophyte author, and to Gary Kremer for his sensitive reading of the manuscript. To Rosemma Wallace, who does not realize the extent of her assistance, I owe special appreciation, as well as to William M. Banks, Barbara Brooks, Norman Brooks, Lisa Brooks, Margaret Lewis, Audrey Oliver, Joshua C. Theriot, Paul Thompson, and Reverends Hamilton Boswell, Robert Hill, John Doggett, Jr., Amos Cambric, Charles H. Belcher, Charles H. Lee, Sr., and Douglass Fitch. I wish also to thank Marguerite Banks, Gloria Bayne, Dorothy Bryant, George Faulks, Catherine Prater, and Carmelita Logan Prince, Jacqueline "Jackie" Bryant Smith, who supplied information, Janet Livingstone for technical advice, Jonathan Eubanks for the photographs, and Velma Lord and Ruth Nichols for their help in recalling names from the past. I thank Polly Law, my editor, for her caring and perceptive work with this book.

I am grateful to each of the Downs people for sharing their lives with me. Frank and Nell, my husband and my daughter, share my enthusiasm for Downs Memorial United Methodist Church and encouraged me to undertake the project. Frank gave his love, prompting, and constructive criticism. Nell was always available with professional advice and loving words of reassurance when my self-confidence needed bolstering.

The
Unsung Heart
of
Black America

Introduction

The Unsung Heart of Black America is the story of a black church in Oakland, California, and forty of its members. It focuses on the fifties and early sixties when Bishop Roy Nichols was pastor, which is the same time my family and I were integral parts of the church's activities. The Downs Memorial United Methodist Church has the reputation of being the religious home of some of the most influential, best-educated, and most prosperous African-Americans in the San Francisco East Bay Area. Critics who are less than flattering in their appraisal of Downs describe it as "snooty," "hankty," and "stuck up"; others call it the "black silk stocking church." Even so, the harshness of these terms is tempered by respect for the church's active participation in political and social issues, its function as a forum for community concerns, and the extent of its humanitarian programs.

African-American literature and theater have documented the sizable contribution of the black church as a place of spiritual nourishment and social and political interaction for black people. The long tradition of motivation and inspiration that clergy and congregations have for their youth is well known, but there is a dearth of biographical information about people in the social status of those who were in this particular church during the time of this book. My purpose is to record the phenomenon of Downs church and to highlight the lives of forty of its members, whom I refer to as the "Downs people," and their place in the Bay Area, and to show that in spite of their origin at a local church setting, they had a far-reaching impact upon the total African-American community.

We are familiar with Mary McLeod Bethune, Sojourner Truth, W. E. B. Du Bois, Booker T. Washington, Martin Luther King, Jr., and Paul Robeson at one end of the spectrum, and the share-croppers, lynch victims, and underprivileged families at the other end. Somewhere between the famous and the persecuted are the unsung and usually unnoticed multitude who are as much a part of black America as those whose actions are widely renowned. Within this group, the bypassed middle level, are the men and women who quietly make a difference in the quality of life for the community and for African-Americans through their careers and public service. *The Unsung Heart of Black America* concentrates upon this group in the East Bay Area and uncovers the similarities among people who share common goals and circumstances but who have developed in distinctive ways. Each person has a unique story to tell, and running through all the stories are recurrent themes concerning family background, family values, commitment to public service, and the importance of each individual's association with this church.

Downs Methodist Church was born out of a change in the demographics of Oakland. The transformation in 1948 of the Golden Gate Methodist Church that had served the formerly all-white neighborhood into one which would accommodate the increasing number of black residents attracted men and women who were service-minded and encouraged the newly emerging political aspirations of black people. Black politicians of that time knew the value of contacts with Downs church and its followers. I remember candidates' nights, political discussions, voter registration drives, NAACP membership campaigns, and Negro History observations as regular events at Downs. The concept of Homework Help tutorial programs in public schools originated there as well.

As I drew up a list of those I consider Downs people, my informal criteria focused upon active churchgoers whom I thought of as doers. I concentrated upon a group that I remembered after thirty years, people who I was convinced have made a substantial contribution to the quality of American life. More-

over, the Downs people share my sense of Downs as an outstanding religious institution of the fifties and sixties and cherish the memory of its community activities and the exemplary
ministry of its pastor, Roy Nichols. They are my friends and
exemplify the spirit of what the Nichols era at Downs meant to
me.

The Downs people fall into two age groups depending upon
their level of maturity at the time under consideration. Of the
thirty-three who were adults, most had completed college, some
were enrolled in graduate course work, and all had careers that
were well on the way. They were active in the civil rights movement, as people who gather in a religious setting with its attendant strong leadership and role models tend to be. These adults
had chosen their life's work and were doing their part to claim
or share power with the white power structure, not necessarily
in the well-publicized, militant, activist fashion, but in their
individual way through community work or other vital people-
oriented endeavors. The remaining seven were schoolchildren
within the sphere of the Downs church and showed the promise
of productive adulthood.

To paint my pictures of the Downs people I will first look at
the group as a community, the factors inside and outside of the
family that helped shape their lives, and the contributions the
forty made to Downs as individual members and their reactions
to the church. The final section of this book, its "heart," is
made up of personal accounts of the Downs people. I conducted
these interviews with the forty Downs people in their homes or
offices. In a few cases they came to my home to talk with me.
For the most part I asked the same questions but let each person discuss and explore other incidents or ideas that may have
been suggested by my initial questions. People talked about a
broader scope of issues than I expected, so the topics of their
concern ranged from the plight of young male African-Americans, to AIDS, to Buddhism, to the factors that should be considered in the placement of adopted children. I invited them to
add a personal assessment to complete the stories.

This community of people and their stories can be duplicated all over the United States wherever there are supportive

black parents whose home training is augmented by the attention of caring school officials and by the inspiration of a church that supplies motivation for growth along with its spiritual teachings. Downs had a high percentage of congregants who were committed to public service and continued their education to prepare for professions that could change the quality of life in their community. Their profiles will add to the store of knowledge about the bypassed middle level of black people and call attention to their thousands of counterparts.

ONE

The Downs Church and the East Bay Community

Downs Memorial United Methodist Church is located in Oakland, California, less than a half mile from the Berkeley city limit. It draws its members from a metropolitan area that includes Oakland, Berkeley, and other cities of the East Bay Area. The contiguous cities of Oakland and Berkeley are the largest population centers. Their proximity makes them appear to be one community. Despite the autonomy of local governments and services, there is no difference on a people-to-people basis; we travel from one municipality to the other without knowing the difference. Of the two cities, Berkeley is better known in some respects. The University of California, famous for its fourteen Noble Prize winners and for the Lawrence Radiation Laboratory's ties to the development of the atomic bomb, assures Berkeley a notable place in academic and scientific circles. Berkeley's renown as the seat of student protests centers upon the Free Speech Movement of the sixties and the student strikes for the creation of the Ethnic Studies Department. Through wide media coverage, the nation saw the protests and disruption of classes during the Vietnam War and the birth of "People's Park" after student-police confrontations resulted in the regents' decision to free that vacant campus site for a variety of community uses.

Oakland is as equally important as its companion city Berkeley in terms of its role in the arts, sports, education, politics, and business, and the activities of its multiethnic citizenship.

My pride equals that of the Downs people in Oakland's enactment, in July 1985, of the most comprehensive South Africa divestment ordinance of any city in the United States. It placed effective restrictions on purchases, investments, and professional services contracts. We were rewarded with a visit by Nelson and Winnie Mandela in June 1990.

Oakland gave this country the Black Panthers, an organization of young black people (notably Huey Newton, Eldridge Cleaver, and Bobby Seale) that gained national notoriety because of its gun battles with the police of Oakland and other cities, and which was the object of explicit persecution by the FBI. Less attention came to its breakfast program for young children. The Afro-American Association, also conceived in Oakland, but not as widely known as the Panthers, emphasizes motivation through the study of black history and related philosophies and the acquisition of political power through business opportunities.

We have an opera company, a symphony orchestra, and several little theater groups. The Oakland Museum has a comprehensive collection of California art and displays the work of artists from the multicultural communities of the city. Our students may attend Holy Names College, Mills College, or California College of Arts and Crafts. For those who choose a two-year curriculum, there are Laney and Merritt Community Colleges.

Oakland has produced its share of famous people: writers Jack London, Bret Harte, Joaquin Miller, and Edwin Markham; the dancer Isadora Duncan, and sports figures Bill Russell, Frank Robinson, Joe Morgan, and Curt Flood. In the last decade of the nineteenth century, Charlotte Perkins Gilman lived here and continued writing and speaking as a forceful advocate for women's rights and for radical political concerns. Oakland sent actor Clint Eastwood and director George Stevens to Hollywood, and Sen. Joseph R. Knowland, former publisher/owner of the *Oakland Tribune*, to Washington. Chief Justice Earl Warren and Attorney General Edwin Meese were Alameda County district attorneys working in the county courthouse in Oakland. Tony Martin, Sheila E., the Pointer Sisters, Dave Brubeck, Tramaine Hawkins, Edwin Hawkins, and Hammer represent the East Bay city in the entertainment field.

Oakland was a pioneer in the conversion to containerized shipping and is one of the busiest seaports in the nation. The giant cranes of the Port of Oakland dominate the skyline like stationary giraffes. Oakland is a center for army and navy installations and is the location of a major hospital that serves active and retired service personnel.

Situated in the midst of Oakland's downtown city square is a sculpture, "There," our rebuttal to Gertrude Stein's uncomplimentary reference to the city as having "no there there." Workers from nearby offices use this structure as a comfortable place to relax and eat lunch while they enjoy a free outdoor noon concert.

Sports lovers (like me) can enjoy professional baseball and basketball seasons as well as beautiful sites for recreational sports: The Oakland Athletics won the pennant in the 1972, 1973, 1974, and 1989 World Series and were the runner-ups in 1990. Our Golden State Warriors won the NBA championship in 1975. We cherish the memory of the excitement and success of the Oakland Raiders and still smart from its move to Los Angeles. Recreational sports enthusiasts have the beauty of the coastal range hills, the San Francisco Bay, and the Pacific Ocean. Lake Merritt in midtown offers a 3.2 mile scenic perimeter for walkers or joggers.

The East Bay, particularly Oakland, has recently attained a certain tragic notoriety due to the drug menace. It has taken an appalling toll on the lives of young African-American men who have been thought of as the inheritors of better working and living conditions. Our city has been the scene of drug murders and drive-by homicides of innocent victims, who had the misfortune of being in the wrong place at the wrong time or who were misidentified as the target for the bullets. In 1986 the funeral cortege of a local drug czar, a horse-drawn caisson followed by fourteen limousines in procession through the streets of east Oakland, attracted the admiration of people who, to our dismay, thought of the deceased as a successful businessman. Young boys, lookouts for drug dealers, pocket hundreds of dollars each week and bring home sums that exceed the wages of their hard-working parents.

In the Bay Area as a whole, a distinction between whites and nonwhites is articulated by the geographic terms for their places of residence. "West Oakland" is generally recognized as a reference to the portion of the city that is occupied primarily by African-Americans with lower incomes and as the location of older, lower-priced, and less desirable housing. The "hill area," the central and eastern parts of Oakland, are the most aesthetically pleasing sections where the better-off, predominantly white residents live. We refer to the less attractive parts where the ethnic minorities and poorer people have their homes as the "flat lands." The "hill area" is more scenic with gently curving streets and views of San Francisco Bay and the lights of the flat lands below. The houses are bigger and nicer and more expensive. It is still true that more affluent whites live in the "hill area" than in the "flat lands." Despite the movement of financially secure nonwhites to houses in the hills, the designations effectively call attention to contrasts of the two residential divisions. Downs is in the flat lands of Oakland, but a large percentage of its congregants live in the hill area.

Prior to 1950 the ethnic minorities of Oakland and Berkeley had very little political power. Mayors, city councils, local school boards, and directors of county, state, and city agencies came from the white, upper-middle-class, male, business-oriented sector of the population. As in most American cities at that time, this was the point of reference for decisions that affected all of the people. It was not easy to knock down the barriers into city council or school board meeting rooms. Again and again, elected representatives resigned in midterm, at which time the seat was filled by direct appointment. The appointed official then had the advantage of running as an incumbent in the following election, effectively shutting out the possibilities for new candidates who were not from the old guard. A meaningful resistance to the exclusion of black candidates came about with the advancement of black people into politics in the East Bay.

During the fifties and early sixties the East Bay experienced a political, social, and demographic black power transition that mirrored what was happening in cities nationwide. The black population was steadily increasing and becoming more concerned with a representative level of involvement in civic and educational activities and other aspects of public life. Community groups, political associations, social organizations, and churches engaged in enthusiastic efforts. Some of the most active, public-spirited people of the area allied themselves with Downs church, formerly the Golden Gate Methodist Church. Dr. Hamilton Boswell, former pastor of Jones United Methodist Church in San Francisco, and now retired district superintendent of the Bay View District of the California-Nevada Conference (which includes Oakland and Berkeley), made the recommendation to christen the revived church, "Downs Memorial," in tribute to the late Reverend Karl Downs. Karl Downs was a young black Methodist minister whose life had ended prematurely that same year. He had a well-respected reputation as an activist and speaker for the causes of international peace and interracial understanding during his student days at Boston University and Gammon Seminary in Atlanta, Georgia. His legacy as a man of action was a harbinger of what Downs Memorial Church would become.

In 1937 the Stevens Hotel in Chicago denied lodging to Downs when he went there in the company of some white Methodist ministers. His colleagues did not protest but instead suggested that he find another place to stay. Downs wrote a provocative article, "Did My Church Desert Me?"—which *Time Magazine* published shortly afterward. This essay prompted the Methodist church to examine its policies and to refuse to meet in any hotel that would not accommodate all people. From 1943 until his death in 1948 Downs was president of Samuel Huston College in Austin, Texas. Huston-Tillotson College in Austin, which was formed by a merger of Samuel Huston and Bessy Tillotson colleges, endowed the Karl Downs Chair in Humanities in 1981.

For the newly christened Downs Memorial Methodist Church the Bishop selected the Reverend John N. Doggett, Jr., minister to the congregation of a Methodist church in the Hunters Point section of San Francisco. Beginning in June 1948, Doggett continued his charge in Hunters Point while he undertook the development of Downs. In its infancy Doggett nourished the new church and set the foundation for its future growth by actively pursuing potential members who shared his interest in the total concerns of the community.

In February 1949 an unexpected opportunity came for Doggett to leave Oakland and go to a Methodist church in southern California. By that time the Bishop had noticed thirty-one-year-old Roy Nichols. Nichols's background and preparation was just what was required for the politically changing Oakland. He was a forward-looking graduate of Lincoln University in Pennsylvania and Pacific School of Religion in Berkeley. His interest in community affairs as well as theology was already well known in the East Bay because of his work with several of the churches in Oakland and Berkeley. Large numbers of African-American families (including mine) were coming into the city and were looking for churches, jobs, and schools for their children. Nichols's sensitivity to the needs of the community made it easy for him to communicate his interpretation of the gospel in ways that had immediate meaning for his listeners. He was an inspirational speaker who challenged congregants to learn about issues of the times and work for positive change. He served Downs as pastor for fifteen years until 1964 when he went to Salem United Methodist Church in Harlem; it was a large congregation of about three thousand. The moderately small Downs had less than eight hundred members. Salem was the next step toward Nichols's election four years later as bishop of the United Methodist Church.

Since its formation as the rebirth of Golden Gate Methodist Church of north Oakland, Downs Memorial United Methodist Church has been the religious center for a congregation of African-Americans in the East Bay Area who are committed to a tradition of human service. When the time came for grass roots campaign activity, Downs was in the forefront. Our first venture as an active political unit began when Nichols first ran unsuccessfully for the Berkeley City Council. We then renewed our efforts for the next campaign that resulted in his seat on the Berkeley School Board. We contributed to the "Nickels for Nichols" fund from our own pockets and solicited additional donations from the broader community. Many of us, adults and younger people, rang door bells, distributed literature throughout the city, and rejoiced when he won the election. Then we followed his part in Berkeley's steps toward integration of its schools and knew that this was an important part of history for the country as a whole. Warren Widener won a place on the Berkeley City Council with the help of his Downs family. We were active workers in that campaign, which he entered when he was two years out of law school, and we supported him later when he ran for mayor and won.

The members of Downs encouraged Congressman Ronald Dellums when he took leave from the Berkeley City Council to deliberate whether he should enter the race for the United States Congress. Our first introduction to him was as a young man before he entered politics. Dellums participated in a counseling program at Downs where professionals on a voluntary basis offered advice in a variety of areas to people of our community to help them cope with their problems. We knew that he considered the advice and the feedback from individuals at Downs before deciding to enter national politics. Downs let him know that we had complete faith in his understanding of the needs of the country and his approach to the solutions. Knowing his record in local government and his integrity as a person, we welcomed the new presence that he would bring to Washington, D.C.

Scarcely a week passed when Downs did not sponsor or host an activity that was politically oriented. Our Commission on Social Concerns organized discussion sessions, held candidates' nights, carried on voter registration drives, and provided transportation to polling places on election day. Each year the commission brought in new memberships to the NAACP, and when the Afro-American Association was established Downs gave permission for the young people to meet in the church to teach Negro history and to explore their ambitions to achieve independence through the business and financial world. Downs nurtured the development of its members and offered a spiritual home for newcomers to the area and a base for their part in the struggle for social justice. Following the tradition of participation in the black church, there was opportunity for the schoolchildren, from elementary grades to high school, to sharpen their skills as public speakers and as performers in dramatic presentations. At Downs, the young people associated with their peers who had comparable backgrounds and aspirations and sat in the company of their elders who were models of social and political awareness and concern for the welfare of the community as a whole.

The Downs People
as a Community

SOUTHERN ROOTS

My exploration of the lives of the forty Downs people began with the World War II mass migration of African-Americans from the South to California. United States census figures reveal a gigantic growth in the black population of Alameda County (which includes Oakland and Berkeley) from 12,335 in 1940 to 203,612 in 1985. Black migration out of the South following Pearl Harbor was not a new phenomenon; World War I had initiated a similar movement to Illinois, Ohio, Indiana, New York, Michigan, and New Jersey. In the midforties, however, the migration changed direction. Jobs were available in the wartime industry on the West Coast, and Los Angeles, San Diego, and the San Francisco Bay Area attracted thousands of newly arrived black workers and their families in search of improved economic and racial conditions.

In Texas, my home state, the news came by way of friends and relatives who had preceded us and from recruiters who promised wages of $1.25 an hour as opposed to $0.40 in Houston. There were jobs for skilled and unskilled workers at Moore Dry Dock, Kaiser Shipyards, Naval Supply Depot, Army Supply Depot, the port of embarkation, ammunition stations, and scores of related industries in the area. We were enticed by the prospect of pay checks of $100 for one week's work and the freedom

13

to live wherever we chose—on well-lit, regularly maintained streets in nicely painted houses, free from the racial restrictions that were endemic to our existence in the South. Our dreams were founded on financial as well as social aspirations for ourselves and our children.

Never again would Oakland and Berkeley have a small number of black people who were predominantly native Californians and most likely knew each other. With the new arrivals, native Californians merged with the migrants. Attendance soared at churches, social and civic organizations, schools, and wherever African-Americans came together, giving evidence of the increasing numbers. The black population continued to grow until the majority of students in the public schools of Oakland were African-Americans. My family of three was part of this change, as were many of the Downs people. The majority of us arrived in California during the forties and fifties, the greatest number coming from the South.

Twenty-eight of the forty Downs people were born in the South. Four came from Texas, six from Mississippi, four from Louisiana, and three each from Oklahoma and Florida. Both Alabama and Arkansas were the birth states of two, and a total of four began their lives in Virginia, Maryland, Tennessee, and Georgia. Minnesota and Kansas were the birth places of two. Ten of the Downs people were born in California. Whether the move came about when they were children or after they were adults, the motives for the migration were similar. California promised a better life, increased employment opportunities, superior schools, and the chance of more equal treatment under the law. World War II brought more lucrative jobs, and the enforcement of the Fair Employment Practices Commission kept alive the hope that full economic justice was attainable.

Charles Aikens was eight when he, his father, and three brothers took off in their Henry J. Kaiser car to make the trip from Mississippi to Oakland in 1951. They were en route to join his mother and other siblings who had left four months earlier. The young boy was happy with thoughts of the Golden Gate Bridge and the gold that could be easily earned in California.

But fresh in the mind of the elder Aikens was the disruption of a family in their hometown of Lampton, Mississippi, when a white woman accused one of his friends, Mr. Sipes, of being a peeping tom. Fearing a lynch mob, Sipes fled leaving a wife and five children whom the Aikens family befriended. And Aikens's father had not forgotten the threats to one of his older sons who had stared, with natural curiosity, at his first sight of a person making his way in a wheelchair. He offended the invalid, a white youngster, who reported the perceived encroachment upon his privacy to his equally resentful father.

When her parents left New Orleans to go to Oakland and begin war industry work, Ramona Maples was just about ready to finish high school and expected to remain there and attend Dillard University. The studious Maples did not think it possible that any college could surpass Dillard, but she was unable to convince her mother and father to allow her to stay in Louisiana. At her father's command, the fifteen-year-old newly graduated Maples reluctantly left Louisiana to come to Oakland in 1943 to complete the family circle.

Wesley Jones, Katherine Drake, Ruth Love, Nell Irvin Painter-Shafer, Vera Pitts, and Ruby Osborne were no more than five when their families left the South. Before she was school-age, Ruby Osborne's father and mother and her two uncles left Mississippi because of the racial conditions. They chose Colorado because an ad in a newspaper solicited workers for a creosote plant. The men had been landowners in Mississippi, had run a saw mill, and were thus interested in a similar type of work. Colorado did not offer relief from all of the discrimination and segregation, but it was surely an improvement over the Mississippi situation.

Most of the Downs people who were migrants from the South came as adults, as did Laurence Bolling in 1946, Roy Nichols in 1941, and Milton Combs, Sr., in 1952. The parents of Laurence Bolling would have been happy to have him return with his bride, Letitia, to Richmond, Virginia, and continue his work with the NAACP and the Southern Aid Society, a black life insurance company. But the well-established business that was owned and operated by Letitia's father, the W. J. Carter Box

Company in Oakland, beckoned much more enticingly than did any of those who spoke in favor of his return to the South. After weighing the attractiveness and the potential of the Oakland opportunity, Bolling made the decision to remain in the Bay Area after his discharge from the army. Roy Nichols (from Philadelphia) and Milton Combs, Sr., (from Minnesota) came to Berkeley as beginning seminary students. Combs was a recent graduate of Macalester College in St. Paul, and Nichols had finished the first four years at Lincoln University in Pennsylvania. They were devoted young men who were ready to prepare for the professional side of religion.

Two of the Downs people left the South when they were children to live in the North as the result of parental decisions but made permanent migrations to California by their own choices after they had reached maturity. Walter Morris and Isham "Ike" Buchanan, both from Alabama, lived and attended school in the North before they came to California. Because of the encouragement of the principal of the Mobile, Alabama, school Walter Morris attended, six of the nine children in his family went to public schools in Boston. It was Morris's turn to go to Boston in 1930 when he was nine. The principal had convinced Morris's father that the quality of education in Boston was far superior to Mobile's. Morris did not live in Alabama subsequent to that time. Having completed undergraduate study in the state of Washington, and medical school in Washington, D.C., he came to Oakland and began his career here in 1959.

After the death of his father in 1940, Ike Buchanan's mother sent him at age thirteen to Cincinnati, Ohio, to live with his older sister. When he graduated from college he did not know where he wanted to seek his fortune, but he was certain that he would not remain in Cincinnati where opportunities were not as great as he would have liked. While he wrestled with the question of his future and waited for a call from the draft board, Buchanan went to California in 1951 to visit his sister. The notice of induction into the armed forces did not come immediately. At the suggestion of a friend he entered the University of San Francisco to study for a California teaching certificate and ultimately began a career in the educational system of the Bay Area.

Some of the Downs people did not settle in Oakland as a result of careful deliberations. In these instances they came because of conditions that were expected to be temporary but became permanent because they found the promise of a better quality of life. When Curtis Bowers finished his tour of duty in the navy in 1952 he left Georgia to visit his brother in Berkeley with the intention of returning home within a few weeks. This plan was changed by one incident. His brother took him sightseeing down Sacramento Street in Berkeley and told him that this street, which appeared spacious and clean to Bowers, was in the heart of a California slum. To the newcomer this sight meant the Bay Area was in reality a prosperous place. Without delay he got good paying jobs doing house repair work, and Oakland has been Bowers's home ever since.

Phillip Raymond is another of the Downs people who originally came to California for a limited period of time but eventually became a permanent resident. In the summer months between his junior and senior years at Tuskegee Institute, he worked in a World War II shipyard in Richmond, California, at the height of the fighting. He returned to Tuskegee for his bachelor's degree but was later stationed in California as a soldier and was discharged in this area. From the service he went to the University of California–Berkeley for graduate study and has made his home here since 1952.

Practical considerations of the differences in climate in the East Bay when compared to that of Jacksonville, Florida, made it easy for Charles Furlow to stay in California after his stint in the navy. He found that he could wear a navy-issue wool pea coat comfortably in June and July. There were no flies or mosquitoes to combat nor did he have to deal with the constant high humidity. He could not see any reason to leave; "If there is any way I can make a living, I am going to make it here." However, Furlow was not greatly reassured by the racial situation in California. He had lived in New York City and had seen the advantages and disadvantages of life as a black person in that so-called "liberated" place. He felt that he could accept California as he had New York by attending to his own affairs and not paying too much attention to the injustices around him.

Coming to California in the forties and fifties, as most of the Downs people did, they faced no employment problems because of the effects of the booming economy of World War II. It was easy to find work—that reason for the migration was totally realized. Even though the racial restrictions were not nearly as overwhelming as in the South, they saw a shift in the manifestations of discrimination and segregation that were more subtle and in some ways more difficult to cope with. They appreciated the absence of the more obvious signs of segregation but quickly learned to interpret facial expressions and clever ruses, such as the withholding of efficient service, which in reality meant similar constraints. This knowledge added to the real overall improvement in the quality of life in California and made it possible for the Downs people and their parents to escape total disappointment with their move to this state. The general feeling was that California allowed them to live in a much freer society with less racial humiliation.

SOCIO-ECONOMIC BACKGROUNDS

The majority of the Downs people describe themselves as poor during their childhood. The struggle was harder for some households than for others, but no one grew up in abject hardship or want. Most of them were not aware of their family's socio-economic standing until they reached college where they learned to evaluate and see beyond their immediate circumstances. Generally, the subject was first introduced in social science courses with such terms as *upper, middle,* and *lower class* and came as a surprise because it had not been necessary to define the quality of their lives in socio-economic terms before. They had had no television to dramatize daily and repetitively the gratification and happiness that can come with more money, or to emphasize the large gaps between their homes and those of the dominant, more affluent culture. Their only points of reference were the people they saw around them—neighbors, schoolmates, and fellow church members who were in the same condition.

Slight variations on the theme of "we were poor, but we didn't know it" emphasize the relative unimportance of material wealth within the family unit. Almost everybody in Nora Vaughn's hometown of Utica, Mississippi, was connected with Utica Institute, a boarding school that was founded by a graduate of Tuskegee and patterned after that college. The school's finances depended upon the fund-raising skills of its president, and the parents of the students made good use of the boxes of clothing that northern patrons sent periodically. Vaughn's father was the agriculture teacher at the Institute. Her family was "very poor, but I don't remember feeling poor. We had nice clothes, plenty to eat, but we were living in this community where everybody was the same."

In Texarkana, Arkansas, Cleophas Williams's family was hit hard by the depression. For years his parents were teachers in rural one-room schoolhouses for grades first through eighth. Of that period Williams remembered, "Economically we saw some real hard times. Even though we were dirt poor, we didn't seem poor." He attributed this to the atmosphere that was created by his father in the diverse roles of head of the house, teacher, preacher, and problem solver for people who had difficulty in dealing with governmental agencies.

There was an air of genteel poverty in Hazel Kyle's home in Pensacola, Florida, even though her family was "as poor as church mice." Her mother brought home linen napkins that her employer had discarded and carefully darned them for her family to use with the nice cups and saucers she had purchased. Having a piano in the home to practice her vocal and instrumental lessons was a luxury Kyle remembered; her parents wanted to encourage her musical talent, which was evident before she was old enough to go to public school.

Logan's Heights in San Diego, where Wesley Jones's family lived, was the section that the African-Americans, Mexican-Americans, and the poorer white folks lived in. Jones considered it a ghetto of San Diego, but he thought that his family was somewhat different from others in that community. They were better-off financially because his father's trade as a contractor was more lucrative than the average man's employment. The family's economic standing made it possible for each of the ten children, who chose to do so, to continue their education beyond the secondary level. Jones could not say that he grew up poor (he recalled the joy of a new bicycle for Christmas and ample food and clothing), but "I didn't know that I was poor or disadvantaged until my second year in college when I read it in a psychology book, and I recognized that they were talking about me."

Laurence Bolling never had any questions about the financial resources of his family either. He spoke of his mother's hard labor as a washer woman to supplement his father's income and his part in the pickup and delivery of the clothes. Bolling has not forgotten the sight of his mother laboring over the washtubs in the backyard and the small compensation it earned. And still fresh in his mind are the detours he made to avoid being seen by certain girls as he took clothes from one place to another. Bolling, however, was well accepted by his peers just as others had been in the black social circles of Richmond, Virginia, in spite of his family's limited financial status. He associated freely with girls and boys whose parents had more money at their disposal, and whose occupations were higher on the scale of respectability than those of his father and mother. Bolling was convinced that, for the most part, his social standing did not suffer because of poverty; he was invited to dances and parties at his high school by virtue of his family's integrity and character. Both of his parents were prominent workers in a large Baptist church in Baltimore. His father taught a Bible class that attracted three hundred people each Sunday morning. On the day of his funeral, the pack of snow on the ground did not prevent four thousand people from filling every pew in the church.

The families of Vertis Thompson and Walter Morris were more prosperous than others in their hometowns because their fathers' highly skilled occupations earned more than the work of other men. In Muskogee, Oklahoma, where Vertis Thompson lived, skilled workers who were employed by the railroads earned higher wages than the majority of black men who were unskilled and who worked in other industries. As a machinist for the Missouri, Kansas, and Texas railroad, Thompson's father could take care of all of the needs of his six sons. When the ravages of the depression reached Oklahoma, his father came to the aid of relatives who could not withstand the crisis. Because of his father's standing in the community and his modest prosperity, Thompson always thought he had a good life growing up in the black middle class.

Walter Morris's characterization of the socio-economic status of his family was much like that of Vertis Thompson. The black community of Mobile, Alabama, was poor, but Morris's family had more security because of his father's work as a combination lumberjack and longshoreman for the local paper mill. His was a dangerous occupation, directing rafts of timber from the river basin to the deep water port where it was loaded aboard ships headed out to sea. The rafts were made from huge logs held together by wire, and free-floating logs balanced in the center. He jumped back and forth from log to log to see that the load stayed on course.

Several of the Downs people who indicated that they began their lives as members of the middle class interpreted the designation in terms of values, attitudes, and exposure to activities outside of the home, as well as in an economic connotation. They talked not only about the freedom from want but also about the importance of education and a life-style where they could enjoy some things beyond the daily needs. The childhood environment and emphasis upon upward mobility afforded an added incentive to get on with the business of doing their part for the good of the race.

Vera Pitts grew up in west Oakland with her parents and two sisters. She knew very early that she enjoyed the comfortable life-style that was made possible by her father's work as a Pullman porter and by her mother's used furniture business. These advantages let her know that she did not want to be poor. She wanted the material things that money could buy—a nice car, attractive clothes, and the sort of home that went along with them. Getting a good education was just as important to her. Vera Pitts did not know if her parents could be defined as middle class in economic terms, but she was sure that the values the three girls learned from their mother and father were middle-class values. "Lower-class values are to get by, middle-class values are to get ahead, and my values are definitely upper-class: leisure and gracious living." At one time Vera Pitts heard Andrew Young's family described as lower-class. She knew that Caucasians and African-Americans used different standards in assigning people to a social caste, but this instance was particularly confusing to her because Young's father was a dentist. In her thinking this would qualify as a middle-class profession, just as her father's occupation as a Pullman porter in the mid-thirties (a steady job that had a high degree of social status in the black community) allowed her to think of herself as coming from a middle-class background.

In junior high school Nell Irvin Painter-Shafer considered the question of socio-economics and asked her father whether the Irvins were poor or rich. She never felt poor nor was aware of any deprivation, but she knew that she was far from rich. He gave her what she recognized years later as a sermon to convince her that the Irvin family was really poor to discourage frivolous use of his hard-earned dollars; however, his well-intentioned homily did not satisfy her curiosity. A more acceptable explanation had to wait until much later when she and her adult peers compared their impressions about their youthful experiences. She was then assured that she had grown up in a middle-class setting.

Elizabeth Pettus's father was a bishop and owned a grocery store, both of which assured her preferential treatment in her hometown of Wasco, California. She described her family's status in two ways: economically middle-class, but socially upper-class. Her home was a well-furnished, attractive house. Her father's traveling all over the country on church business afforded the family rare opportunities, such as dinner at Fisherman's Wharf in San Francisco and trips to the museums there. On Easter Sunday mornings they went to sunrise services at the Hollywood Bowl.

Bishop Clarke's South Gate Garden Grocery Store sold meats, vegetables, fruits, and canned goods. Each morning delivery men brought milk from the dairy and fresh bread and pastries from the bakery. The store occupied one of the Clarkes' four lots. It was an aluminum building that had been built as a garage to house the trucks that belonged to the former owner. The four lots with the store, the family home, and two rental houses formed a little community within the one yard.

Until he and his mother left Jackson, Mississippi, to come to Berkeley when he was ten years old, James Howard lived as part of a prominent, well-to-do black family, which was allowed privileges that were denied to other African-Americans in Mississippi. His family was "different"; it included four generations of college graduates who were financially successful and owned the biggest house in town. The best stores in Jackson permitted the women to shop for clothes, and his mother was the only student who had a car when she graduated from high school in 1936. She drove Cadillacs. When she went to Tennessee Agricultural and Industrial College for graduate study, she wore a full-length Hudson seal coat. In 1946 his grandmother bequeathed the thirteen-room family home in Jackson to his mother. She sold the property and came to California where, unfortunately, things were different. Because of failing health she was never able to gain a real foothold in Berkeley. A severe case of hypertension caused several strokes and kept her from holding jobs that would have allowed her to sustain the quality of living that had been her wont. Howard had to find work to contribute to the day-to-day expenses and earned from two to three hundred dollars a month cleaning offices along Sacramento Street. Throughout these hard times, however, her middle-class values persisted. Until the time of her death, Howard's mother kept constant pressure on her son to prepare for the doctorate that was her ambition for him. She called him "Doctor" while he was still an undergraduate. When she died she felt assured that even though he was not yet in a doctoral program, the degree would surely follow, as it did.

A lack of money was never a limitation for the important things in Wilma Johnson's family in the San Joaquin Valley of northern California. Whenever it was time for one of the ten children to enter college, her mother would say, "It's time for

Clarence to go," or "It's time for Paul to go," or whoever was finishing high school that June—and the money was found somehow. In terms of values and expectations Johnson classified her family as definitely middle-class. Her parents had the background of owning property in Mississippi and a dedication to the concept of better living conditions through education and preparation for higher employment proficiency. However, if finances alone were considered, she would choose the term poor.

More than half of the Downs people (thirty of the forty), were raised in houses that were owned by their parents, and it was not unusual for the families to collect supplementary income from rental units. Four of the Downs people received long-lasting lessons of the value of land and real estate for income, speculation, or rental. Dorothy Pitts and Curtis Bowers took note of their fathers' activities, and Dorothy Lee and Katherine Drake observed the business acumen of their mothers as they added to their incomes after getting divorced.

Memphis, Tennessee, was a growing lumber capital when Dorothy Pitts was a child. The Ford Motor Company was slated to build a plant there, and the street that she lived on was to become a state highway. Her father knew this, and he also knew that the purchase of land in that section of the city would be a shrewd investment to accrue more capital. With this knowledge he accumulated other property to add to the land on which the family home stood and used it for income. As fortune dictated they were not able to realize the gain from this business venture. Dorothy Pitts's father was fired from his job as a straw boss at the lumber yard after an unhappy incident.

One evening in the late twenties, Dorothy Pitts's father and his white boss were sharing a drink of whiskey on the side porch of the family home. The boss asked, "Oscar, what would your landlord say if he knew you were sitting here with a white man drinking whiskey?" Her father answered without thinking of the possible consequences, "I don't have a landlord. I own this property and I have some more property down there." He was fired the next working day and banished from the only work he knew how to do. Money became a problem. At the beginning of the depression, money was not nearly as easy to come by as before. Pitts's father was too proud to accept relief. He did the only kind of work he could get to bring in money: he became a numbers runner and a bootlegger. Her mother traveled with vaudeville actresses, working as a seamstress. Sometimes it was necessary for the children to pick up coal from the railroad tracks to tide them over until either their father hit the numbers or their mother returned home with her paycheck. Dorothy Pitts described her two parents as "strivers" who were deeply interested in land ownership and entrepreneurship.

The numbers business was conducted in a building that stood on the same piece of property where the family residence was located. Pitts's parents worried about their daughters being in proximity to the men who would come to do business. They did not allow the girls to come near the male patrons and cautioned them, as they sat on the swing or in the chairs on the porch, to "keep your knees together and your dress down." The family survived intact with the help of relatives, but without the anticipated benefits of the railroad land venture.

Curtis Bowers grew up on his father's three-hundred-acre farm in rural Georgia where cotton was one of the important crops. Bowers had clear memories of his father's interest in acquiring land and his conviction that land ownership represented the answer to the black man's search for independence and respect in this country. The example of his father bore fruit when Bowers, as an adult, began his practice of searching out old houses to remodel for rent.

The year that Dorothy Lee was born was the year that her parents bought the first real estate they owned. Despite the fact that their income was not large, and they were "very poor," and their existence was "just about hand-to-mouth," her mother was a very good manager and saved faithfully. Lee recalled her mother's philosophy: "We got this little bit, now we are going to get a little bit more." The family home was built in the center of two large lots in Oklahoma City, Oklahoma. By diligent money management they secured the funds to build duplexes on the unused area of the lots, which brought the total to three structures. After Lee's mother came to California in 1949 she continued the tradition by buying a building that had eight units.

Thelma Scott-Skillman and Charles Furlow learned prudent money management from their parents. The income in Scott-Skillman's Oakland home was ample to purchase the things she needed and many extras, but her parents wanted their children to understand the value of money and how to handle it efficiently. By the time she was ten, she had taken over the chore of preparing the family's income tax returns. Two years later, at age twelve, with her father as cosigner, she opened a charge account to purchase a tape recorder and set up a payment schedule from her weekly allowance.

Charles Furlow's father gave him a similar lesson in economics when he told him that he would have to earn the bicycle he coveted. The arrangement was for Furlow to work after school for a druggist in Jacksonville, Florida. From his $2.50 weekly salary, he would pay $1.00 to the man from whom he bought the bike, give $1.00 to his mother to help with the household expenses, and save $.25. The remaining $.25 could be used as he saw fit. From this regular savings Furlow had a bank account when he was in the sixth grade. Furlow's father instilled in his children a knowledge of good management of money. He combined that with his continued search for better-paying jobs and maintained a good standard of living for his family.

Ella Wiley's mother and stepfather showed ingenuity in her upbringing. Since her parents were divorced when she was a very young child in Louisiana, her formative years were influenced to a greater degree by her mother, who set the tone of a good life. Her summation of those years: "We were poor but happy. We didn't have money to do things, but Mother gave me the values that money can't buy." When her mother remarried, her stepfather set aside a spot of cotton on his forty acres of farming land and earmarked its profits for Wiley's school expenses. She did the weeding, and her stepfather picked and baled the cotton.

The range of financial security presented here is a sampling but representative of African-Americans in many other similar situations in the Bay Area during the fifties and early sixties. I found within my group the gamut from a sharecropper family that depended temporarily upon public welfare to a fortunate household that occupied a thirteen-room house and enjoyed Cadillac cars and fur coats. The median seems to be a comfortable way of life with money enough for all of the creature comforts and for some of the pleasures that remain fond memories of childhood. Now, with the total development of their careers and the choice of their way of life intact, all of the Downs people can be placed unequivocally in the African-American middle class where they must deal with all of the privileges, responsibilities, and disadvantages of that group in American society.

COPING WITH RACISM

No matter what section of the United States the Downs people lived in as children or before they migrated to California, how well educated their parents were or how high the family rated on the social or economic scale, each of the forty knew that they existed in a racist society. They also knew that their mothers and fathers encountered discrimination in some form. It was not possible for the parents to avoid completely the dilemma of teaching their children to cope with its effects. They wrestled with thoughts of challenging the status quo, which carried a likelihood of economic retaliation or physical harm, or suffering the psychological damage of silent acquiescence in the face of indignities. Walking this potentially dangerous tightrope was a common concern for the parents of the Downs people.

Mothers and fathers knew that white people had financial and political power and could withhold jobs and cripple the family security. Still, the parents were not happy with the degradation that comes with quiet acceptance and in some cases adopted a middle ground that included teaching realistic survival skills designed to protect both the life and property of the family unit. The fact that the racial climate was not a typical topic of conversation between parents and children did not diminish its importance or the major position it held in the thoughts of the adults and in their discussions with other adults. The omission was more an attempt to shelter the young people and provide a place where the oppressive situation could not claim such dominance. Fathers especially found it difficult to admit to their children their sense of frustration in resisting the discrimination. Instead, a number of parents chose to emphasize the concepts of self-respect, self-confidence, racial pride, and good behavior.

Long before I reached high school I heard my parents in Houston, Texas, discussing in hushed voices an alleged tarring and feathering of an outspoken local African-American who had somehow overstepped the bounds of black-white relationships. At another time I wondered whether my brother Charles's severe punishment for fighting was based upon the aggressive act itself or more upon the fact that his opponent was a white boy.

Jack Costa in Alameda, California, and Pete Taylor, Jr., in Houston and in Oakland did not hear in explicit terms the unpleasant facts of race relations, or the rules of conduct that were set specifically for young black boys. Their parents' lessons had to do with the general standards of good behavior and the nurturing of self-esteem. It was not necessary to caution Taylor to be sure to sit on the back of the bus in Houston—that was self-evident. Growing up in California, Costa did not attend segregated schools. He went to the same movies as the other boys, used the same rest rooms, and entered through the same doors, but at times he "could hear a little resentment" when he accompanied his white schoolmates to places of amusement.

Across the continent in Minnesota, Milton Combs, Sr., learned much the same lesson. He discovered that certain schoolmates, girls who were not black, were "off limits" to him. His education about the racial situation in his state did not stop there. Combs saw the painful attempts of his father, a butcher, to deal with his union's discriminatory practices toward black workers—men who had been recruited to broaden the union's base of power during negotiations with the employers.

Looking back over their experiences as young girls, two of the Downs people, Elizabeth Pettus and Phebia Richardson, had no illusions that they escaped completely the consequences of racism. But they felt that they were not exposed to as much of the tension as many African-American children because of their standing as daughters of well-known church officials. Due to her father's position as a minister, bishop, and unofficial mayor of the black section of Wasco, California, Pettus could associate with white girls of her age, and she could sit at the counter of the local bakery on a hot day and be served by the attendant. As a young girl in Louisiana, Richardson played with the children of the white postmaster who lived next door. She sensed that her family was treated differently because the local people respected her father, a well-educated minister in the Methodist church. Yet both girls knew that they were controlled by the overall customs of race relations in their towns.

The women of James Howard's family had the unusual privilege of being able to try on dresses in the best stores in Jackson, Mississippi, to test the fit of the garment before they made the purchase. (Other African-American women were not allowed to do this.) The family commanded more respect by virtue of their land holdings, their independent air, and the history of four generations of college education. This did not ensure complete immunity from racial discrimination, however, because they, like all other African-Americans in Jackson, were restricted to one day of the week when they could attend the county fair. To Howard, one of the joys of coming to California was not having "to wait until Monday to go to the fair anymore."

In Opelika, Alabama, Ike Buchanan learned to live within the racial restrictions because he perceived "this is the way things are, and this is the way things have to be." There was no discussion of change, nor any efforts to effect change. When Buchanan was thirteen, his father died, and he went to Cincinnati to live with his sister. Soon he joined the Kenyon Avenue Christian Church and became involved in a series of civil rights activities. Under the aegis of Mrs. Devine, the minister's wife, Buchanan and a group of high school students from the NAACP mounted a boycott that resulted in the desegregation of restaurants in the heart of the city. In his senior year he and four classmates lodged a protest about the football team playing on the home field of a rival school in the state of Kentucky where the spectator stands were segregated. His school did not play again in Kentucky until that state changed its restrictive policies. They took further action that led to the cancellation of the school's annual ferry boat excursion down the Ohio River to Coney Island, an amusement park that was completely segregated. Never again was Buchanan able to accept the status quo placidly.

Living in Virginia, Laurence Bolling saw firsthand evidence of racial injustice very early in his life. There were the Saturday night rallies of the Ku Klux Klan, with a show of strength aimed at controlling the African-American community through intimidation and fear; they also meant to demonstrate to the black men the folly of trying to protect their women and children. He remembers his father's frustration when he was not able to move into certain sections of Richmond, Virginia, where he wanted to rent a better house for his wife and son.

Another unpleasant recollection for Bolling was the distribution of food during the depression. When Herbert Hoover was still in office, the city attempted to relieve the congestion of food lines in downtown Richmond by establishing centers in the outlying districts so that people could get food from locations close to home. In the white parts of town the city officials rented storefronts, and whites could go to the neatly stacked packages and draw their allotment. In the sections that were mostly black, however, city officials drove trucks down the middle of the street and threw boxes of food onto the sidewalks. There was no assigned place to accept the boxes; there was only the indignity of going to the sidewalk and picking out your share.

Bolling's parents were determined to qualify to vote in the state of Virginia. Black people not only paid the poll tax but had to pass an examination that was given only to nonwhites. This included reciting portions of the Bill of Rights and giving the exact dates of admission of each state to the Union. Bolling saw his mother and father prepare for this examination with hours of intense study. For him, it was a lesson in the dedication to the diligent pursuit of a goal.

Life on a farm brings a certain amount of insulation from racial affronts if the family owns the land. If they are not share-croppers, they are not dependent upon the white boss for employment and are not subject to his whims for all items of subsistence, including food and clothing. Such was the life of Curtis Bowers in rural Georgia on his father's large farm. His lot was far better than that of his neighbors. He shared with me an event that caused him to think of race relations in terms of economics. One year Bowers's father used black and white farm hands to pick the acres of cotton. He started the white workers in one field and the blacks in another, at opposite ends of the planting. As they finished one field, they would move to the next. Near the end of the reaping they were left with only one area to harvest. The father began the whites on one end of that field and the blacks on the other. As they moved toward the center of the section, Bowers watched in anticipation of what would happen when the two supposed antagonists met in the middle. To his surprise, absolutely nothing untoward occurred. They did their work and when it was all done, they turned around and left the picking area. To Bowers the moral was that when faced with economic need, people will put survival first. Earning a living was uppermost in their minds; they did not have time to fight.

I can describe Mary Ellen Rose Butler as a child of the YMCA. During Butler's youth her father was executive secretary of the North West Branch YMCA in Oakland, and the YMCA served as the focal point for all of the affairs of the family. She saw the frustrations of her father as he faced the task of administering a public agency meant to serve the needs of black people in a large city. There was the inevitable recurrent lack of sufficient funds and staff. After years in the YMCA, Butler's father was confronted by the new challenges that came with his appointment to the city council as Oakland's first black councilman.

When Butler entered the job market she found that unlike the average black applicant she had a double possibility for unfair treatment. On the one hand she could be denied employment by companies that did not wish to hire black workers. There was also the chance her light complexion might give the impression that she was not an African-American. If she were inadvertently hired as a nonblack, she could be accused later of misrepresentation. Butler was a staff member of the Public Relations Department of Blue Cross in Oakland in 1961 and 1962. She and the custodian, with whom she developed a friendship, were the only nonwhite employees in the building, and she was the only one in a professional status. In one of their conversations they discussed her precarious position in a job where her racial identity might be a liability. He told her, "Those folks don't know you're black." After that, to avoid any unforeseen prejudicial action in this respect, if she was not certain that a potential employer knew her ethnicity, she would say, "I am black, in case you don't know it." Without fail, they would reply, "Why, that's no problem."

Through the span of their years all of the Downs people have come into contact with racial discrimination in the United States and have felt its influence upon all areas of their lives. Specifically, they have felt the effects upon where they or their parents worked, the wages for their labor, the availability of acceptable, affordable housing, the quality of public education, and the general conditions of life. Having thus been seasoned by this type of prejudice, the Downs people chose service-oriented careers and joined the struggle for social justice through their work and in community involvement. They welcomed the advancements that came with the civil rights movement but have been troubled by the setbacks and challenges since the Reagan and Bush administrations. The lack of commitment to civil rights and affirmative action, coupled with the prevalence of drug abuse, has made it difficult for the Downs people to be completely optimistic about the future of black youth. But they have retained a significant degree of hope and are continuing to work for the good of the young people.

RELIGIOUS ORIENTATION

Religious activities have always been an integral part of the week for the Downs people, as equally important as going to school. Sixteen of the Downs people have roots in the Baptist church, and the same number in the Methodist church. The

Episcopal church contributes one to the group, and two of the forty are former Catholics. The remaining five come from fundamentalist churches that are strong in the South: the Church of God, the Church of God in Christ, and the Christ Holiness Sanctified Church.

The pattern of my church life as a young girl in Houston, Texas, which was not unlike that in the homes of most of the Downs people, was well established before I discovered Downs church. My family spent most of every Sunday and many hours of other days in our Baptist church. On Sunday mornings we rose early, almost as early as on a week day, and after my father's Sabbath prayer ate the special breakfast prepared by my mother. Then the children left home to walk to Sunday school and remained for the 11:00 A.M. service. When it was over, everybody went home together to ingest a midafternoon dinner, a meal prepared with more time and care than during the week. The young people returned to church in the late afternoon for the youth organization meetings and then waited for our parents to join us for the evening service. Finally the day ended, and we all went home to sleep or prepare for the week ahead. There were midweek choir practices, organization meetings, and programs to observe religious and community holidays. Our social life as well as religious life revolved around the church.

Every generation in the family of Eugene Tarrant had at least one Baptist minister. His great grandfather, a circuit preacher who ministered to Baptist churches in small towns in the vicinity of Ennis, Texas, said to young Tarrant, "Boy, you're perfect for a Baptist preacher. I know you're going to be one." Tarrant intended to fulfill this prophesy but abandoned the idea when he went into the navy after high school and sailed the Pacific Ocean in World War II. His thoughts about the relationship of life and death were terribly shaken when he witnessed the suffering and the slaughter of men in the naval battles. The sight of ship decks running with blood, the cries of the wounded and dying, and the curses directed at God and at all mankind caused him to reconsider his beliefs. His enthusiasm for the church and its teachings cooled greatly. By the time he left the service and resumed civilian life, the desire to become a preacher had dissipated, and he was satisfied to return to lay attendance in a church.

When Vertis Thompson was a senior in high school he was the general director of the youth training program in his Baptist church and assistant superintendent of the Sunday school. The people of the church wanted to send him to the Baptist Congress that was being held in Cincinnati. He declined the offer, saying that they should send another person who would not be leaving for college the following September, and who could use the lessons of the Congress for the good of the church. The older members were emphatic that he should take the trip and utilize the benefits of the experience for his own growth without thinking of the value to the church.

As he approached graduation, he thought about career possibilities in religion, dentistry, law, and medicine. He narrowed the choice to medicine and the ministry, areas that he saw as two aspects of the same thing: Jesus healed bodies as well as spirits just as the medical practitioner does. He seriously considered becoming a preacher until he had a long talk with his minister just before he was inducted into the navy. To encourage Thompson toward a church career, the minister tempted him with the proposal of a telephone call that would immediately admit him into a seminary and automatically exempt him from the draft. Thompson resented the implication that his religious convictions could be used as a means to escape military service, and life as a church leader lost its appeal. He went into the navy and was assigned to the medical corps and upon discharge from the service entered medical school.

Vallejo, California, had a Baptist and a Methodist church for African-Americans when Gertrude Hines was a child. She, her mother, and her eight siblings were members of the Methodist church. On the other hand, her father felt no need to join any church group. "He believed in the golden rule, that was his religion"; however, he had no objection to his family's practice. His appearances at the church were limited to the times when one of his children participated in a program, or when the Vallejo Ku Klux Klan made threats against it. Then Hines's father led a contingent of men from the NAACP who sat outside of the church all night to guard it from assault.

The Second Baptist Church of Riverside, California, was the focus for the religious life of Etta Hill's parents and their ten children. Her father was a trustee and sang in the choir, and her mother took part in many of the organizations. Hill started out as secretary of the Sunday school when she was nine or ten years old and retained that office for five years. She then became superintendent of the Sunday school, sang in the senior choir, and held a variety of offices. Because of her extensive involvement in the church's programs, she thought of herself as "Miss Second Baptist," a true representative of her beloved church.

As would be expected, the reasons for the Downs people's introduction to our church reflects the diversity in ages and family status. Some of the Downs people came simply because of the convenience of getting to and from a church location. They had to take into consideration the juggling of work hours and home responsibilities before making the initial trip that was the start of their integration into the Downs family. Others, like the young men who came when thoughts of courtship were of the utmost importance, were drawn by the prospect of meeting attractive young women. Charles Aikens followed his high school sweetheart to Downs. Jack Costa came at the invitation of his lady friend. In the course of time Nichols officiated at the wedding ceremonies of both couples. One of their friends who heard about the youthful social group at Downs was Wesley Jones, then a student at San Francisco State College. The prospect of seeing "nice chicks" was as enticing to him as it had been to Aikens and Costa. What Jones did not expect was the pastor, Roy Nichols, whom he found to be youthful, inspirational, and willing to offer the kind of direction that made sense to him.

Jones gave credit to the minister's early counsel for the success of his career. As the two sat on the ground behind the structure that was then the church, leaning against the frame building, they could hear the cool wind blowing. Jones would position himself so that he could feel the warm rays of the sun.

It was almost like a garden. Nichols was talking, not lecturing, to Jones: "Man, all you got to do is to get you a little old port- folio. You don't need to have anything in it yet, but build on it." Jones understood that the minister was telling him, the naive young undergraduate, to develop a clear idea of what he wanted to pursue and then act on it. His first reaction was, "I don't have a portfolio," but the seed had been sown, and it cultivated his determination to be the first black person to serve as the director of a social welfare department in a California county. He had the idea, and he knew what the challenges were: prepa- ration and an advanced degree.

Laurence Bolling and Eugene Tarrant found their way to Downs because of the church's membership drives. Bolling's wife, Letitia, was one of the first members, but he had not yet made the connection. He first accompanied her to a Sunday service in response to the invitation from representatives of the church, Clarence and Beatrice Shirley, who came to his home as part of an evangelism team. Knowing that the visit was evan- gelistic rather than financial made Bolling more inclined to go to see for himself what Downs had to offer. He was not disap- pointed, and on the day of his first visit he began an affiliation that has lasted since 1949.

What brought Eugene Tarrant to Downs was its Sunday night radio program, "The Christian Answer." His attention was cap- tivated by Nichols's invitation to take part in the church's build- ing project. Tarrant was intrigued by the radio program, and since he was on vacation he went to the construction site the following Monday morning and soon found his niche as a part of the work crew. It was not long before he became a member of the church.

Unlike the sensitive topic of race relations, religious doc- trine and practices was not a subject that the parents con- sciously avoided in the presence of their children. It was part of the families' lives and dominated their households. The Downs people came from this sort of background, and for various rea- sons, such as filling a personal need, their paths led them to this place of spiritual nourishment. Again and again they made ref- erence to the charismatic personality and the leadership of the young minister, Roy Nichols. He was the strongest single force that attracted the Downs people to their church.

EDUCATIONAL ACCOMPLISHMENTS AND CAREERS

The Downs people present an impressive array of academic accomplishments. Most of them attended segregated southern schools at some point during their education and are examples of the successes in an educational system with the inherent disadvantages of Jim Crowism. They were upwardly mobile students who were well motivated and supported by parents, extended family, and church. Their minds were fertile grounds for the dedicated African-American teachers and school administrators whose interest in the pupils extended far beyond the classroom and into their off-campus life.

Those who went to high school and college in the South pay tribute to their segregated schools that taught black history and racial pride and insisted the students study higher mathematics and other demanding subjects. In spite of growing up in an era of oppression and legal segregation, they learned the importance of academic preparation toward the solutions of social problems. While they recognize the stigma of segregated schools and the inferiority they represent, the Downs people praise their black teachers for the care they gave to their students and for their overall appreciation of and dedication to the African-American community. In an effort to recapture this perspective, some of the Downs people are now encouraging their children to attend black colleges.

The father of one of the Downs people and the grandfather of another were founders of schools for black students. In 1915 Walter Morris's father and five other men established the first public school in Alabama, the Mobile County Training School. Previously there were only private schools for blacks and whites, but attendance was dependent upon the ability to pay the fees. The men saw the need for a free public school for all of the children in their community. They banded together and through political action secured a subsidy from the county to buy the land and build the school. Initially it was limited to the elementary grades in a converted house, but they added other structures until it was developed into a modern building that could accommodate all of the school grades. The Mobile County Training School was ultimately taken over by the county superintendent of education, and the six men acted as advisors to the superintendent. In 1975 the founders were honored in a ceremony by the mayor, congressmen, and other dignitaries. Morris's father was the only survivor present.

Frederick Douglass School in Lawton, Oklahoma, was started in 1907 as the first school for black students by the maternal grandfather of Ruth Love. He was a slave boy who ran away after being punished for helping his mother with heavy chores. His unhappiness with the lack of educational facilities for black children set him on a search for a place for their instruction. The Frederick Douglass School began as an elementary school for eighteen students with Love's grandfather as the teacher and principal. As the number of students increased, so did the grades, and it became an elementary and secondary school. It was integrated in 1966 and as a result lost its secondary grades.

Most of the Downs people grew up with the guidance and encouragement of parents whose formal education did not exceed the secondary grades, but the parents of twelve of the forty had some college training. All of the Downs people have had at least two years in college, and twenty-six completed courses beyond the baccalaureate; several have more than one graduate degree. There are seven doctorates, fifteen masters of arts, two doctors of law, and two medical doctors. Two of the Downs people earned the bachelor of divinity. One man earned the CLU designation after extensive study into the intricacies of the insurance industry well past his first four years of college. Although the educational level of the members of Downs church is above the local average, it cannot be said that all of the eight hundred had academic achievements that were comparable to those of the forty Downs people. Nor can it be claimed that the majority of the black population in the East Bay Area during the fifties and sixties could match their noteworthy records.

I examined the record of the progeny of the Downs people, the ninety-three men and women, boys and girls, that I refer to as the Second Generation. Even though at this stage of their development their accomplishments are not quite as spectacular as their parents', their academic and career history is certainly worth noting. Eight of the ninety-three have not yet graduated from secondary school. Many of the remaining eighty-five have enrolled in college, and some are still studying for a degree. Although some dropped out before the fourth year, the majority have completed a first degree or more. Within the Second Generation there are seven masters of arts, two masters of business administration, four doctors of law, one doctor of divinity, two medical doctors, one masters of pharmacology, and one doctorate in psychology.

While the Second Generation has not had time to demonstrate whether they will duplicate the scholastic attainments of their parents, some of the Downs people are not convinced that their children who grew up in very secure, middle-class homes share their high regard of, and willingness to sacrifice for, education. One of the Downs people, a mother of three who obtained her master's degree while working a full-time job and caring for her family, expressed disappointment in her children because they do not realize the importance of continued education, nor have they been willing to sacrifice the time and energy to prepare for employment beyond entry-level positions. She is unhappy because they do not take seriously life beyond immediate gratification; none of them are working toward advancement. Another mother is unhappy that her son, who has finished high school and found a job that pays a respectable salary, also has shown no interest in further study.

The Downs people who have surpassed the educational level of their parents work in professions that were formerly not open to black people. Their occupations demand more scholastic preparation and finely honed skills but in turn bring greater salaries than their parents thought possible. Fathers were the main economic support in the families of the Downs people. Eleven were professionals (ministers, teachers, attorneys), and others made their living as civil servants, farmers, and skilled or unskilled laborers. Fourteen of the mothers were not employed outside of the home. Of those who left home to earn money, one was a social worker and one a seamstress for vaudeville actresses. Five of the women were teachers or administrators in the local school district, and one was a practical nurse. There was a Hollywood actress, a beautician, two caterers, ten domestic workers, and four women who were "industrial operatives," or factory workers. The majority of the Downs people are in a division of human service; sixteen of the forty are engaged in some phase of public education from elementary grades to university. Those who are in education expressed thoughtful concern for their students, particularly the ethnics, who may be "lopped off" unless special efforts are made to rescue them.

Other Downs people work in social welfare, medicine and public health, insurance, recreation, housing, theater, fine arts, religion, psychology, journalism, and the judicial system. One man operates his own business, another is retired from his own business, and a third has retired from his position as legislative representative of his waterfront union. I found multiple work combinations with specific Downs people operating at the same time in the areas of housing, law, and politics; journalism, teaching, and writing; and religious services and education.

The Second Generation has chosen similar areas for their life's work. The corresponding interests are in medicine, education, and the judicial system. They include two physicians, four attorneys, two architects, three businessmen (including a bank vice-president), three nurses, one pharmacist, and a public health administrator. Another seven are employed at some level of public education. Improved opportunities for black people opened vocations that had been closed to them, so the Second Generation had a wider range of careers to choose from than their parents did. Despite the fact that the Second Generation has not yet duplicated the remarkable degree of progress that their mothers and fathers made, they have maintained the upward trend. Growing up in California in an atmosphere that was not tainted with the pervasive racial barriers of the South, in homes that were decidedly middle class, it is not surprising that in some instances they lack the added spark of motivation that was such a propelling force for their parents. Regardless, the Second Generation includes young people who are in the by-passed middle level of African-Americans whose work in human service is making a difference in the life of their communities.

THE DOWNS PEOPLE AS PART OF THEIR CHURCH

The forty men and women whom I have designated the Downs people, in addition to being my friends and coworkers at the church, were among those who did more than merely sit in the pews on Sunday mornings. They were among the people whom Nichols sought out to assist with the administration of Downs in its day-to-day activities. Eugene Tarrant recalled with pleasure that Nichols described him as a person who met without reservations the four requirements of the Methodist church: he served Downs with his prayers, his presence, his gifts, and his services. Jack Costa began the first Boy Scout troop at Downs in the midfifties with a cadre of five boys. It had grown to thirty-five when Calvin Jackson took on that responsibility in 1962, serving boys from the church and the neighborhood. Dorothy Pitts's duties at Downs included fund-raising and program planning and implementation and were almost an extension of her daily occupation in social services. She chaired the Commission on Social Concerns and took on obligations that related to the personal, civic, and political welfare of the community. She, along with Ruth Love, Dorothy Patterson, Juanita and Alfred Simmons, Wilma Johnson, and Elizabeth Pettus, set up the Homework Help Program, which became a prototype for similar projects all over the nation. With the help of professionals in a wide range of disciplines, this tutoring program offered instructional assistance to students.

Each of the Downs people who were public school students in the fifties and sixties were regular participants in the Methodist Youth Fellowship (MYF). Charles Aikens held offices and James Howard was a speaker on the Sundays when the youth had charge of the services. Gordon Baranco was a star on the MYF basketball team that, under the direction of Wesley Jones, competed successfully with teams from other churches. The boys and girls participated in MYF sponsored activities—picnics, summer camps, and leadership sessions.

Nora Vaughn produced and directed Easter and Christmas plays for Downs, forming the nucleus that later became the Black Repertory Group, the little theater group in Berkeley. Her late husband, Birel, and Irvin Fuller (also deceased) were the moving forces behind the building program for the present sanctuary. This required him to be away from home many hours each week. Vaughn said, "My husband was living at that church, and I was doing his work at home, like looking after the children all the way through [the construction]. He built that church. There isn't a single block in there that he didn't lay."

When it became apparent before 1954 that the Downs building could no longer accommodate its growing attendance, the trustees voted to embark upon a building program. The bids that came in for the construction ranged from $80,000 to $140,000, astronomical figures for the budget. When the board met to wrestle with the financial dilemma, Ivora Peazant, a staunch member, took the floor and said, "You wait until my Daddy comes to California; he'll build you a church." The trustees waited for three months until her father, Irvin Fuller, an experienced carpenter, arrived from Louisiana. At about the same time the board made contact with the Questad Construction Company, which agreed to deduct six to seven dollars from the contract price for every hour of donated labor. Birel Vaughn, a journeyman mason, convinced the Alameda County Labor Council to waive the regulation for union labor with the understanding that all of the volunteer work would be under his supervision. Fuller and Vaughn assumed the burden to guarantee the quality of the work. These men who are no longer alive left a monument to themselves in the beautiful sanctuary, and in our memories of the hours that we spent in the work force. They were at the site every day during the months of construction.

We all came, men and women, boys and girls, after the close of the regular school and work day, and we reported on Saturday mornings and stayed all day. There were jobs for all levels of capability—general clean up, hauling, moving and stacking lumber, sanding and painting, and carpentry chores. Phebia Richardson did a lot of pulling nails before choir rehearsals, and on Saturdays and Sundays too. She and Marylese Mitchell still reminisce about the times when they and other women put glue on boards, and they point to the locations where they filled nail holes with putty. There is a camellia bush near the Idaho Street entrance to the church that blooms each year to remind Elizabeth Pettus of the days when she, her three children, Nichols, and a few others planted the flowers and shrubs for the landscaping.

The youth contingent was well represented in the hard work. Wesley Jones, director of Youth Activities, organized the teenagers into work teams. The boys helped Birel Vaughn pour cement blocks, and the girls cooked for the crew and did odd carpentry chores. Herman Bossett recalls the time when he held the rope to help Birel Vaughn put the roof in place.

Some of the women were as physically active as the men when we attacked the piles of lumber, scaled the ladders, used hammer and saw. While the more adventurous females did actual construction work, other sisters prepared the midday meals each Saturday. The food preparation added to the incentive to relinquish hours that would have been taken up with personal matters. Ramona Maples came practically every Saturday to coordinate the food detail, as did Dorene Walton. Hazel Kyle downplayed her role as not doing "too much but cook, or hand somebody something, not too much physical stuff. Marylese and the others were up there nailing."

Laurence Bolling, using equipment from his box company, hauled away three to four truckloads of debris each week. Standing on the scaffolding inside the sanctuary, Nichols applied paint to the ceiling high above the altar—a symbolic location for the minister to work. It was a large area with an intricate design that required concentration as he worked with his paint brush on spaces high above his head. This was an exciting period, a time when we felt a sense of ownership, and we knew that it was something that we were doing together. When it was finished in 1956 everyone joined in the celebration: *The church was ours.*

A combination of Nichols's analytical discourses, the quiet litany, and the sedate hymns, anthems, and Negro spirituals of the Chancel Choir created a style of worship that was appropriate to the way of life of the Downs people. We did not want to express our emotions openly in our hours of worship; the peaceful atmosphere was a logical extension of our life-style. It corresponded with our material success and reflected the image of Downs as a prestigious church with a progressive program. Our members were influential and well respected in the business and professional worlds of our community, and expressive religious observances would not have been compatible with the Downs members' status. Spirited singing and shouting was more typical of poorer churches, of less-educated people, and for those who live in the rural South. However, the Downs people were careful not to appear overly critical of demonstrative services.

In the fifties the congregation of Downs was not ready to accept an official Gospel Choir. During the Nichols years Zephyr Ward appeared as gospel soloist only at the early morning Sunday service. It was not until after Nichols left and the Reverend Amos Cambric took over in 1964 that the change took place. By then the musical revolution of the midfifties had exploded musical standards in both the secular and the spiritual worlds, and the inspired new freedom of expression changed the traditional vocal and instrumental renditions for Catholic and Protestant hymnody. And with the civil rights and black power movements, African-Americans gained more self-confidence and were more disposed toward accepting in our churches music that many of us enjoyed over the radio or on the record player in our homes.

Cambric's new leadership signaled that the time was ripe to add a new choir devoted exclusively to gospel music with Ward as the organizer and director. The Gospel Choir under her direction was welcomed by the congregation and became an integral part of the church program. There was one voice definite in its disapproval of any departure from the standard selections. Eugene Tarrant cherishes enduring memories of singing Negro spirituals with choral groups in his high school. Tarrant thinks

of spirituals, anthems, and hymns as sacred art forms that add
to the beauty of worship and should be retained but not adul-
terated with "jazzed up" interpretations. He loved the purity of
the music at Downs in the Nichols era. Other of the Downs
people were lukewarm in their acceptance of gospel music.
Their comments ranged from, "a little goes a long way" or "not
as a steady diet," to the less-than-enthusiastic statements, "I
like it at times" and "it's OK." Ruby Osborne was much more
enthusiastic in her appreciation of gospel music. She thought of
it as part of the total black experience—of knowing and identi-
fying with African-American culture and being at ease with its
components. These were attributes that she associated with the
benefits of having attended Hampton University, a black school.
Osborne liked the hymns and anthems of the Chancel Choir but
welcomed gospel as a worthwhile new dimension to the music
of her church.

To the Downs people there was an overlapping of the benefits they got from Downs. They put a high value upon the spiritual rewards of the religious teaching of the minister and the
music of the choirs, but they placed almost as much emphasis
on the social growth from personal support, fellowship, career
and educational motivation, and increased self-confidence. For
many of the forty, the religious instruction was not a new part
of their lives; it merely reinforced the early training that they
had gotten at home.

Wilma Johnson feels that the spiritual nourishment at Downs
and at her previous church gave her courage to meet the challenges of her personal life and her career. In the sixties Charles
Aikens was dazzled by the promise of a professional baseball
player's high salary rather than the route to the delayed rewards of a college education. He also found support at Downs:
"There were people [there] who actually needled me about not
just being an athlete. They let me know that I had a brain to do
something else." With a law degree from the University of California, Warren Widener knew that he had the professional qual-
ifications for a career in law and politics. But more importantly
than that, Downs gave him "the confidence to know that I had
the right kind of moral ideas and commitments and that I could

stand up and hold my own in any religious or atheistic environment and feel comfortable."

Thelma Scott-Skillman credits Downs for her ability to build a foundation of religious and spiritual orientation that applies to all facets of her life. She feels that she gets a comprehensive foundation from a combination of Sunday school, worship services, and her home training. Ruth Love's statement about her daily needs rings similarly true. Love says that she does not precisely differentiate between spirituality and the secular world, but she knows that in order to function each day she needs both spiritual and emotional support—and she feels that she gets a suitable mixture of support from Downs. Many other Downs people admit that they knew there were Bible classes and prayer meetings going on at church, but they did not take advantage of them. More than one regret that they did not do so and wish for more formal religious instruction to aid their understanding of the Bible and the beliefs of the church. They see this as an inadequacy in their lives that they should have filled at the time.

The Downs people talked about lasting friendships that began at the church but did not depend upon church affiliation; they withstood changes in church membership or new places of residence. In the fifties a group of women who were part of the Mothers Circle at Downs made friendships that transcended the concerns of the church and continue into the nineties. Their children were infants and toddlers, and they wanted to relate to mothers who, like themselves, were not working outside of the home. These women formed a second club, "The Delights," which was not an official part of the church but was made up almost entirely of Downs members. "The Delights," an early manifestation of the consciousness-raising feminist groups of the seventies, offered companionship and enrichment to the women whose days were spent at home with small children. Their conversations were almost exclusively about their problems as parents, but they held workshops on the development of self-confidence as women, preparation to reenter the job market, and financial investment skills. The club maintained an atmosphere of confidentiality that allowed free discussion of personal difficulties without fear of betrayal. The Delights have continued their activities without interruption for four decades.

Now there are significant changes in the churchgoing habits of the Downs people and in the way they seek spiritual fulfillment. Slightly more than half (twenty-three of the forty) are still at Downs. Twelve left Downs to embrace different doctrines and denominations: Baptist, Episcopalian, Buddhist, Catholic, congregational, religious science, or nondenominational churches. For a variety of reasons, five are not active in any church setting. In the majority of these five cases, the disassociation does not reflect a rejection of the basic tenets of the home training; it is more a matter of a rearrangement of priorities and the failure to find a church home that meets the individual and personal needs of the family and the demands of the work-a-day world.

One of the five who is not a churchgoer is Nell Irvin Painter-Shafer. She classifies herself as an atheist and is concerned about the role of the Christian church in world history. Her questions have to do with the church's sanction of war and the alliance of white Christian churches with bigotry and segregation. When Painter-Shafer visited Canterbury cathedral, she was struck by the flags from battalions and tombs of dead warriors from England's wars. To her it meant that God was the God of national battles with the church and arms all together. At the same time she feels that she lives her life in a christian way (Christian with a small "c") by the golden rule, doing unto others as she would have done unto her. Christian with a capital "C" represents to her people who start Christian schools to segregate and who are filled with bigotry. Painter-Shafer says she was taught the value of a decent life and a concern for the welfare of her fellow man by example, both at home and at Downs.

Included in the seventeen who have discontinued membership in Downs church are four who said that they did so because they were unhappy with the minister's leadership. It did not take Wesley Jones long to discover that Downs would never be the same for him after Nichols left. He thought that maybe he was worshipping Nichols, but this did not disturb him because of the value of the experience when the pastor had served as his mentor and counselor. Jones was candid about his dislike for the Reverend Mr. Cambric as a pastor because of the totally different philosophy that he brought to the church.

Three of the Downs people left during the tenure of Rev. Charles Lee. Dorothy Pitts changed her church affiliation after she was party to an incident between Lee and several youthful members, students at Laney Community College. The young people came to the pastor for help when they had a problem with their college administration. Lee's refusal to enter the dispute indicated to Pitts that he was not willing to help with needs that were not strictly clerical in nature. She did not want to remain at a church with a minister who, in her opinion, "couldn't face reality." Phillip Raymond and his wife, Jessie, had been active at Downs for more than twenty years under four different ministers, having served as cosuperintendents of the Sunday School for fourteen of those years. After a period of dissatisfaction, the husband-and-wife team concluded that they were not getting the support they needed for the administration of the church school, and furthermore they were not satisfied with Lee's attitude in his relations with lay people. Finally and reluctantly the couple made the decision to leave Downs.

In the years that Calvin Jackson was at Downs he held leadership positions with the Boy Scouts, the Methodist Men's Club, and the board of trustees. Things went smoothly for him under Roy Nichols, Amos Cambric, Charles Belcher, and for a while with Charles Lee. But the time came when Jackson was not able to function as chairman of the trustee board because of the differences in opinion between himself and Lee. Jackson chose to resign the chairmanship so the minister could fill the position with someone who agreed with his philosophy. Rather than remain as an inactive bystander, Jackson left Downs in 1974 after thirteen years of full participation.

Of the twenty-three who remain at Downs most are not as active as they were during the period of this study. With few exceptions they attend services regularly but have relinquished the leadership roles. Now they want to enjoy the spiritual nourishment without the obligations of official duties. In some cases their interests in career, community, or social areas demand more time than before and leave fewer hours for Downs. Burn-out has led others to step down and allow new members to take over the reins.

Each of the Downs people who are no longer associated with the church—including those who left because of unhappiness with the pastoral leadership—spoke with love and enthusiasm about their experiences at Downs, and each has maintained uninterrupted contact with more than one fellow Downs member. Regardless of the reasons why the seventeen discontinued membership—choice of a different worship style or denomination, a move to a new city, or a disagreement with the ecclesiastical climate—they retain friendships that began at Downs. From time to time they return to the church, just as I do, for special events or to bring back pleasant recollections of an earlier period in their lives.

THREE

The Downs People as Individuals

INTRODUCTION TO THE PROFILES

This section, the profiles of the forty Downs people, is the heart of the book. By glimpsing into their lives I want to picture each of the Downs people as an individual who, in the company of the other thirty-nine, and the more than seven hundred members not profiled here, was one of the people who composed Downs Memorial United Methodist Church in the fifties and sixties. For me, and for the Downs people, our church was a comfortable environment that met our religious and social needs at the time. We were in the company of people who had similar backgrounds: strong parental support, familial church involvement, emphasis on higher education, and commitment to public service. At Downs our ambitions were nourished through spiritual channels, and our participation was encouraged in political and social activities that were important to black people. This is the setting in which I first met the Downs people and began an association that has lasted in some ways to the present, although I am no longer officially affiliated with the church.

The similarity in the backgrounds of the Downs people is balanced by differences in personality and ultimate self-development, which preserve sufficient autonomy in their thoughts and accomplishments. The profiles reveal an extensive interaction among the forty members that goes beyond the church and does not depend wholly upon regular association with Downs. They share interests in things having to do with careers, politics, community concerns, and social activities, and many have made long-lasting friendships.

Gertrude Hines and Wesley Jones are concerned about the adoption of African-American children. There is a specific inter-weaving of the responsibilities of Dorene Walton, Ella Wiley, and Dorothy Lee as teachers and administrators in the elementary schools of Richmond, California. Dorothy Pitts and Warren Wide-ner worked together for the city of Berkeley. Walter Morris and Vertis Thompson were classmates in Howard University School of Medicine and pooled their resources in 1959 to construct an office building in Oakland for themselves and other health prac-titioners. Dorothy Lee and Elizabeth Pettus share a commitment to Delta Sigma Theta sorority, which brings them together in times and places that are independent of church in projects that do not necessarily have a religious orientation. Becoming a mem-ber of the Church of Religious Science makes me again a fellow worshipper with two former Downs people, Phillip Raymond and Jack Costa. Their spiritual evolution parallels mine.

Downs was the spawning ground for two informal groups of women, the Delights and the Eight of Us. Both include women whom I have selected as Downs people and others who are mar-ried to men included with the Downs people. The impetus for their alliances came as friends who enjoyed each other's company and wanted to extend their camaraderie beyond the regular church services. The Delights and the Eight of Us still function with their basic goals intact and only a few changes in their rosters, generally due to death or a member moving away from the area.

With one exception all of the Downs people readily consented to being part of this collection. The exception could not believe that anyone would be interested in what he had to say, or that his life, which he did not consider exceptional, should be put along-side others that he thought were much more interesting. When he consented to participate, he was very gracious with the hours that he gave me from his crowded work days. At the end he repeated what I had heard from almost all of the Downs people— that he had found it personally rewarding to relive memories that had long been dormant, and to articulate ideas and feelings that he had not taken the time to examine.

The profiles begin with a picture of my life, from Victoria, Texas, to Houston, Texas, to Oakland, California, and continue with summaries of my conversations with each of the Downs people.

DONA IRVIN
Born 1917, Victoria, Texas

"From Victoria, Texas, to Houston, Texas, to Oakland, California, and Downs Memorial United Methodist Church."

In the early fifties my husband, Frank, and I realized that we needed to find a church for our family. I had begun to feel the urge to continue the tradition of church affiliation that was part of my childhood and my adult life before I came to California in 1942. Frank remembered a talk by Roy Nichols, then a student at Pacific School of Religion in Berkeley, who had since become pastor of Downs Memorial United Methodist Church. One worship service there made the choice for me. I liked the emphasis on current topics and the general atmosphere of warmth and friendship. Right away I began an association that would continue for nearly fifteen years and made my first acquaintance with the men, women, and young people whom I now identify as the Downs people.

From our house on Sixty-first Street in Oakland it took twelve minutes by car to cover the three-mile distance to Downs church. First we turned onto Alcatraz Avenue, and before long we crossed the city limit into Berkeley. After driving several minutes more, we reentered Oakland and continued until we reached the intersection of Sixty-first Street and Idaho Street where the church stands. We had gone from one part of Sixty-first Street in Oakland to another part of that same street, still in Oakland, having traversed a section of Berkeley before returning to Oakland. It was a nice ride.

We passed homes that looked much like our own and small places of business, some black-owned, closed for the Sabbath. Near the corner of Alcatraz and Grove Street (now Martin Luther King, Jr., Way) there was Cramer's Style House where I had regularly gone to "Mr. A. G. Cramer, II, Stylist," on Saturday mornings so he could do my hair. Nearby was the office of Leonard Wallace and his staff of real estate brokers and salesmen. Years later an agent from this office helped us purchase the house that we now call home. Farther along was the shoe repair shop owned and operated by Mr. Hooper, a Tuskegee graduate. His machines repaired the soles of our shoes and put on new heels.

From the fifties when I first went to Downs Memorial Church until 1963, it was the single most influential factor in my life besides my family. It was a young congregation; few people were older than thirty-five, and I can recall only one funeral. There were other parents whose goals corresponded with those that I had for my child, and the youth program offered opportunities for her to interact with her peers in a way that I approved. The young people had social hours, and they had opportunities to sharpen their skills in program planning and implementation and by presenting well-rehearsed reports to the congregation on Sunday mornings. I liked the satisfaction of knowing that the center of my daughter's social life was in the company of boys and girls who went to Downs. Their parties were chaperoned by parents, and the outdoor activities were in the company of advisors who were representatives of the church. Before she was licensed to drive a car, I did not think of driving her from place to place as an unwanted chore. I was an usher and helped organize church programs—those that were religious, political, or purely social—but my greatest pleasure was the Wednesday potluck dinners.

In my mind the designation *Downs church* has a double significance. The name *Downs* stands as an honor to the late Reverend Karl Downs. But the word *down,* as in goose down, conjures up an image of a soft and warm envelopment, a reassuring and comforting situation, a place of love and intimacy where I was nourished by the ministry of the pastor and embraced by the fellowship of kindred souls at the church. This marvel was made tangible to me when Frank and I had concluded our two-year stay in Ghana, West Africa, and were on our way back home to California. We had a brief visit in Zurich, Switzerland, immediately after leaving the African continent and its hot tropical climate. Zurich was cold and dreary and dark when we arrived; we knew no one in the city and did not speak any language other than English. Finally, after a delay in customs the taxi driver deposited us at our hotel. I was ready for the night's rest. I snuggled into a bed with a divinely soft, huge, goose down comforter, and I lay my head on a pillow stuffed to capacity with goose down feathers. Here was an awakening of the memories of Downs Church and the friends who awaited me in Oakland. It was the literal incarnation of all of the good feelings of my young days—the love of family, the endearment of friends, and the warmth of my life at Downs. I did not return to Downs but I readily resumed friendship with some of its people.

I am the youngest of five children, all born in Victoria, Texas, to parents who had met in 1900 when my father was my mother's teacher at Straight University in New Orleans. She was pretty, light-skinned, and an undergraduate from Opelousas, Louisiana. He was from Lake Charles, Louisiana, a dark-skinned, handsome man of regal bearing. His five children were much closer to him in skin tones than they were to Mama and would never be mistaken for white, as she often was. After Papa's graduation from Straight, instead of returning to his hometown he remained at the college as an instructor. When Mama got her degree they were married and went to live in Victoria, Texas, where he taught in the segregated "colored" schools.

Shortly after my seventh birthday Papa resigned his position as principal of Victoria Colored High School and moved his family to Houston to become National Grand Secretary of the United Brothers of Friendship and Sisters of the Mysterious Ten (UBF & SMT). This was in the heyday of the secret benevolent societies that offered social activities, life insurance, and sick benefits to black people prior to the advent of social security and welfare payments, and before this country's insurance industry was ready to sell protection to black folks. There were business meetings, programs, social events, special observances, and secret initiations of new members. The rituals and panoply were respected and coveted. I was very proud of my father's position.

So much of what happened in my young life was dictated by the church. Papa held many church offices, and Mama played the piano to accompany the choir in which all of the family except me sang. The dominant influence of the church and its people was repeated much later at Downs. Because of my father's position as teacher and principal of a school and later as an official of a national organization, our family was included in African-American middle-class society. This was acceptable only to the degree that it did not conflict with the dogma of our Baptist church. I could make full use of the local colored YWCA and the segregated library, but dancing, card playing, and other frivolity were taboo. Few of Hollywood's productions passed the strict inspection of my parents. Only a limited number of my schoolmates were worthy of my association; they had to conform to Mama's appraisal of their social and moral integrity. I envied the easy friendships my schoolmates shared and their casual visits from one home to another.

Papa died when I was 16, just before I entered college. The magnificent display of his funeral procession that marched from the Hammond Funeral Parlor on Swartz Street to Mount Corinth Baptist Church, some six blocks away, did much to allay my adolescent grief. First came the all-male band, resplendent in their navy blue uniforms, followed by the men of the UBF and then the women of the SMT, all dressed in the formal regalia that was reserved to honor a deceased member. The well-attended services at the church and at the grave site were a perfect blending of Christian and fraternal ceremony.

I spent my first two college years at Prairie View, fifty miles from Houston, and the next two at Texas Southern University in Houston. There I met Frank, fell in love, and eloped with him in my senior year. When I graduated in 1937 it was called Houston College for Negroes. We stayed in Houston until World War II. Then, Frank and I, with Frank, Jr., (who died when he was five) and our ten-week-old infant daughter, Nell, joined the migration of blacks to California. We were in pursuit of a life that would be free from racial insults and would allow us to work

toward financial security in the high-paying west coast shipyards. I came with dreams of a pink stucco house in the ideal
situation of a Hollywood movie. I did not get the pink stucco,
but years later we bought a brown shingle house of the architec-
tural design that is still popular in the East Bay Area and began
a new life.

Beginning in 1963 Frank had the opportunity to work as chief
technician in the chemistry department at the University of
Ghana, and the contract allowed me to accompany him. We
were in Ghana for two years and had a part in its development.
It was a wonderful introduction to the variations of culture,
political thought, and economic evolvement that exist outside
of our own country. While we were there, I taught English as a
second language to junior staff of the university—Ghanaians
who did semiskilled and unskilled work. They were adults who
spoke English well enough to operate successfully in that English-speaking environment, but their English reading skills
were on a primary level. My classes were part of the country's
mass education drive to eliminate illiteracy. The textbooks provided by the Ministry of Education for adult classes contained
material that fit in with the everyday lives of my students. I
revelled in the chance to be part of the racial majority of Ghana.
It was good to do all of my business with people who looked like
me—from the man who cut our grass to the president of our
bank. Like everyone else standing on the side of the road, I
waved my white handkerchief to greet the Ghanaian president,
Kwame Nkrumah, as he drove by on Achimota Road in Accra.

When we returned to Oakland from West Africa in 1965,
Nichols had left Downs for New York City and took away all
incentive for us to return to our former church. Sundays became the time for other forms of activity and relaxation. I used
those hours to prepare for the next week's work, go on bicycle
rides, enjoy sports programs, or visit friends. The spiritual side
of my life was dormant for nearly twenty years. Yet all the while
my interaction with friends from Downs continued without any
break. In 1968 my life changed distinctly. At age fifty-one, after
working on a series of unfulfilling jobs, I wanted more of a challenge. The civil rights movement had made it easier for a black

woman my age, who had been out of the job market for five years, to be considered a viable candidate for an administrative position. At the same time, the University of California was adding to its small number of black employees. I took a job as head counselor in the Student Personnel Office of the Division of Teacher Education in the School of Education. Five years later I went to Oakland Public Schools and worked as a personnel assistant until I retired in July 1982.

Retirement brought a need to grapple with thoughts of a very serious nature. By that time three of my four siblings had died, and I was forced to contemplate for the first time thoughts about my own mortality. And there was an awareness of a persistent vacuum in my life—an absence of spiritual nourishment to bring peace to that part of my being. Frank had discovered the Church of Religious Science, and because I saw in him an increased self-assurance and the acceptance of a healthful, prosperous future, I began to listen to their teachings. Along with some others that I had known from Downs, I joined that church.

My personal impact upon my community centered around the education of public school students. At the University of California I assisted potential teachers in developing the skills they would bring to the mostly ethnic minority boys and girls in the inner city. I worked in Oakland Public Schools at a time when affirmative action was a serious part of personnel selection. We were concerned with the candidate's knowledge of subject matter and teaching methods, the applicant's understanding of the needs of the students at the specific school site, and the effect the assignment of that individual would have upon the total ethnic and social composition of the school staff.

It was inevitable that the course of my life would lead me to Downs where I could bring my talents and gifts to its well-grounded program that was directed toward the betterment of the community. Even though I am no longer a part of the congregation, the Downs influence continues in my ongoing involvement in community efforts and my friendship with individuals from the church. I include myself with them as part of the bypassed middle level of African-Americans who are not usually heard from but whose experiences and accomplishments have made a difference in the total community.

CHARLES AIKENS
Born 1943, Columbia, Mississippi

"I wanted to call attention to the fact that all kids can learn; it's just that the pursuit of excellence seems to be missing among the flat land kids."

From secondary school into young adulthood Charles Aikens was a part of the youth contingent at Downs. He participated as an officer of the Methodist Youth Fellowship and as an actor in Easter and Christmas pageants. The counsel of the minister and members of the church after he graduated from high school had a strong influence on the development of his adult life.

The glamour of life as a professional baseball player had been a longtime dream for Aikens, but the actuality did not fulfill his youthful expectations. After he graduated from Oakland's McClymonds High School in 1959, he signed a contract with the Baltimore Orioles. He was appalled by the treatment of black players and organized a protest and presented a list of grievances to management along with the statistics of each of the players. Although he was considered the number one prospect in the Orioles' minor league, having had two seasons of .330 and .278, he was immediately shipped out. The protest experience proved to be a costly one: it signaled the finish of his brief career in sports.

With the professional ball episode behind him, Aikens returned to Oakland and to Downs in 1961, having only a high school education and no interest in continued study. In response to Aikens's complaint that times were "getting real hard" with no jobs available, Nichols told the young man that this would always be the case for people who did not prepare themselves for career opportunities. Fellow members of Downs encouraged him to enter college, telling him that the sports world was not the only avenue open to him. This advice, coupled with interacting with successful fellow church members, made it easier for him to enter college. He developed an interest in journalism, in teaching and writing, and in public service. By the time he was a senior at California State University, Hayward, he was a Ford Foundation fellow studying political and urban affairs and reporting in Washington, D.C., under Supreme Court Justice Thurgood Marshall, Senate Minority Leader Gerald Ford, former Secretary of State George Schultz, and television journalist Eric Sevaried. He attended seminars and visited the White House, the Pentagon, the Supreme Court, and the Press Club.

As a fellowship student, Aikens was assigned to help with the research for the book *Repression of the Black Panthers.* In the Oakland segment of the research, he interviewed David Hilliard (one of the founders of the Panthers) and saw the sand bags that the Panthers put up as protection from the gunfire of the Oakland police in their raids upon the group's headquarters in west Oakland. With Hilliard he shared the emotions of the young men who were challenging the system and who knew the physical dangers that faced them. Then he interviewed Oakland Police Chief Charles Gains, Judge Cecil Poole, and instructors at Merritt Community College who had taught Huey Newton and Bobby Seale when they were organizing the Panthers. During the New York segment of the fellowship, Aikens attended the trial of the New York Twenty-One, Panthers who were charged with threatening to blow up the Statue of Liberty. In contrast to the alleged radical actions of the Panthers that were emphasized at the trial, Aikens had seen firsthand the beneficial effects of their breakfast program for children in Harlem, which fed children breakfast before they went to school—often the only hot food the children had for the day. The exposure to the governmental operations in Washington and researching the book project convinced Aikens that he wanted to become a journalist.

When he completed the fellowship, instead of going back to school to finish the course work for his degree, Aikens became an intern reporter for the San Francisco bureau of *Newsweek* magazine. *Newsweek* wanted a "diamond in the rough" whose potential had not been developed and whose skills they could

sharpen. Within a few months Aikens realized that his future in
the media would be more secure if he had a degree. He went
back to Hayward State and received a bachelor's degree in journalism in 1971. Seven years later in 1978, he was awarded a
master's degree in educational public relations from the University of San Francisco.

Aikens worked as a reporter for the *Oakland Tribune* and
the *Oakland Post* newspapers. He taught journalism and creative writing and served as newspaper advisor at North Peralta
and Merritt community colleges. He was newspaper advisor to
student activists who had high visibility on campus and in the
community, and who were anxious to bring their political ide-
ologies to the public. Aikens's responsibility was to assist them
in using that forum to disseminate information about their
causes in ways that did not offend the majority of the readers,
but at the same time he wanted them to develop a seriousness
about education comparable to their political devotion. In one
instance he convinced them that they could be effective without printing the picture of a naked woman on the front page of
an edition.

From 1976 to 1984 Aikens worked in public information and
public relations, first at Oakland Public Schools and then at the
Oakland-Alameda County Coliseum. At the coliseum he soon
became disillusioned with his position as director of promotions and public relations. He found himself surrounded by
false prestige and occupied with chores that he termed trivia—
writing news releases, developing policy statements for employees, leading tours of the facility, and arranging speaking
engagements for the staff. Aikens left the coliseum to write a
book about the sprinter Jim Hines, who became known as "the
world's fastest human" when he set the record for the hundred
meter dash in the 1968 Mexico City Olympics. The book highlights the background and aspirations of Hines and other African-American athletes, including Aikens himself.

Now Aikens wears four working hats, all in career areas of
his choice. On a part-time basis he teaches public relations and
journalism at DeAnza Community College and works as a scout
for the Milwaukee Brewers baseball club. In journalism he is

news editor for the Oakland-based weekly newspaper, the *California Voice* (published by Ruth Love). Aikens operates National Promotions and Public Relations, an enterprise to promote clients, predominantly in the entertainment field, by developing complete press kits about them and securing performance bookings. He also helps his clients manage their finances.

After giving serious thought to the differences in the test scores in hill area schools and those in the flat lands, Aikens entered the race for election to the Oakland School Board in 1986. He remembered the change in the learning habits of his sisters when they transferred from schools in west Oakland to another part of the city where the learning atmosphere was more stimulating. Aikens wanted to proclaim loudly that all children can learn if they are given the right learning environment with teachers who have both an understanding of their cultural traditions and good motivational tools. His goal was to prevent students in the Oakland schools from graduating high school without knowing how to write a sentence. His first bid for election was unsuccessful, but Aikens was grateful for the number of votes he received in comparison with those his opponents received with far larger campaign funds. Aikens has vowed to run again.

Aikens describes himself as a late starter. He began as a young boy whose almost exclusive interest in sports caused him to waste valuable time, which delayed his metamorphosis into a man with a desire to read book after book and explore all avenues of learning in an attempt to make up for those squandered hours. He is now reading, writing nonfiction, and trying to help other people from his vantage point of having had experiences and having made contacts in the school district, the larger community, and the political arena.

Charles Aikens is one of the Downs people who progressed from teenager to adulthood during my years at Downs. I first knew him as a high school student, pleasant in manners and faithful in attendance at youth activities and Sunday morning services. It was obvious that as a young person he had been taught well at home and was receptive to further tutelage by role models at Downs.

GORDON BARANCO
Born 1948, Oakland, California

"I decided at an early age that I really liked the political aspect of being a lawyer. Plus, I have all of those relatives from Louisiana who would come out every summer and say, 'Boy, what are you going to do with yourself?' I would have to give them an answer."

Gordon Baranco went to Downs because he was obliged to accompany his parents. The family of five attended Sunday services regularly, but Baranco was not part of the religious activities for young people. Even now when he and Wesley Jones, the director of the youth organizations and coach of the church's basketball team (of which Baranco was a star player), talk about the Downs experience, they remember that the team was the main thing that kept the boy coming to church. Baranco has fond memories of having to put one dollar out of his five-dollar monthly allowance into the collection plate, of the lasting friendships from that time, and of the games the team played under the mild-mannered Jones. He continued at Downs until he went away to college.

Baranco's mother and father told their sons and daughter to choose occupations where they could be of service to other people and convinced them that this need not be a dull way to make a living. He considers being a judge in the superior courts of California and his volunteer community service as repaying the assistance that he has received. It was not difficult for Baranco to choose a career. He thinks of himself as an argumentative, independent person who makes his own decisions, and he had been taught that he had to have a career goal firmly in mind. From junior high school he was determined to be an attorney, so the logical step after high school was for him to enter the University of California–Davis where he earned both his bachelor's and law degrees.

Baranco spent the first year after law school as a legal assistant in the California state attorney general's office in San Francisco. He worked as an attorney representing the state licensing board in administrative hearings to determine if an applicant was suitable for a particular license, or if there was a record of a criminal conviction that would make the candidate a poor risk. For the next three years he was deputy district attorney in San Francisco, a trial attorney in that large urban area. Still in San Francisco, Baranco next became managing attorney for Neighborhood Legal Assistance in the Hunters Point district. This office advocated for mostly poor black people in civil matters such as landlord-tenant disputes, marital dissolutions, probates and wills, and conservatorships and guardianships. From Neighborhood Legal Assistance Baranco returned to Oakland in 1980 where he worked for five months as assistant city attorney handling general civil litigations and lawsuits for the city and advising the city attorney and the city council in legal matters.

On September 18, 1980, Baranco received a telephone call from Gov. Jerry Brown's office with the offer of an appointment to the bench of the Oakland-Piedmont-Emeryville Municipal Court. According to Baranco, a municipal court judge generally deals in people-volume work in which legal preparation is certainly required, but at times the position calls for a combination of clerical skills, social work, and judicial expertise. He heard cases having to do with misdemeanors, which include drunk driving, hit-and-run driving, and driving with a suspended or revoked license. For the last two years in the municipal court, Baranco acted as presiding judge of that arm of the judicial system of the East Bay Area. The present step in Baranco's career began when Gov. George Deukmejian called to inform Baranco that effective April 23, 1984, he had been appointed judge of the Superior Court of California. Baranco was gratified to know that someone thought that he was professionally qualified for this appointment. In superior court Baranco hears cases that are of a more serious nature and draw from more diverse areas of the law.

Baranco thinks he has made a significant difference in the quality of the lives of a large number of people in each of his jobs. He agrees with Victor Hugo's belief that every man or woman, on the basis of his or her own suffering and experience, builds for everyone else. Each experience has given him a chance to make a difference in his community. Although he acknowledged that it is good to have the power and the authority of a superior court judge, Baranco wondered if he is actually doing any more for humanity now than he did when he was an attorney for the legal aid group in Hunters Point. There he offered professional legal services for poor African-Americans, people who were conditioned to think of black attorneys as inferior to white ones. They thought that black lawyers did not read the same law books and were not as well trained, and they shared a prejudice against legal aid attorneys.

He also remembers when he was the only African-American in the district attorney's office in San Francisco; he made an effort to communicate to his coworkers the sensitivity that was needed in the courts where the majority of defendants were poor and black. The office at that time was run like a fraternity house whose brothers were from the Irish and Italian Catholic population that had little contact with or understanding of the black community.

Sitting as a judge in the courts in Oakland, Baranco is saddened by the overwhelming imbalance of the large number of black defendants in criminal matters and the small representation of African-Americans in decision-making positions in the judicial system. He sees defendants who went to school with him and who offer as defense the terrible circumstances of their lives. He is sympathetic to their general plight, and having been raised in the city, he knows the obstacles of that environment. However, he is aware of a broader picture that includes the criminal's responsibility for him or herself. He rejects the explanation that the high crime rate is the result of a genetic aberration among black people and sees the reasons as having to do with a combination of the effects of poverty, the lack of formal education, the pervasive racism of our society, and exploitation; all of which provide fertile breeding ground for frustration and crime because the situation limits the defendant's world where expectations cannot be realized. Baranco is not surprised that people who are victims of these circumstances often seem to feel that the way to solve problems is by antisocial actions: money can be easily earned by selling cocaine, sexual gratification is best achieved by relations with children, and the only way to retaliate against women is to rape them.

From the start of his legal career Baranco's community service has encompassed an interracial, intercultural, and interfaith aspect. His membership on the board of the Chinese Community Council in Oakland's Chinatown came about because of his interaction with the Chinese community through his Chinese-American wife, Barbara, whom he married in 1980 after a courtship that had begun in high school. He also served on the boards of the Young Community Developers in the all-black Hunters Point section of San Francisco, the Northern California Conference of Christians and Jews, the University of California–Davis Alumni Association, the Alameda County Red Cross, and the Black Lawyers' Association.

Serving on the board of governors for the Conference of Christians and Jews has been a learning process for Baranco. Here he was in the company of fellow directors who had expertise in corporate and money matters, and who spoke in what he termed a foreign language about their extensive financial dealings. Baranco's assignments for this board were to help conduct seminars on affirmative action for local business people, and to assist in setting up programs where urban young people visit rural areas for exposure to different life-styles. Baranco especially enjoys the involvement with the Chinese Community Council, a long-established social service agency that is concerned with refugee and relocation problems, employment training, and bilingual education. This gives him the opportunity for cultural exchange and a chance to take part in board meetings that, due to the council's excellent organization, are free from the typical yelling and fighting about money.

Throughout the four years Baranco served on the board of University of California–Davis Alumni Association, he chose the nominating and membership committee so he could get more African-American representation on the board. Traditionally the alumni association was run by predominately older white agribusinessmen, graduates from the days when Davis was an agricultural college. As he expected, their memory of the campus and their outlook upon the best ways to meet the financial, social, and educational needs of an ethnically and socio-economically changing student body were far different from his.

The year 1982 brought two distinguished awards to Baranco. He was named Berkeley Jaycees Young Californian of the Year and University of California–Davis Young Alumnus of the Year. Both recognitions were in appreciation of his donation of time to community service and his standing in the professional world. Gordon Baranco is also one of the alumni of the Oakland Public Schools whose portrait hangs in the meeting room of the board of education to motivate and encourage students and staff by his successful career and his commitment to public service.

In Judge Baranco's chambers there is a portrait of "The Supreme Court," fifteen young men dressed in basketball uniforms (instead of black robes) surrounded by basketballs and other basketball paraphernalia. I thought of Baranco on the basketball team at Downs two decades ago and savored this portrait as proof that he had not lost his love for basketball. I found a happy blending of the devoted family man, serious servant of the courts of the law, and athlete, one who enjoys the exhilaration of spirited exercise and good natured competition.

LAURENCE "LARRY" BOLLING
Born 1918, Richmond, Virginia

"I just want people to use me up to the hilt until I die."

In appreciation of Laurence Bolling's more than forty years of unselfish service, Downs sponsored a "Salute to Laurence Delaware Bolling" in December 1990. The event, which was held only a few months after the death of his wife, Letitia, was an outpouring of love from both the church and the community with ecumenical and interracial representation. For Downs this was the chance to thank Bolling for his work as financial secretary, chair of the Pastor/Parish Committee, teacher in the Sunday School, singer in the choir, and regular attender of Bible classes and prayer meetings.

The success of Laurence Bolling as a community and church activist is the result of his parents' training and the example of their lives. Money was scarce and came through hard labor.

Bolling's mother took in washing to supplement his father's wages, which never exceeded twenty dollars a week. In high school Bolling enjoyed a popularity that resulted from his outgoing personality and the esteem with which his family was regarded. And he was welcomed into the homes of friends who were more affluent than he and included in their social activities. He knew that he was not limited by his reduced financial status. With encouragement from his mother, Bolling vowed to become an ordained minister. She felt that the honorable vocations for a man were medicine, the ministry, or letter carrier, ranked in that order in terms of respectability.

To prepare for the ministry, Bolling enrolled in the school of theology at Virginia Union University after he graduated from high school in 1934. The struggles of the depression interrupted his study, and his plans for a career as a minister were aborted. He then went to Van deVyver Institute, a Roman Catholic business school, where he studied economics, business management, typing, and Gregg shorthand. The shorthand was useful in the army because his assigned duty was to transcribe and record the proceedings of court martials. The other training was of value when he went into business after he left the army.

The romance between Bolling and Letitia began when they met at the USO in Oakland in 1942 during World War II. They spent as much time together as possible during the six weeks Bolling had before he was shipped overseas to the Pacific Theater. Thoughts of the waiting Letitia made the three years in the Russell Islands, Guadalcanal, the Hebrides, the Imari Islands, and the Philippines more tolerable for Bolling. "We had never spent more than that month together, but somehow we just knew that we were going to get married." They wrote each other daily and were married in 1946, three days after he returned to California.

Bolling's parents were convinced that the South's need was greater than California's for the service that Laurence could offer his community. Mrs. Mary McLeod Bethune, educator, member of President Roosevelt's "Black Cabinet," and champion of Negro rights before the civil rights movement, offered to find employment for Bolling if he would return to the South after the war and take up the leadership of the NAACP branches in Maryland. Bolling had worked with the NAACP in the thirties and forties and had experienced the adversities of public service in an unfriendly environment when he helped to found new chapters throughout Virginia, North and South Carolina, and Florida. NAACP workers were often run out of town in the middle of the night.

Bolling's decision after the war was to settle in Oakland with his bride and assume the management of the W. J. Carter Box Company, the well-established business that was owned and operated by his father-in-law. Mr. Carter had begun this innovative enterprise in 1906 soon after the San Francisco earthquake. He salvaged used boxes from ships at San Francisco's booming port, repaired, and resold them. With time Bolling's parents came to understand his motives for staying in California and were happy with their son's ability to successfully operate his commercial establishment.

Bolling feels that he failed to respond to a divine call to the service of the Lord as a minister. He regrets that he did not make the financial sacrifices to continue seminary—instead he let his desire to reap immediate rewards take precedence over his commitment. I suggested that his service to Downs, to the religious life of the community, and to the broader concerns of the East Bay might satisfy the call to the ministry. He could accept it as compensation for half of his obligation, but not as total fulfillment.

From the beginning of his public service with the Virginia NAACP, Bolling has continued to respond to the needs of his community in a variety of ways. For more than ten years he has been associated with the United Way, a portion of that time as chairman of the executive committee of United Way of America, and with its international group. He sits on the board of the Bay Area Black United Fund, a public agency whose raison d'etre is to respond to the societal needs of the African-American community. Bolling supports it wholeheartedly, but he would welcome its obsolescence if it came about by United Way's more meaningful attention to the critical needs of African-Americans, such as the drug menace and the accompanying slayings in Oakland.

In the sixties Bolling was president of the Metropolitan YMCA of Oakland, the first black person to occupy that position in a metropolitan YMCA. Currently he is a member of the city's recreation commission, the same commission Joshua Rose served on as the first African-American member. There was a hint of resentment in Bolling's voice when he spoke about his involvement with the public schools of Oakland. He had been a resource person during the administrations of superintendents Marcus Foster and Ruth Love. Bolling chaired a committee that explored the question of whether to close some underused school sites. Their report detailed well-defined steps that could be taken in the instance of each of the contestable physical plants. When the succeeding boards and administrations arrived, they did not appreciate what had been researched previously and wanted data that had been collected by their own appointees. Bolling wondered whether their unwillingness to give Love credit stemmed from the fact that she was the first female leader and a black woman.

Bolling's reputation as a speaker brings a flow of requests for appearances. His biggest thrill in this role came in 1975 when he addressed the annual prayer breakfast of the late mayor of Chicago, Richard J. Daley. He received VIP treatment as a guest of the mayor: limousine transportation with a police escort, palatial accommodations in the Hilton with a guard at the door, and exquisite food. Bolling spoke with humor about the vigilant protection, a shielding so efficient that if he had wanted to sin a little bit in the big city, it would have been impossible. Another rewarding appearance was in October 1983 when he appeared as keynote speaker when Milwaukee, Wisconsin, honored its black achievers, young men and women who make a difference in the social climate of their city.

The partnership of Bolling's commitment to public service and his religious beliefs is illustrated by the struggle he faced in his unsuccessful candidacy for the Oakland City Council in the seventies. The Police Officers Association supported him and made a contribution of twenty-five hundred dollars. The Concerned Citizens of Oakland (CCO), an all-white, conservative, right-wing, law-and-order group gave their endorsement initially. However, when Bolling told them that the books of the city should be open to citizens for review they withdrew their support. He learned about their action the following day when the *Oakland Tribune* informed its readers that the CCO had "dropped Bolling."

The defeat at the polls taught Bolling that without the financial resources to run as an independent he needed powerful backing, and that there are some things you do not say publicly until after you are elected. He learned that it is difficult to be a politician and a Sunday school teacher at the same time. Sometimes honesty forbade him from saying and doing the things that were expected of him as a candidate. His assessment of the experience is that he was too naive and too new to the political arena. "The influence of parents and the church background and the teachings of the Bible made me have to tell people honestly what it is. They say you can't do that if you want to be elected."

If I were asked to name the people who epitomize the spirit of Downs in the Nichols years, I would rank Larry Bolling right after the pastor in the company of B. L. Vaughn and Irvin Fuller. Bolling was there every Sunday in the bass section of the choir. He presided over the offertory, and after we had put our envelopes into the collection plates he led the congregational response, "All things come of thee, oh Lord, and of thine own have we given thee." It was reassuring to know that Laurence Bolling was taking part in the monitoring of the fiscal matters of our church.

HERMAN SEBASTIAN BOSSET
Born 1938, Los Angeles, California

"Vaughn was more than a builder of material things. He built me. He built something in me that was concrete, like the concrete he poured in the ground."

In addition to cherishing his relationship with B. L. Vaughn, who introduced him to Downs church at a crucial time in his young life, Herman Bosset has fond memories of the camaraderie with his boyhood friends there. The young people attended different schools during the week but were part of the same meetings, programs, picnics, retreats, and "good clean fun" at Downs. They loved each other.

Herman Bosset was lucky to fall under the influence of the late B. L. Vaughn during his preteen years and to have Vaughn take the place of his father, a bartender whose death had been hastened by heavy consumption of alcohol. His mother was a Hollywood actress who played the maid in Charlie Chan movies with Mantan Moreland and had a role in *Stormy Weather* with Lena Horne. Bosset was born in Los Angeles and lived there until he was about ten years old. When his parents divorced he came to Berkeley to live with his grandmother on Boise Street very near the home of the Vaughn family. By his own admission, Bosset was a "pretty frisky little boy." He first met Vaughn when he was hurling rocks at a barn next door to the lot where Vaughn was building his house. Vaughn told Bosset to stop, and the ten-year-old boy ran home full of shame and resentment. However, he was curious enough to return the next day to see what the builder was doing. Vaughn asked him, "Do you want to help?" He answered, "Yeah." The man and boy worked side by side with shovel and pick and became friends. Vaughn took an interest in the spirited young boy. His firm, yet loving discipline and care helped to shape the future man. Vaughn taught him to pour concrete and to make bricks, and later under his direction, Bosset and his friends from the Methodist Youth Fellowship invested their physical strength in the construction of Downs's sanctuary. Bosset drew an analogy between his part in the building of the church edifice and the simultaneous building of his personal character. He thought of Vaughn as more than a builder of bricks, houses, and churches; he helped to build Herman Bosset, the person.

Bosset spent fifteen years, from 1959 to 1974, in the Marine Corps. Within that time he was in Vietnam from 1966 to 1968 where he saw horrible, brutal actions. One such incident occurred in the Aschow Valley where demolitions had blown up the tunnels of the Vietcong. After the destruction was complete, the next chore was to "bring up the bodies, torsos with entrails coming up out of the top of their heads, heads blown off, pieces of legs, just human meat." They stacked the remains in piles, and soon dogs, birds, and flies started to feed on the carnage—this a mere fifty yards from the waiting marines. A member of Bosset's unit was so shaken that he took gasoline and set the pile on fire.

On a med cap patrol, which involved marines going to villages to give medicine, aspirin, or salves as a gesture of friendship, in the Danang area there was a carpenter, his son, a daughter, and a grandchild. The man asked the marines to spend the night with them because he feared for their safety. The officers in charge would not allow the troops to stay but promised to return the next morning. They ate Vietnamese duck and drank Vietnamese whiskey with the family and could see that the man was desperate for them to stay overnight, but the decision was not left to the enlisted men. The following day they found the bodies of the family with the heads placed on top of their chests.

When the news of the assassination of Martin Luther King, Jr., reached the African-American marines they wondered aloud, "What in the hell are we doing here?" They were fighting a war in Vietnam and other people were fighting a war at home. *The Stars and Stripes* carried a picture of a twelve-year-old African-American boy lying in the street with a white cop standing over him holding a shotgun. Bosset read about riots and killings in Newark, New Jersey: African-Americans and whites fighting each other while he was in Asia fighting a man and a woman and a child he did not know.

After Bosset had seen the madness in Vietnam, he said to himself that there had to be something more, something that he could do to help unify humanity to compensate for the killing. He had seen the reduction of human beings to the level of animals, the victims as well as those who represented the military power of the United States. The human relations program of the Marine Corps was the answer. He volunteered for that section and was assigned to the Japanese-American Friendship and Cultural Association (JAFCA) in Japan. JAFCA attempted to bridge the gap of misunderstanding by teaching American servicemen about Japanese culture and customs. It offered a human relations course to help the men get along better with the people of different cultures within their own units. JAFCA sent the men to orphanages, jails, and restaurants in Japan. Students at Hiroshima University, the site of JAFCA, and the American GI's interacted with each other. Because of the effectiveness of the program there was a decline in disruptive incidents.

An unfortunate episode did occur, however, one night in 1972 when four servicemen were drinking underneath the oldest bridge in Japan, the Kentai Bridge. This bridge, a cultural symbol to the Japanese people, is thousands of years old and made without nails or iron, only Japanese rosewood, the heaviest, hardest, and most beautiful wood in the country. In a drunken condition, the men chopped some of the wood from the bridge and burned it for warmth. Their action caused a great furor. The emperor wanted all of the American troops to leave the country immediately. It took a lot of diplomatic action involving high level representatives of the army and the diplomatic corps to ease the tension. JAFCA did its part by talking, negotiating, and understanding. The incident was not fully forgotten, but it is unlikely that such a thing will happen again.

When Bosset was in the service he was a coach of a boys' football team in the Pop Warner organization. He worked first with seven- and eight-year-old boys and then with twelve- and thirteen-year-old boys. It was more than the game of football; it was coaching, scouting, camping, and crafts because he wanted to give the boys experience in a wider area of involvement. Since 1978 Bosset has been an Alameda County probation officer and a group counselor working with young boys. He has learned that young people who are in trouble need love most of all and a sense of recognition. One boy told him, "Man, if just somebody gives a damn," an eloquent expression that relates directly back to what he has heard from parents: "Oh, I don't care anything about him. He's no good anyway." The children need love, support, and guidance from the adults who are part of their lives—factors that are missing for most of these troubled boys. Some of his charges have asked Bosset, "Would you be my Dad?" He has to be on guard not to become too emotionally involved and to maintain a balance of being tough when that is required, but soft when the time comes for a show of concern.

Bosset fears that without a restructuring of the family to show children that they are loved and recognized as individuals, there will be a generation of violent, antisocial people who are detriments to the community. He thinks that the change must take place within the walls of the homes and within the hearts of parents. Sometimes Bosset gets discouraged when he considers the conditions at his work or when he thinks about the years in Vietnam. Then he remembers the fate of his father and two uncles who drank themselves to death. He is thankful that he does not need to seek solace from the bottle or drugs or vent his feelings by cussing out his neighbor. He is thankful that his young children are healthy, physically and mentally. Bosset often thinks of B. L. Vaughn and the strength that he derived from him. He remembers his association with the young people at Downs and knows that growing up the way he did, he could have developed in a totally different direction. He accepts his shortcomings and the mistakes he has made but knows he is on the right road. In the words of a popular song of many years ago, Bosset has learned to, "pick yourself up, dust yourself off, and start all over again."

My conversations with Herman Bosset were in my home. When he came the first time I was surprised to see a man on a motorcycle ride up to my house wearing the full regalia of a cyclist: boots, goggles, gloves, and helmet. After a moment I recognized him and could again see the lively, energetic boy atop the uncompleted roof of the church, working with B. L. Vaughn and the other men and boys, but at the same time looking for an opportunity to play a practical joke on a fellow worker. He had become an adult, a family man, but there was the same sparkle in his eyes, and the same gentleness that made it easy to appreciate his playfulness.

CURTIS BOWERS
Born 1928, Emanuel County, Georgia

"My brother took me down Sacramento Street, and it was clean, and he told me that this was the slums of California. I got a couple of little jobs doing repair work, and I got rewarded very well, so I decided that this was the land of opportunity."

Swainsboro, Georgia, was the closest town to the farm where Curtis Bowers was born and lived the first years of his life. He was born on his father's three hundred-acre farm in Emanuel County, Georgia. People who lived in the vicinity were farmers or worked at the local sawmill. Both of Bowers's parents paid poll taxes and took the examinations to vote in local and national elections. The foremost concern of Bowers's father was buying land and operating the farm efficiently so that he could provide for his family of three boys and five girls. He was a smart man who ran the cultivating and sowing and reaping as a business.

Bowers's father had little formal education; his wife taught him to read and write. He showed his business acumen at the onset of his married life when he convinced his wife's siblings to sell him the land that they had inherited from their parents. These fields, added to the share that had come to his wife, gave him a start toward the large farm that Bowers knew as a child. From time to time he purchased additional land to reach the total of three hundred acres.

Bowers attended Fort Valley State College in Fort Valley, Georgia, for two years and was then drafted into the army. He was discharged twenty-one months later in 1952 and came to Berkeley to visit his brother who had taken up residence there. He liked what he saw in Berkeley—the streets, houses, people, and the availability of work. Bowers returned to Georgia just long enough to marry his longtime sweetheart, Geraldine (now deceased). They returned to the East Bay, assured that they could live well here, financially and socially.

Within a month, with the encouragement of Nichols, Bowers went to work at the University of California–Berkeley. From his first position as a laboratory assistant whose chief duty was to set up and sometimes perform demonstrations of experiments to accompany the professors' lectures in large classroom settings, he rose through the ranks to his present position as management services officer in the College of Chemistry. In short, if Bowers should fail to carry out his duties of securing materials and space, the repercussions would affect the course offerings for students in chemistry or chemical engineering.

With amusement Bowers recalled the statement of the man who was superintendent of buildings and grounds during his first years on campus, "I will die and go to hell before I see a nigger sweep the floors of the university." Prior to his retirement, that person witnessed the beginning of Bowers's climb up the career ladder to his present status as third in command of the nonacademic administration of the College of Chemistry. The academic staff in the chemistry department includes more than one Nobel Prize winner. Bowers feels free to knock on the door of any one of these learned men and walk in to discuss the business of the day without feeling intimidated by racial differences.

In July 1990 Curtis Bowers was one of the honorees at the Fall Convocation of the University of California–Berkeley, the annual prestigious and dramatic display in the campus Greek theater. That year's observance was more exciting to the Downs people because David Dinkins, recently elected the first black mayor of New York City, was the keynote speaker. Bowers was recognized for his exemplary record in outfitting and staffing the laboratories and in monitoring and reducing the chemical hazards in the College of Chemistry. Through his position at the university, Bowers is visible to African-American students in a way that may counteract the effects of the underrepresentation of African-Americans at all levels of the university community. He keeps himself open to talk with students about collegiate or personal matters. He spends a large part of his day solving the kinds of problems that are inevitable when people with different needs and different approaches work together.

Bowers learned from his father that black people must have something of value to offer in order to gain the respect of the establishment in this country. This is a capitalistic society, so capital in the form of land and property is one of the best things that a black person can present. Bowers does not discount the importance of education as an enabling factor in the amassing of capital, but he also likes the personal satisfaction of creating a lamp or a table or something tangible with his own hands. Throughout the building of the Downs sanctuary, Bowers gave scores of hours to the project. His experience in building and construction was of great value and made him the righthand man of B. L. Vaughn and Irvin Fuller, the craftsmen in charge of the volunteer workers. Bowers did carpentry work, loaded trucks, hauled debris to the garbage dumps, and worked as general assistant to the builders. He continues to help with the upkeep of the building by painting and doing other repairs.

Bowers's interest in real estate stems from the example and the teachings of his father, and his desire to accumulate property, combined with the pleasure he gains from working with his hands, has led him to renovate houses for rent. His first venture into house renovation was born out of his own need to find a place for his family to live without paying what he considered exorbitant rent. The idea was spurred by his brother's assistance in finding a house that was a good investment for a buyer with carpentry skills and the inclination to use them. Bowers bought a small house, and with the help of his brother and friends (some from Downs), he enlarged it by adding living quarters for two additional families below the upper floor, which the Bowers family occupied. The work crew came after the regular eight-hour work day and on weekends. They used long extension cords to string lights to illuminate the area after nightfall so that they could dig trenches for the foundation and the sewer lines. The finished product was an attractive, functional residence that was financially rewarding for Bowers.

Bowers's friends know of his interest in real estate and they kid him about his desire "to own the world." But behind their gentle gibes they admire his energy and drive, and they will admit that they wish that they could duplicate his accomplishments.

Bowers and Geraldine, until the time of her death, were faithful members of Downs. When I first saw them at celebrations at the church, their oldest daughter, Denise, was a self-assured little toddler, making her way on legs that were not quite secure enough for her to run as she would have liked. Vida and Stephanie were not yet born. Denise knew that she was loved by her parents and by the people around her. This has been my picture of the Bowers family since I met them in the fifties.

ISHAM "IKE" BUCHANAN
Born 1927, Opelika, Alabama

**"My mother was the stalwart, steady support for the family.
She was always there to give us support and whatever assistance she could."**

The best thing that happened to Ike Buchanan at Downs was meeting his future wife, Flora. Mutual friends had told one about the other, made arrangements, and set dates for them to attend church together; however, the plans kept falling through because of repeated schedule conflicts. Finally they met at a musical program and started a relationship that culminated in a beautiful marriage at Downs more than thirty years ago.

For the first few years of his life, Ike Buchanan lived in Opelika, Alabama. The family was poor; his father was a laborer, and his mother was a domestic worker. Neither made more than one dollar a day, which did not go very far in the thirties or the early forties. When he was in elementary school Buchanan was encouraged and motivated by his fourth grade teacher, Mrs. Zuber, who detected that Buchanan had talent beyond reading, writing, and arithmetic. She saw his interest in music and offered to give him piano lessons. Before that he would sit on the steps of the back porch of his house and put his feet through the step below, imagining that he was a great pianist giving a concert at Carnegie Hall. When he began the lessons he would go to a neighbor's house or to a church to practice. He studied piano for five years before he lost interest. Even though he no longer plays the instrument, he has sung in choral groups since his early school days.

Following the death of his father when he was thirteen, Buchanan's mother sent him to live with his older sister in Cincinnati, Ohio, to improve the overall opportunities for him. In a chain migration pattern, each member of the family left Alabama one by one until the entire family relocated to Cincinnati. After he graduated from Morehouse College in 1951, Buchanan had to cope simultaneously with an unsuccessful search for work in Cincinnati and the expectation that he would be drafted into the army any day. To change his luck he decided to seek his fortune elsewhere. The first step was to visit another sister in San Francisco, look for work there, and await the call to service. When September came around and he had not been inducted, Buchanan enrolled in a teacher training program at the University of San Francisco to become certificated to teach English, sociology, and mathematics. The induction did not materialize until 1954, after Buchanan had taught in Vallejo, California, for a year; he then served two years in the army in Okinawa.

During his tour of duty Buchanan was a psychiatric intake technician, who assessed the need for patients to consult with a psychiatrist. To his delight the assignment did not require him to carry a gun. After basic training he never saw a weapon. When he was scheduled to go out on the range, he avoided it by begging off other more important duties. From the standpoint of his work in the army and his relations with fellow servicemen, Buchanan thought of those two years as a valuable learning experience. His roommate in Okinawa was a psychologist from whom he learned a great deal. They discussed mental illness and the state of American society in general. At that time Buchanan was not opposed to the draft; he would go if called, but he would not volunteer. Years later when his son reached draft age, it became a much more personal issue with him. He did not want to see his son called to military service where the possibility existed of being killed fighting for a cause that may or may not be of any relevance to him. When his military tour ended, Buchanan returned to his teaching job in Vallejo in 1956.

After teaching in the high schools of Vallejo and Emeryville for more than a decade, Buchanan went to Laney Community College in 1971 as financial aid counselor and later as director of special services. Both positions were with the Extended Opportunity Program and Services, which recruits and brings disadvantaged ethnic students into the community college system and provides financial aid. The Veterans' Upward Bound Program, which Buchanan also supervised, trained veterans who had not finished high school or whose basic skills were not sufficient for them to survive in college-level classes without tutoring.

As director of special services, Buchanan influenced large numbers of students. He was the one who held the financial aid purse strings, and he used them to lead the poorly motivated ones to realize that it was through their own efforts that they would be successful; success was measured in terms of the goals that they set for themselves. Students and his staff saw Buchanan as a goal-oriented person who tried to help other people become goal-oriented as well. He had a special interest in trying to see that ethnic students prepared themselves to get their fair share of the things that America has to offer. Beginning in September 1987, Buchanan gave up the assignment as director of special services and became a counselor to disadvantaged students. He made this change because of the stressful conditions at work, caused mainly by a general lack of support from the college administration. The effect of the intolerable state of affairs manifested itself by an alarming rise in his blood pressure, which threatened his health.

Buchanan is concerned about the financial condition of the nation's schools and the need for a new national pledge to make the status of the educational system a definite priority. A friend who teaches at a local school recently told Buchanan about the closing of the library at his site because of budgetary cuts, in a school where the reading level of the students is already very low. This closing eliminates another avenue of learning for those children, and Buchanan and his friend see it as a problem that will be difficult, if not impossible, to correct.

In Buchanan's estimation the most significant contribution of California community colleges is their open door policy that admits students who want to study while they determine whether they will pursue a higher degree or a vocation. Admission does not depend upon an entrance examination or a high school diploma; applicants need only be eighteen years old and have the ambition to engage in further study. Buchanan welcomes the trend toward an entrance assessment that does not deny admission to anyone but gives the student access to information upon which to build future study plans.

One of Buchanan's community interests is the East Bay School of Performing Arts where he served as president and member of the board of trustees. This community-based school gives private and group lessons by professional artists in music, drama, dance, and filmmaking. The scope ranges from classical, jazz, and folk music to ethnic and classical drama. His interest in the school began when two of his children were enrolled in the music classes. For a while Buchanan acted with the Black Repertory Group, the community theater that was born at Downs church with Nora Vaughn as its creator.

Buchanan found people at Downs who were in the teaching profession just as he and Flora were. Through his association with them he could exchange ideas and get support for his own thoughts. There were mothers and fathers who had children the same age as his, and they discussed parenting as well as career values. Although Buchanan never became an official member of Downs, he attended, made financial contributions regularly, and was part of the activities of the church to the same extent as a person whose name was on the church rolls. Flora sang in the choir, and their children went to Sunday school and to the Vacation Bible school. The Buchanans were involved at Downs until they moved to suburban Danville in the seventies.

Having been a student at Morehouse College, Buchanan learned the philosophy of its president, Dr. Benjamin Mays: to hold his head high, to be his own man, and to be independent and self-confident. Dr. Mays's lessons were an important part of the training that shaped Buchanan's life.

Recently Ike Buchanan has grown a thick beard that is mostly white with a definite mingling of black, just enough to add distinction. There is no hint of the hypertension or any other worry that he may have. Soon Ike will retire and devote his time to his hobbies: fishing, gardening, and finding new ways to barbecue foods. Perhaps, as he says he will, he will write a book about his experiences at the community college.

MARY ELLEN ROSE BUTLER
Born 1940, Berkeley, California

"As a race we have come this far, and I see no reason why we won't continue to survive as long as the world survives."

Mary Rose Butler grew up in a home where she was surrounded by things that had to do with service to the community. She saw her father's commitment to the YMCA and to the political life of Oakland, and in her early life she learned about the contributions of her mother's uncle through the publication of his newspaper in Boston. The example was set in her childhood for her to continue the tradition of public service.

One of the clearest memories Butler has of her years at Downs is passing out leaflets door to door in the sixties under Nichols's direction; they had to do with fair housing. She and her college roommate were particularly interested in this issue because they had experienced overt racial discrimination in getting an apartment near the University of California's Berkeley campus. Butler has held on to the benefits of learning from the pastor's sermons on biblical history that make present-day life relevant politically and sociologically.

When Joshua Rose, Butler's father, died in 1987, the high regard that people in the East Bay had for him and his accomplishments was perfectly reflected in a comprehensive story about his career in the *Oakland Tribune*. People remember him as a longtime executive secretary of the northwest branch YMCA in Oakland, and as the first African-American on the Oakland recreation commission and the Oakland City Council. Butler grew up in an atmosphere where the Y was intimately involved in the social and political activity of her community.

From the elementary grades Butler had access to *The Pittsburgh Courier, Ebony Magazine,* and African-American history books. *The Boston Guardian,* a paper that was edited by her mother's uncle, William Monroe Trotter, came to her home regularly. Butler heard her mother's accounts about Trotter and his sometimes fanatical dedication to the militancy of his newspaper. He was an adherent to W. E. B. Du Bois's academic approach to solving the problems of black people and espoused it in his paper. Butler took pride in knowing that this historical figure in African-American journalism was part of her family.

Following graduation from Oakland Technical High School in 1957, Butler went to the University of California–Berkeley, where she received a bachelor's degree in 1961. When she was an undergraduate Butler joined the Afro-American Association, which was established by Khalid Al-Mansour (formerly Don Warden). In this period of the awakening of black awareness, Al-Mansour, then a law student at the university's Boalt Hall, talked about the need for black people to read their history and develop business opportunities in their communities. After college Butler spent one year in the public relations department of Blue Cross using her journalistic skills to write employee newsletters, speeches, and pamphlets. For the next two years she was employed by Bank of America as a business writer, composing the monthly *Small Business Report,* which discussed specific businesses in relation to what the bank could do for potential borrowers. The report would end with the statement, "And if you would like a loan from Bank of America to start such a business, come and see us." Butler liked this job because of the precise, explanatory type of writing it required.

Butler's next assignment was as the first black reporter employed by the *Berkeley Gazette* newspaper. She covered the school board from 1964 to 1968 when Berkeley was planning and implementing its desegregation program. Nichols served on the school board during this period, and although they never discussed it, Butler thought that Nichols opened the door for her to work at the *Gazette.* For the next year and a half Butler was a reporter and editor for *The Post,* a paper published by attorney Tom Berkeley, a prominent figure in African-American political circles in the Bay Area. Here she learned layout skills and covered a wide variety of events including social news and the aftermath of the murder of George Jackson at San

Quentin in 1971. In one instance Butler interviewed Fania Jordan, sister of Angela Davis, when Davis was on trial for her alleged part in the shoot out at the Marin County courthouse.

Butler was awarded a congressional fellowship with the American Political Science Association in 1972. She went to Washington, D.C., to work in the offices of Rep. Shirley Chisholm and Sen. Alan Cranston of California and observe Congress in action. At the end of the congressional fellowship Butler stayed two years as a reporter for the Alexandria, Virginia, bureau of the *Washington Star Reporter*. Alexandria is a historic town across the Potomac from Washington, D.C., where George Washington lived after he left Mount Vernon. It has plush sections of old, restored colonial houses for the rich residents, but there is a sizable black population. Butler did general reporting—school board, city council, crime, accidents, anything that was newsworthy. She wrote stories about African-Americans in the city and covered the television miniseries *Roots* from there. It was a good feeling to know that her material was being read by people in the nation's capital, by opinion makers and decision makers to increase their knowledge about black people.

Having ended her first marriage prior to the start of the Washington fellowship, Butler met and married Donald, an electrical engineer, in that city in 1978. When he received a job offer in San Francisco in the same year, they returned to the Bay Area with their new family of her two daughters and Donald's son. It took an agonizing amount of time job hunting before she found employment. She was sure that she was discriminated against because she was a thirty-eight-year-old applicant. With her extensive experience she was qualified to be an editor; her peers who had equal records were in managerial positions, but newspapers were looking toward younger reporters and not veterans. In about five months she went to work for Oakland Public Schools as a public information writer. Butler went from the school district to the *Oakland Tribune* in 1979 as a features editor, supervising thirty reporters, columnists, and editors; she was responsible for several sections of the newspaper: Daily Lifestyle section, Sunday Lifestyle section, Sunday Travel, TV Book, Sunday Calendar, and the Wednesday Foods section. She attributed her assignment to the influence of Robert Maynard, the black man who is the owner and publisher of the paper. He has used his leadership to bring people like Butler into the administrative level, people whose managerial potential was not recognized by previous editors because of race, sex, or age.

Being a features editor demanded long hours and a lot of hard work and brought with it the classic conflicts of the working woman who must balance her time between family and career. Such was the tightrope Butler had to walk, and she thought she met the challenge successfully. Her family was progressing well, and during the four years she was features editor her sections continued to improve. In 1983 Butler became an editorial writer for the *Oakland Tribune,* writing editorials that discussed pertinent issues from the point of view of the publisher. Here, Butler spoke out on current issues of the day, such as the political situation in Lebanon, the shooting down of the Korean jetliner, and the resignation of the first black woman to be crowned Miss America. The most recent promotion for Butler was effective in August 1990 when she took over the job as editorial page editor. This came after her long experience with the paper and after she had received the John Swett Award for Media Excellence. Butler's goal is to continue to discuss issues that concern Oakland and the East Bay Area in a professional manner through her editorials on the opinion page.

Butler participates in the affairs of the black community in Concord, an East Bay suburb. She takes an active role in the Concord-Pittsburgh chapter of Alpha Kappa Alpha sorority, which has a Reading Is Fundamental project in an elementary school in Pittsburgh, another East Bay suburb, and a Teen Parent program. The sorority has sponsored black history programs and held their first cotillion as a fund-raiser for three scholarships for graduating high school seniors. She is involved in the activities of the Black Families Association of Central Contra Costa County, which was formed a few years ago to address the fears that resulted from the suspicious death of a young black man.

I remember Butler at Downs from just about the time she

was ready to graduate from high school and admired her total demeanor. She had come to my home with the young people for the entertainment part of the evening after the meeting of the Methodist Youth Fellowship. I have included her as one of the Downs people who were students during the fifties and sixties, because I think of her as a young person who at an early age showed the promise of a successful career and a dedication to public service.

MILTON A. COMBS, SR.
Born 1928, Minneapolis, Minnesota

"Be ye doers of the word, and not hearers only."

Roy C. Nichols and Milton A. Combs, Sr., pastor and assistant pastor of Downs Memorial United Methodist Church, made a perfect combination; each complemented the other and thus gave the Downs people increased benefits of spiritual care. At the same time Combs, in the dual capacity of seminary student and pastoral leader, profited from formal classroom study and from practical interaction with the pastor and lay people in the church membership. His duties included assisting in the rituals of the Sunday service, administering the rites of communion, and counseling individual members.

The atmosphere of love in Milton Combs's boyhood home in Minnesota came from both of his parents. Having been raised on a ranch in Omaha, Nebraska, where black families had to fight literally for their existence, his father took a more pragmatic approach toward raising his children. Combs's father learned to do whatever was necessary to survive and developed the philosophy, "fight, curse, and not kowtow to anyone." He wanted his sons to learn to box so that they could defend themselves: turn one cheek, but if that cheek is hit, then "give them hell."

Combs chose to enter the ministry because of factors that started to come together when he was a teenager. His family lived across the street from the Hallie Q. Brown Community Center, the hub of activity for black youth in St. Paul. It provided cultural events, athletics, and other entertainment. Combs became an unpaid assistant, working with the Boy Scouts and other community services in the company of the role models there. This experience stirred his first interest in community service. He was scout master of the troop at Pilgrim Baptist Church and developed a close relationship with Dr. Floyd Massey. With training and encouragement from Dr. Massey, Combs obtained a license to preach.

Directly from high school Combs went into Macalester College in St. Paul, Minnesota, "The Harvard of the Midwest." After he graduated in 1952, he came to California to enter the Berkeley Baptist Divinity School. While he was a seminary student Combs worked as the youth minister at Beth Eden Baptist Church in Oakland. He liked that church and its people but wanted to be where he could assist with adult programs as well. Nichols invited him to come to Downs as a student assistant pastor, and it was Combs's first relationship with a Methodist church, having grown up a Baptist and attended a Presbyterian affiliated college. He learned to appreciate the meaning of the ecumenical church and gained an introduction to the diversity of the Christian religion.

Combs began to think about service out of this country where he could offer his talents in a meaningful way. His interest was initially sparked by fellow seminary students from Asia and other parts of the world who spoke with him about their homelands. The challenging spirit at Downs and Nichols's sermons also seemed to say to him, "Be ye doers of the word, and not hearers only." He and his wife, Edna, applied to the American Baptist Foreign Missionary Society and received appointments to Burma in 1957. Even though Combs felt that there were opportunities for him to help the people he would be working with, he had no intention of staying in the field for thirty or forty years as some of the older missionaries had, "having the Bible in one hand and preaching condemnation." He wanted to serve as a coworker to facilitate the means to meet the needs that were not being met by the people of the country. Combs was careful to maintain the philosophy of the "new missionary"—to never allow himself to be "top dog," but to work with and train local leadership so that they would not be dependent on the missionaries. He rejected the paternalistic relationships of the past.

Combs had several roles in Burma. Once in the country, he was employed by the Burma Baptist Convention and one of his main responsibilities was to coordinate the youth activities with young Baptist leaders from all over the country. A target program was to pool their resources to build a national campsite for the students. Combs helped locate land and materials and worked with local contractors and laborers on the construction of three bamboo buildings with thatch roofs. With other youth leaders he sponsored volleyball and badminton tournaments for church groups and for Baptist Christian schools. In addition, Combs helped to develop the publication, *The High Call*, mainly for Baptist Christian youth but which would eventually be circulated on an interdenominational basis. It was a monthly paper in English and Burmese with articles and information related to Christian youth. Along with the work as youth secretary of the Burmese Baptist Convention, Combs taught in the Burma Divinity School and discovered that he had a talent for teaching. This proved to be a useful source of satisfaction when he returned to the United States.

The five years that Combs was in Burma were part of a transitional period in American overseas missionary work. After World War II some countries that had been fertile ground for missionary service became independent and extended their political freedom to other areas. They reclaimed the responsibility of making determinations about what their religious programs should be rather than having foreign missionaries make those decisions for them. This led to conflicts between missions and governments. Combs could see that missionaries were not relinquishing control or giving jurisdiction over certain matters to indigenous people. There were well-trained Burmese people in the church who could take over the leadership that was in the hands of missionaries.

By 1962 the political changes that had been taking place since 1948 when Burma gained independence resulted in the nationalization of all institutions in the country—including those

that were religious—and the deportation of foreign missionaries. The Combs family returned to America in April 1962.
Combs shared his observations about the failings of missionary
service with their associates and incorporated the suggestion
that more emphasis should be placed on training religious leaders from other countries, but he was not sure of the ultimate
effect of his expressed recommendations.

As the end of his mission work in Burma drew to a close,
Combs had to think of his future work. There were no church
openings in the East Bay for him to go into. He remembered
the positive feedback from his students at the Burma Divinity
School. He went to San Francisco State University and took
courses for a credential to teach in a community college. After
a few years Combs completed work toward a master's degree in
education with emphasis on African-American studies. For
more than twenty years Combs has been teaching history, sociology, psychology, philosophy, and religion at Solano Community College. He especially enjoys teaching the courses that explore the major religions of the world—Hinduism, Buddhism,
Shintoism, Christianity, Judaism, Islam, and Sikhism. To honor
his development of well-received courses in comparative religion, the college named Combs its Distinguished Faculty Member of the Year in June 1990. Combs has been rewarded by the
personal satisfaction of his two career areas, the ministry and
education. As a pastor and as a teacher, he has been in a position
to suggest goals and objectives for the lives of other people, and
he has had the satisfaction of hearing a young person tell him
about the impact of his leadership; how something he said or
did helped that individual move along the line of achievement.

In the past fifteen years Combs has not been involved in a
continuous assignment as a minister. Prior to that he had a variety of positions as interim pastor in a Presbyterian church, a
Baptist church, and a Community Reformed church. He has not
completely closed the door for the future; he knows that perhaps he will be pastor or associate minister somewhere in the
Bay Area. For many years Combs worked closely with the Northern California Center for Afro-American History and Life, formerly the East Bay Negro Historical Society, as a member of the

executive board responsible for developing the black history month observance and the organization's annual program. He has been in the forefront of the production of a slide and audio cassette program and the setting up of a speakers bureau.

The Macalester College Alumni Association selected Combs in June 1987 to receive its Distinguished Citizen Citation. This honor is bestowed upon "Macalester Alumni who in accepting the privileges of a college education, clearly assume the obligation to exercise leadership in those civic, professional, social and religious activities that are essential to a democracy." The college felt that the work in Burma, the community involvement in the Bay Area, and Combs's teaching record made him an excellent candidate. He is the only African-American male recipient in the almost forty-year history of the citation.

The entire Combs family, parents and children, have been involved in the construction of the trihexagonal house that is now complete after five years of physical labor. They conceived the plans and set about building the house from foundation to roof with the help of friends (some from Downs). They sawed the wood, hammered the nails, mixed and finished the concrete for the retaining walls, and sanded the beams for the ceilings. It required hard work, sacrifice, and faith, but they now have a beautiful, comfortable home that is the fulfillment of their dreams. Combs does not regret the money or the time that went into the home; he believes that the returns are always in direct proportion to the investment in any type of undertaking.

I met Milton and Edna and their three young children when they first came to Downs in 1954. Milton, Jr., was four years old, Karyn was three, and Kristina was two. Downs loved all five immediately, and thought of Milton, Sr., as a perfect counterpart to Nichols. When they left to go to Burma the church maintained contact with them, wrote letters, and sent boxes of clothes for the Burmese people. At the end of the missionary service we welcomed Roy, who had been born in Burma, and John, who was born after they returned to Berkeley. Frank and I have more of a personal interest in the Combses: Milton, Jr., is our godchild.

JACK COSTA
Born 1921, Alameda, California

"My Dad always said that whether a person is black or white, you treat him as a human being. If you could take the blood and pour it on the table, it is all red. There is no difference."

Both of Jack Costa's parents came to the United States from the Cape Verde Islands where Portuguese is the indigenous language. Costa and his brothers and sisters spoke Portuguese at home with the family but were comfortable with English when there were other English-speaking people present or when they were outside of the home. His father was a seafaring man who started off as a child sailing with whaling boats. He worked his way up by going to navigation school to receive his papers as a skipper, but during World War II he was not given the command of a ship because he was classified as a black man. Instead he worked on the waterfront as a carpenter repairing the barges and as a mate on the Delta King and Delta Queen, boats that plied the waters of San Francisco Bay and the Sacramento River between San Francisco and Sacramento.

From early childhood to adulthood Costa attended a Catholic church in Alameda, California, where he participated in catechism classes and served as an altar boy. Costa lives by his father's training that taught him that everybody, no matter what their race, has the same levels of sensitivity and deserves the same degree of respect; his children were taught to say, "Yes sir," and "No Ma'am" to adults. Costa's father stressed that members of their family would not resort to illegal means to obtain material goods. The family name and reputation took preference over a personal wish of any one person.

As a boy Costa attended the Alameda public schools. Almost immediately after graduation from high school he went to work on the waterfront in San Francisco and has remained there for more than forty years. With steady upward reclassification he is now a yard superintendent in charge of longshoremen who load and unload containers and prepare them to be put off or onto ships. His responsibility is to see that everything is put in the right place and recorded into the computers correctly so that any inquiries about departure, destination, en route status, or arrival time can be answered accurately. Costa must make sure that he has sufficient manpower on hand to perform the tasks of a specific day. The satisfying part of Costa's job is that he deals with a different group of workers each day. He must make a judgment about the temperament of each man in the first instant to determine how much work he can expect from him. Having made his evaluation, Costa then assigns the individual where he is best fitted. He remembers to say to each worker at the end of the day, "Thank you very much, you did a beautiful job today."

Jack Costa started the first Boy Scout troop at Downs. Over a period of five years he nursed it from the original five boys to thirty-five. Costa remembered with great pride the year that he and the Reverend Henry Bayne took twelve scouts from the troop high up into the Sierra mountains for a ten-day camping trip. Costa spent many nights of the week with the scouts—at the district level and with the Downs troop—and with other community activities. One of his children once said to him, "Daddy, aren't you going to be home some nights?" The scouting obligations included backpacking trips into the mountains, newspaper drives, and regular visits to the Richmond swimming pool. Costa arranged with Nichols to schedule Sundays when the Downs troops could take over the ushering duties.

Costa's first visit to Downs was the result of an invitation from Beverly, his girlfriend at that time, and who became his wife in 1950 in a ceremony that was performed by Nichols. Costa and Beverly and their children remained at Downs for more than thirty years. Along with their regular attendance at Sunday services, Costa's leadership in the Boy Scouts, and Beverly's membership in the women's circles, their children took part in the Sunday school and other youth activities. Even after they had chosen Religious Science over Methodism, they continued to make periodic visits to Downs for "refueling," to satisfy a remaining need to return to the warmth and friendship of their former place of worship.

Costa is a prominent member of the Oakland Lions Club,

having begun as treasurer and risen to the presidency. Through the Lions he has been involved with vision- and hearing-test projects in mobile units at selected locations for free screening of residents. Costa drove his truck with its trailer hitch to haul the units all over the East Bay Area. He has been involved when the Lions promote donations to the Alameda County Blood Bank, and when they play Santa Claus at Children's Hospital.

Being first of all a family man, Costa is unequivocally proud of himself and his family. He is satisfied with his contribution to the community, and he takes pride in the guidance that he has given to his children and their response to his home training. He holds the name Costa in reverence and teaches his children as his father taught him: protect the family reputation by maintaining good citizenship. There is no doubt about the family emphasis in the Costa home. Although my conversation was primarily with Jack, Beverly added to the warmth of the evening by joining in the talk. She has now become the victim of a debilitating illness that requires concentrated attention. Jack has provided everything for her comfort—the material things and care that she needs and his continued love. I have seen the tenderness of the time and the part of himself that he gives to her.

KATHERINE DRAKE
Born 1916, Shreveport, Louisiana

"At my age I like to keep in contact with young people so that I know something about them."

With the encouragement of her sisters from Delta Sigma Theta sorority, Katherine Drake joined the Downs family when she returned to the Bay Area after an absence of several years working, studying, and teaching in the field of nursing. She found that it was just the sort of church setting she wanted and without delay started to work in the church office. At the same time she took part in the women's groups and participated in other programs and observances. For many years Drake was the guiding force in the church office while she raised her children in the shelter of Downs.

After her parents divorced a friend suggested to Katherine Drake's mother that she and her five-year-old daughter migrate to California from Louisiana to begin a new life. Mother and daughter came to Berkeley and had the good fortune to meet Frances Albrier, a politically active pioneer African-American woman, a Berkeley resident who knew all facets of the social and political demands upon black people in California. She helped the newly arrived mother become oriented into her surroundings and had a substantial influence on Drake as she matured.

Drake and her circle of young friends were good students who used the public library for homework preparation and spent hours there reading books just for fun. The girls formed a vocal trio, which they thought was as good as "Diana Ross and the Supremes," with Drake as the lead singer. The group sang in church programs and wrote and performed skits. When Drake was in public school her mother worked as a maid for a family who was generous with frequent gifts, and who made it easier for their employee to work and raise her child at the same time. They allowed Drake's mother to take her daughter when she went with them to Lake Tahoe and other places where black people were normally not accepted and gave them both attractive clothes that they could wear without humiliation. The employers would ask Drake to join their children when they made music to entertain guests and offered additional financial assistance when she went off to college.

Drake learned early about the class and color distinctions in the black social hierarchy of the East Bay. The lighter skinned young people were more admired and respected and had their exclusive group that did not include people who were darker complexioned. Drake and her friends did not qualify for the lighter group and sought pleasure within their own social set. There were other nuances of status besides color. Berkeley residents feel superior to their peers who live in west Oakland. They think that they rate higher in the caste system because they go to Berkeley High School and not McClymonds in west

Oakland or Oakland Technical in north Oakland. Drake grew up in a setting where young people as well as adults are ranked in regard to color, place of residence, occupation of parents, and the reputation of one's school, all within the broader context of discrimination based solely on race. She knew that it was not unusual to face prejudice and discrimination based merely on ethnicity—to have to deal with a negative attitude that had been formed before there was any hint of her personality, or her financial or social status.

Albrier suggested that Drake attend Tuskegee Institute to prepare for her chosen career, nursing. Drake had gone from first to twelfth grade in the Bay Area and had no knowledge of black colleges. Albrier told her that nurse training in Tuskegee would give her exposure to other serious African-American students in an all-black situation, as well as excellent preparation for a career where employment opportunities were always plentiful.

Drake finished the three-year program at Tuskegee with a diploma but no degree. She registered at the University of California–Berkeley to complete a bachelor's of science. The year at Berkeley was a completely different situation; Tuskegee Institute had an all-black student body, and Berkeley had only a small percentage of nonwhite students. After Drake received the degree in 1940, she returned to Tuskegee to work as a nurse, first at the Institute Hospital, and then at the Veterans Administration Hospital in charge of the orthopedics ward and teaching orthopedic nursing. Eighteen years later Drake came back to California.

Because of a coronary condition Drake retired in 1974 from the Veterans Administration Hospital in Martinez, California, where she was head nurse and supervisor of medical and surgical services. Before and since retirement Drake has been a volunteer for the Richmond schools in the preenrollment physical examinations and eye tests of school children. She has been associated with the El Cerrito Democratic Club and a veteran member of the board of directors of the University YWCA. The Negro Business and Professional Women conferred upon her the Sojourner Truth Award in 1983 to recognize her longtime service as publicity chairperson.

Delta Sigma Theta sorority asked Drake to write a play for its annual Black Family Symposium in 1987, one that would address the subject of teenage peer pressure in relation to drugs and sex and expose some of the myths that cause innocent confusion. With the help of her daughter, a practicing physician, Drake created a two-act drama that was performed by students of a local community college. It included alcoholic beverages as substances that can be abused and showed scenes of a parent giving unintended approval of overindulgence by constantly sipping from a bottle of beer—an action that is socially acceptable, but potentially harmful. To Drake it is unrealistic to expect parents and educators unilaterally to create an environment where young people will take full advantage of educational and career opportunities. Children need the cooperative efforts of schools, the home, the extended family, and the community, especially from those who have "made it," such as Frances Albrier.

There could not have been a better role model for Drake than Frances Albrier. Albrier's and Drake's mother's advice guided her through the Berkeley public schools, and Albrier directed her toward Tuskegee. In Tuskegee, Drake continued to exercise her gifts of singing and writing skits as she had done in public school. In the course of thirty-four years of the practice and teaching of nursing, Drake continued writing for her church, sorority, and service organizations and participating in their activities. Despite health problems, which forced her into early retirement, she continues to do volunteer work and to use her writing skills, both directed toward the benefit of young people.

Katherine Drake was one of the pillars of the church in the fifties and sixties. She was always there for worship services or other observances or social occasions. Even though she is not as active now as in that time, she is still a devoted member of Downs.

CHARLES FURLOW
Born 1908, Americus, Georgia

**"Except for being in the right place at the right time—God in action—
I would say that I'm just an ordinary Joe."**

When Charles Furlow thought about his early years at Downs, a wealth of gratifying reminiscences came to his mind. He mentioned the inspirational feeling of the late Ed Stallings leading one thousand men singing "A Mighty Fortress Is My God" at breakfast one Sunday morning just before they departed for home after a retreat for Methodist Men's Club members in the scenic mountains near Santa Cruz, California. He recalled his part in the "Nickels for Nichols" campaign for the Berkeley City Council, and remembers it as the beginning of his desire to do something to improve conditions for black people. With pleasure he described nailing beaver board during the construction of the sanctuary and the lasting friendships that he formed at Downs.

Each change in employment for Charles Furlow's father resulted in more responsibility and a better salary. He progressed from bartender, to shipping clerk in a retail store, to post office clerk, and finally to supervisor of window clerks in the main post office of Jacksonville, Florida. His father stressed the importance of study and hard work to his five children. They saw their father "practice his scheme" for his job using a model that duplicated the letter sorter at work. He spent three or four hours a day at home throwing pieces of paper into the 180 slots to sharpen his skills. Furlow's mother was a "homebody type of person who spent her time with the things that housewives did in those days: cleaning, cooking, washing, ironing, growing flowers, and attending church meetings and teas."

Furlow attended elementary and secondary school in Jacksonville where black people knew full well that they could only drink at the fountain marked "colored," and that they had to pay their utility bills at a window in the city hall that was set up especially for them. He heeded the warnings from his parents to avoid trouble with white people by obeying the law and not associating with law breakers. These instructions comprised what they regarded as the best way to survive in a bad situation. When he first arrived in California, Furlow found that "race was not the come-and-go free situation that a lot of people imagined it to be" in this state. He saw signs in cafes and bars and in Casper's hot dog stand: "We reserve the right to refuse service to anyone."

Before he finished high school Furlow joined the coastal merchant marines and visited cities in the northern part of the country. His observations of New York City, Philadelphia, and Baltimore were not reassuring. Why should he live in a smelly walk-up apartment with overflowing garbage cans filling the sidewalks and unkept community toilets and bath facilities? He saw no advantage in living in those slumlike conditions. Furlow returned to Jacksonville and completed high school in 1929 when he was twenty-one.

In 1931 when the twenty-three-year-old Furlow took time off to earn money for college, he experienced for the first time what he calls "God in action"—being in the right place at the right time. He had been looking for work in New York City for weeks, going to employment agencies, walking up and down the avenues, and knocking on store doors. Finally he came to Morningside Park on the periphery of Harlem and stretched out on the grass with a newspaper over his face. His self-esteem was low; he had exhausted his money and could not pay his rent. There was a sharp kick on the bottom of his foot. It was surely a cop to chase him away from the park. Instead, it was a man who said, "Do you want a job?" The conversation continued: "Yes." "Can you operate a switchboard?" "No, sir, but I don't believe anybody can beat me learning." "Have you ever operated an elevator?" "Yes." "Come on."

That man did not know anything about Furlow and could not see his face when he approached him. Yet he kicked *him* under his foot, took *him* to West End Avenue, and gave *him* a job in an apartment building. In addition to running the elevator and answering the switchboard, Furlow helped the maids in the building with the heavy work in exchange for food. He saved enough money to return to college. Half a century later

Furlow still wondered why that man chose him for the job. His only explanation is that it was "God in action" guiding his life.

Charles Furlow was attracted to the field that would be his life's work by the promise of earnings that were far greater than the amount he was paid to teach in a Florida high school. His salary of sixty-five dollars a month for the eight months of the school year was far less than the twenty-six hundred dollars that white teachers earned annually for the nine months that they worked. A friend who was employed by the Afro-American Life Insurance Company offered Furlow one hundred dollars a week to work as an insurance agent. The friend convinced him to go to the West Palm Beach office of the company to watch the cashier compute the pay for the agents. He saw that each check was for more than one hundred dollars for seven days' work. Furlow learned some of the "finer things" about the insurance business: An agent could earn more money selling than he could collecting. For each dollar that he collected for a life insurance policy, he retained twenty cents, but if he sold one dollar's worth of premiums, he could earn two dollars and fifty cents.

This information struck a responsive chord in Furlow, who was in his third year of teaching. Here was an opportunity to make four hundred dollars a month as opposed to sixty-five dollars. Furlow's mother was unhappy that he left his prestigious job teaching to go into insurance. She reminded him of the expression among black people in the South, "If you can't do anything else you can sell insurance." She had seen men who said that they were insurance salesmen wearing patched pants and shoes with holes. His mother thought he would "go to the dogs."

Furlow proved his mother wrong. His initial prosperity was short-lived, however, because the agency director failed to honor his commitment to let Furlow take a vacation at Christmas time as a promised reward for winning a yearly collection campaign. Furlow told his boss "to take this job and shove it" and ended his initial venture in the insurance industry, but it was not the last. There were temporary detours, the first a year as assistant manager of a migratory labor camp at Belle Glade, Florida, in the center of a rich farming community on land that was drained from the Ochokebee swamps.

The good thing about this period was that he renewed the acquaintance of the woman that he had been attracted to in West Palm Beach. A serious courtship followed, and he and Julia were married in St. Louis in 1943, the day before he left to resume navy duty in California. After his discharge they established their home in the East Bay Area in 1944. Ten years later they began their association with Downs that is as strong today as it was then. Through the years Furlow has held a variety of positions, including a seat on the official board and president of the Methodist Men's Club.

When they first settled in the Bay Area, Furlow took an interim job delivering special delivery letters while he waited for a permanent assignment in the post office. One day while he was making a delivery, his car broke down at the top of the steep hill on Marin Street in Berkeley, and he had the traumatic experience of backing down until he could turn into another street. That finished Furlow's post office career. The next time he went into downtown Oakland he saw a sign in an upstairs window at Tenth and Broadway, "Golden State Life Insurance Company." Somebody had told him that this was a black company, and on an impulse he went into the office and talked to John Payton, manager of the Oakland division, who offered him a job on the spot. Furlow stayed with Golden State for ten years in the positions of staff manager, district manager, and agency personnel trainer. In 1955 he decided to direct his efforts toward his own office; if he could train people to earn money for Golden State, why could not he go out and earn money for Charles Furlow? For the next twenty years Furlow had a very lucrative business in insurance. A year and a half later it had grown to the extent that he moved into a larger office, which he shared with a real estate broker. As business continued to do well, Furlow and Dr. William L. Anderson built an office building on Sacramento Street in Berkeley. All the while Furlow was studying for the Charter Life Underwriter's (CLU) designation, and after six years of diligence, he received it. He was then qualified to display in his office the evidence of his status as an expert in his business—a certificate of completion of the advanced course of study and the passing of an examination administered by the College of Life Underwriters, based in Bryn Mawr, Pennsylvania.

Furlow has contributed to the development of younger people's careers in the Bay Area: Doug Jones, who worked in Furlow's office, is the manager of the Oakland office of Pacific Telephone, and Arrece Jameson, who was Furlow's clerk, is Oakland's city clerk. Harry Jones and Phil Chenier, former agents who worked out of Furlow's offices, operate their own successful agencies. Furlow's greatest ambition in business, however, was to make life better for the people he hired by providing good working conditions and fair salaries. From the example of his father Furlow became a staunch believer in training for any undertaking. He rejects the idea that skills can be learned by osmosis; there must be some organized training set up for a specific purpose.

From 1969 through 1971 Furlow, Roosevelt Carrie, and Lovoia Baker, all experienced agents, conducted a training program to prepare African-Americans for positions as underwriters, claims adjusters, and risk managers. The three devised the curriculum based on their knowledge of what was needed and obtained funding from large insurance companies. They taught most of the classes themselves, but there was a lecturer from the University of San Francisco economics department and one from the Insurance Educational Institute. The twenty-seven-week course covered all aspects of insurance sales and policies and ended with a week of instruction about correct dress and decorum. From a total of forty-eight students, the great majority were placed right away and with rare exception are still working in the industry.

Furlow is optimistic that the present recession in the accomplishments of young black people is a cycle which will pass. He believes the permissive type of guidance and behavior will be discarded, and there will be a return to the basics in education with emphasis on computation and the ability to read effectively.

ETTA HILL
Born 1914, Riverside, California

"Art is a way that I express my philosophy of life and my feelings for people, the world of nature, and the world of humanity."

Early in the fifties Etta Hill came to Downs; she was attracted by Roy Nichols and his ideas for the church and the community. She had known him as a seminary student and knew him to be a person who could give the sort of leadership that the East Bay needed. At Downs, Hill was head of the Vacation Bible school, attended meetings of the women's clubs, and brought her children to Sunday school.

Etta Hill was born in Riverside, California, but her roots are in Georgia where her parents, grandparents, uncles, and aunts came from when they migrated to Riverside in the late nineteenth century. Many African-American families in Riverside were neighbors of Hill's people in Georgia, and this association continued in California as an extended family. Living in Riverside did not insulate Hill from the effects of racial discrimination. Coincident with her completion of two years at Riverside Community College, some African-Americans in southern California initiated action against stores that depended upon the patronage of African-American customers but did not employ them. Leon Washington, a newspaper owner and leader in the black community of Los Angeles, spearheaded a boycott aimed at securing the employment of black workers in the S. H. Kress stores. The result was jobs for eleven African-American women, including Hill, who had taken part in the protest. She worked at the Kress store for three years before she went to Chapman College and the University of Redlands, both located near Riverside.

Hill had decided to become a public school teacher, but there was a problem when the time came for the student teaching assignment. Her white classmates found placements easily, but not Hill; the schools were not ready for black teachers. Even though she got her bachelor's degree in 1939 from Redlands, she had no teaching certificate and had to go to San Francisco State College to student teach for that remaining requirement.

With the certificate in hand Hill taught physical education for ten years at Fremont High School in Oakland, and then went to Franklin Elementary School in Berkeley as a physical education specialist. From Franklin, Hill transferred to Lincoln School in Berkeley after being invited by then principal Larry Wells (a Downs member now deceased) to supervise the student center and tutor underachievers in basic skills.

Hill's years of teaching were within a period of conflict between the older teachers and the ones who were just entering the field. The more experienced teachers had traditional values and attitudes about education that clashed with those of the younger teachers, sixties and seventies graduates whose philosophy reflected a challenge to authority and advocated a more relaxed classroom control. Hill could not accept the younger generation's interpretation of the motivational and disciplinary responsibilities of the classroom teacher. She disagreed with the permissive atmosphere that she thought diminished the constructive guidance from teacher to students. She saw the informal mode of dress (jeans and barefoot sandals) and the student's use of the instructor's first name as major points in undermining the professionalism of the classroom.

The two groups had different thoughts about curriculum and teaching methods. Staff meetings were unpleasant experiences for Hill, and the faculty discord prevented her from enjoying teaching as she had in the past. When she no longer had the heart to try to cope with the differences, she decided to leave teaching and devote her time to painting and drawing; it had been in her mind for three years before she took the chance to do something about it. In 1972 she acted. She gave up her teaching position, sold her spacious home, and moved into smaller living quarters. Fewer living expenses, a wise investment of the profits from the sale of the home, and her pension from the fifteen years of teaching allowed her to live comfortably. One night she looked out of the window of her home, a window that framed a panoramic view of San Francisco Bay and the Golden Gate Bridge. The next day she bought a pad and crayons and began to sketch and enrolled in art classes. In six months she won first prize and honorable mention in a show at the El Cerrito Community Center. A turning point came in 1974 when she went to Texas Southern University and the University of Texas to study art.

Twenty years after she first stepped into art, Hill has shown her work in San Francisco, El Cerrito, Napa, Santa Rosa, Oakland, and Los Angeles, California, and in Houston, Texas, and Hobbs, New Mexico. Her posters of Dr. Martin Luther King, Jr., are shown all over the country. Hill is most proud of her work's inclusion in the January 1988 exhibition of fourteen African-American pioneer artists that was sponsored by the Ebony Museum of Art in Oakland.

Hill spoke of her friendship with the young Roy Nichols who was "pretty much like a part of our family." The seminary student, in addition to his class load, was working several hours each night and came almost every day for dinner with Hill and her former husband. Once she sold Nichols the Model-A Ford that she had been driving. She was aware of his commitment to public service and admired that trait, but she did not feel that she had the personality for active involvement in direct political or community action for herself. Instead, she joined the League of Women Voters to get an understanding of the issues and to learn how to vote intelligently.

Hill lives in an apartment in Oakland, on the eleventh floor of a senior citizens' complex. Her studio looks out over San Francisco Bay with a view of the city much like the one that inspired her to give up teaching and enter this new stage of her life. An easel, paints, brushes, and works in progress are all around and dramatize the courage and strength of commitment it took for her to leave the financial security of a tenured position to enter the unknown world of a full-time artist; she was fifty-eight when she took this major step into a new career. Hill has published a book of moving poetry, *Expressions*. Her poems reflect wide interest in the affairs of the world: the earthquake in Mexico City, the condition of black people in South Africa, the American hostage situation, and the "Iran-Contra Mess." The seriousness of these poems is balanced by a well-expressed joy in life, love for her family, and a delight in the beautiful things around her.

Several months after I wrote about my conversations with Hill, she died at age seventy-seven. I was with her family and friends at a service to celebrate her life in the sanctuary of Downs church. They spoke of the things that I recall most vividly about Hill—the impact of her part in the boycott of the Kress store in Riverside, her love and concern for her family and for the peoples of the world, and the beauty of her art and poetry.

GERTRUDE "TRUDIE" HINES
Born 1917, Vallejo, California

**"Apparently there were a lot of Ku Klux Klan people in Vallejo.
My father would sit outside of the church to make sure that nobody destroyed it."**

Gertrude Hines's father, a carpenter who built the house in which she was born, and her mother, a caterer, were community-oriented people who exposed their children to their civic activities. He was a member of the Vallejo chapter of the NAACP and took part in all of its activities, which included guarding his family's Methodist church from the Ku Klux Klan. He took his children to NAACP meetings and encouraged them to read black publications such as the *Chicago Defender* and the *Pittsburgh Courier,* which were mailed to them from the east. Hines's father's last involvements were with the NAACP. He died when he was seventy-six years old in an automobile accident that occurred while he was driving to a NAACP trial.

Before the desegregation of hotels and restaurants, black people, including persons as well known as W. E. B. Du Bois and the concert singer Roland Hayes, had to accept the hospitality of local African-American families when they traveled away from home. Because of her parents' status as well-respected and important members of the African-American community, Hayes and Du Bois came to Hines's home in Vallejo when she was about six years old to relax after the long train ride across the country and to enjoy meals that had been prepared by her mother, a warm hostess, and a very good cook. Her father impressed upon his children the significance of sitting at the table to share a meal with personages of such importance. Hines was awed by both men. In her young mind, she compared Hayes to a little bird: he was small in stature, and he "hopped around like a little bird" when he performed on stage. Du Bois, the distinguished erudite gentleman, was "King of the Jungle, strong and brave, and very much in charge of the situation."

There were only about twenty black students at the University of California–Berkeley when Hines was there from 1934 to 1938. They met between classes on the "slope," an inclined wall beside the entrance to the main library, or on the broad steps in front of the Campanile. Despite the fact that almost all of them were working during the weekends, they managed to have a social life through their Black Students Club. In 1938 she left the university with a degree in psychology and education.

Unlike any of the other Downs people, Gertrude Hines made the change from her former Oakland church to Downs because it was her daughter's choice. Although they had attended South Berkeley Community Church when Nichols was there, they did not follow him to Downs immediately but waited until Beverly decided to celebrate her sixteenth birthday with an official affiliation with Downs. It was a happy choice for both. From 1958 to 1979 Hines was among the most active people at Downs, since "nobody could be in that church under Roy and not be active." She became involved as an advisor to the high school and college group soon after she joined. Nichols thought that Hines was the perfect selection. She was studying at the University of California for a master's degree in social welfare, which she received in 1960, and could practice the principles of group social work that she was learning.

Hines's career has been as a social worker. In the schools of San Francisco her cases had to do with school adjustment problems that resulted from economic hardships, ethnic differences between students, or from having a teacher who did not like or perhaps simply could not understand the child. She evaluated and made recommendations in instances of child abuse and emotional or mental retardation. In the Alameda County Welfare Department Hines was involved in concerns such as aid to dependent children, foster care, adoptions, and old age security.

She was responsible for taking the newborn babies from the hospital to the adoptive home, or to the foster home until the adoption placement was complete. She also had the responsibility of the more sensitive aspect of the adoption process. She interviewed the natural mothers to learn whether their decisions to give up their babies were on a temporary or a permanent basis, talked with people who were applying for adoption, and made home studies to determine if the homes were satisfactory for the new arrivals. Hines made visits intermittently to make sure that the child was comfortable.

Hines is affiliated with the Black Social Workers Organization, a national group whose commitment is to place children in homes of their own ethnic group. This stand is based on the belief that close personal interaction with its own race will strengthen the child's cultural background and thereby give it a better foundation for coping with outside problems. If Hines were working with adoptions today, she would struggle to find parents of the same racial heritage, but she does not feel as strongly as the organization does about the overriding importance of ethnic uniformity. Her preference would be to put a child in an ethnic environment similar to its own, but Hines would not hold this as an absolute criterion. She would rather place the child in foster care with its relatives before settling on an adoptive home that is unlike its ethnic background. Hines is convinced that we shall, at some time, achieve the stage of one world without racial and ethnic restrictions, and we will only have to think of placements in terms of where the child will have loving, supportive surroundings, and the best opportunities.

When Hines opted for early retirement from San Francisco schools in 1977, she continued to work as a consultant to the schools for five years. During that time she produced programs for the district's radio station, interviewing women of color, third world women who were working in positions that would be of interest to the listening audience and who could discuss timely topics. The guests were hair dressers, nurses, secretaries, doctors, lawyers, and nutritionists from different ethnic groups. Hines took her tape recorder when she traveled about the world and talked with dynamic third world women wherever she met them. Their conversations became part of the radio program.

The image of Trudie Hines comes to my mind when I think of the best examples of social workers as a profession. Her philosophy of life gives her a belief in the unity of mankind without barriers of race or class and is based upon a set of principles that came from her mother and father.

JAMES HOWARD
Born 1940, Jackson, Mississippi

"What made that experience rewarding was actually seeing what I went into the profession for — to see behavioral changes in people."

James Howard was an integral part of the youth group at Downs, beginning in 1954 when he was fourteen years old. His commitment to the church was kept alive by a combination of pleasure in the social life and satisfaction from the more serious activities. Downs had a major part in his development until he entered the air force after he graduated from high school.

It was always just James Howard and his mother. His father, an attorney, left Mississippi three weeks before Howard was born, ostensibly to open a law office in New York City and send for his family when it was established. He never sent for them. Mother and son came to California in 1950 when he was ten "to get as far away from my father as she possibly could." Howard's mother became the dominant influence in his life. With her coaching he was reading Shakespeare and reciting sonnets when he was a young child. He enjoyed showing off when he was seven but felt like a "freak kid" when she asked him to perform once he was a teenager. Howard finally had a male influence when his mother remarried in 1953. He loved his stepfather and developed a relationship with him over four short years; his stepfather died the year before Howard finished high school.

In Mississippi, Howard's family was considered affluent, but when they came to California their fortunes changed because of his mother's ill health. She had a serious heart condition, and much of his memory of her centered around convalescent periods. Howard's mother received disability assistance, but with the death of his stepfather it was not sufficient without him taking jobs after school to supplement the family funds.

With his mother's encouragement Howard joined the youth group at Downs. She thought of it as a place that most resembled what she wanted his world to be like: "It had intelligent people, and kids who were doing something." Under the direction of Nichols and the youth director, Wesley Jones, Howard appeared on the church's radio program and participated in Youth Day observances as a featured speaker from the pulpit. He coordinated a speakers bureau of young people who were available to fill requests to discuss a variety of subjects.

Howard went into the air force from high school. After his discharge he intermittently toyed with the idea of a career as an English teacher, a minister, a mortician, or a gynecologist, and enrolled in several different colleges without completing any one program. Eventually he concentrated on psychology and earned a doctorate from the University of California–Berkeley in 1978. With the support of his wife, Marie, whom he had married in 1969, he found his niche in a nurturing profession where he could be directly involved with the intimate lives of people.

Having earned a doctorate, Howard first worked at the East Oakland Family Health Alliance with Israel Dunn as a clinician doing counseling and therapy. Then as research assistant he was part of the Black Family Research Project with Wade Nobles. Following that, he went to the Christian Welfare Growth and Development Center in San Francisco, a special education school for children three to twelve years old who were thought to have learning disabilities. He diagnosed the children for this school and for the Third Street Clinic, also in San Francisco.

With his background in clinical diagnostics, special education, and research, Howard was well suited for his next position as director of a Red Cross juvenile delinquency project in San Francisco. He was extremely proud of this three-year experience because through it he was able to realize his goal as a psychologist—to effect changes in the way people behave. This federally funded program that accepted third-time offenders, ages fourteen through seventeen, as an alternative to incarceration could be thought of as an expensive operation for the kids that it served each year. Statistical data showed, however, that there was a general 66 percent recidivism rate for juvenile offenders compared to the 20 percent rate of the offenders in Howard's project.

Their success was due to counseling and alternative education classes, which included special education and an employment component. If a job was found for a participant, but the potential employer did not have the money to compensate the worker, the project paid the salary. It provided a support system for young people who in many instances were living with grandmothers, foster parents, or on the street. Once the staff found them a job and furnished a support system so that they could buy some clothes for themselves and had some pocket money, there was positive response.

In opposition to critics who say that the legal system has been too lenient with young offenders, Howard believes that the courts are deficient in the sense that there are not enough qualitative programs like the Red Cross project to effectively impact change in juveniles. He has proof that it is possible to reclaim some lives that seem to be beyond redemption. Judge John Benson of the juvenile court often took advantage of the choice of rehabilitation over incarceration. He would say to the malefactor, "OK, kid, instead of jail, this time you are going into Jim Howard's program. But if you mess up, you are going to jail."

Unhappily, the stress of the operation's financial struggles in its last year and a half brought about a total burnout. Howard has a case of hypertension comparable to his mother's that responded to the adverse conditions with an astronomical rise in blood pressure and an incident of cardiac arrest; so he had to restrict his involvement to situations involving less stress while he took care of his health. When his blood pressure had stabilized and his health had improved enough for him to undertake a full-time project, Howard found the ideal spot for him and his family to relocate. As he drove over southern California he discovered Julian, a small settlement one hour northeast of San Diego in the foothills of the Sierra Nevada mountains. At five thousand feet the air is smog-free, and there is a view of the nearby desert with visibility as far as Arizona. Best of all, it is free from the bustle of urban areas. Howard and his wife, Marie, a nurse, operate a health clinic in this part of southern California with a full range of services, including medical, chiropractic, and Meals on Wheels for senior citizens.

Howard has lent his professional expertise to groups whose efforts are directed toward the welfare of students and athletes. Through his friendship with professional athletes Howard joined with National Sports Career Management, which helps athletes who suddenly go from "rags to riches" survive the transition without exhausting their financial resources and their physical well-being. This organization also extends its services to high school and college students who are potential professional athletes.

Jim Howard is one of a limited number of African-Americans whose family has four generations of college educated men and women. His education is a combination of formal preparation and the commitment to use his abilities in ways that make a difference in the lives of other people.

CALVIN JACKSON
Born 1933, Havana, Florida

"If you just mention nuclear, people go to pieces. It is a lack of knowledge, of information. We haven't done a very good job on that, and we still aren't doing anything on that."

One Sunday morning at the beginning of the sixties, the minister of a Baptist church in Oakland said to Calvin Jackson, "You know, you ought to go to Downs, you look like a Downs man to me. Reverend Nichols is the pastor over there, you ought to try them out." Jackson went to Downs the next Sunday and was not disappointed. Downs was the kind of religious setting he had been looking for: a church that had an environment of public service. During the Nichols years Jackson was the president of the Methodist Men's Club, the leader of the Boy Scout troop, and the chairman of the trustee board. He shared in cutting the church's operating cost by helping to paint the building and make repairs on the structure as the necessity arose.

Toward the end of the nineteenth century Calvin Jackson's grandfather died and left a three-hundred-acre plantation in Florida to his seven children. Besides the timber that grew there, the land produced tobacco, cotton, peanuts, sugar cane, and rice. It yielded crops, but the cash returns could not cover the family's daily needs and leave sufficient funds to pay taxes. The sons lacked the management skills to protect their interests and to withstand the obstacles that were put in the way of African-American farmers. They had to sell the land, which took away a means of financial independence, and let it pass from the Jackson family into the hands of new owners.

With the loss of the family plantation, Jackson's father sought other land to farm so that he could support his wife and five girls and seven boys. He became a sharecropper in Havana, Florida, a small settlement seventeen miles north of Tallahassee. As the boys reached the age when they could help with farm chores, they abandoned their school books and took up the implements of sowing and reaping. The longer the sons were in the fields, the more ground they lost in school; it was impossible for them to keep up with the progress of their classmates or maintain an interest in further education. All of Jackson's brothers dropped out before they finished the twelfth grade. When his turn came to go into the fields, his mother refused to let him and the two youngest sisters leave school as the older children had. Jackson's high school days and those of his younger siblings continued without the interruption of taking time off for farm work.

Jackson's first real job was in the post office in Quincy, Florida, a town near Havana. The first black postal employee in Quincy, he started when he was fourteen. Thirty-six years later he learned that Quincy had had no other black employees since he left. Jackson worked in Quincy for two years before he went to Mobile, Alabama, to live with his brother and finish high school in that city. There he met Ethel, who became his wife in

1955, while he was studying at Dillard University in New Orleans.

Jackson completed a bachelor's degree at Dillard in chemistry in 1958 and then went to the University of Kansas. Two years later he was awarded a master's degree in radiation biophysics and immediately began an atomic energy commission internship, as one of the young managers who was being groomed for positions in the commission offices. The internship began in Washington, D.C., followed by a tour of duty around the country during an orientation period that familiarized the trainees with the agency and its operations. The commission sent Jackson to San Francisco in 1960 for a four-month assignment. It was a temporary appointment that began with the understanding that there were no permanent jobs available in the San Francisco office. He was slated to return to Washington and await placement in an office where a vacancy existed. It happened that in San Francisco he developed the outline of a safety program that would benefit that agency. However, the program could not be implemented unless he was there to get it off the ground. Jackson returned to Washington, but one month later he received an offer to return to San Francisco; thus, he began his career with the Atomic Energy Commission in 1960.

Since 1982 Jackson has worked at the Lawrence Berkeley Laboratory as the head of a one-man office, the Office of Health and Safety Liaison. He is a troubleshooter, a resource person who brings the staff together from the program side of the laboratory and from the safety side. The two groups work on safety issues and resolve problems that affect the laboratory. His input is based upon his knowledge of safety measures that he gained from years of experience with the commission. That experience includes work as staff health physicist where he studies the effects of radiation on people, animals, and plants. He has set up systems to monitor places such as the Stanford Linear Accelerator Center and the Lawrence Livermore and Lawrence Berkeley Laboratories to ensure that they protect workers and people who live in the vicinity.

While answering my questions concerning the widespread fear of nuclear energy and reactors, Jackson said that he was very comfortable with the concept of nuclear energy because of his work with it over the years. He feels that the universal apprehension is due largely to a lack of information, but most of all due to the unfortunate fact that nuclear energy was introduced to the world as a weapon of war. He wishes that the agency would spend more money on educating the populace about the technology and the safety factors. From his vantage point of one who is intimately involved in an industry that remains mysterious to the public at large, he has seen the safety precautions that are taken and knows about the low incidence of accidents. Since the supply of fossil fuel is not infinite, he foresees a time when all countries will have to depend upon nuclear power, the cleanest source of energy that is known to man. When that will occur depends upon how well we manage the remaining fossil fuel supply.

Mendocino County is north of the Bay Area on the coast of the Pacific Ocean. It is a good place to grow timber and Christmas trees. Jackson has purchased forty-five acres of redwood and fir trees in the vicinity of Ukiah, California, nineteen miles off Highway 101 in a scenic area just far enough away from the ocean to escape the thick incoming fog, but close enough to retain the cool breezes that come in from over the water. He has built a geodesic dome, a round house thirty feet in diameter at the base, and twenty-seven feet tall. It is two stories with a seventeen-foot bank of windows on one side. The wood that he used for the house was cut and milled from the trees on the site.

Jackson makes trips to Mendocino County on weekends and vacations. He spends his time on the land thinning trees as his part of a contract with the Department of Agriculture, which is designed to encourage landowners to grow more timber. The idea is to maintain an eight-foot center around the large fir and redwood trees so that they can get sufficient sunlight and grow to full size quicker. He cuts the smaller oak and madrone trees that do not make good timber but merely take up space in the middle of the valuable firs and redwoods. Jackson chops down the unwanted trees, sells the heavier pieces, and cuts the remaining limbs for firewood. The project combines hard physical labor and the exhilaration of working in the open air free from the fumes and noises of the city.

Calvin Jackson is a man whose father was a sharecropper in Florida, and whose family's tradition of having the sons leave school during the times when they were needed in the fields made it impossible for them to finish high school. He escaped this interruption because of his mother's insistence that her three youngest children remain in school for the entire nine months. Of twelve children, he is the only one with a college degree.

WILMA JOHNSON
Born 1931, Batesville, Mississippi

"My style was one of an open door; consequently I worked long hours because people take advantage of that."

When Wilma Johnson's parents moved from Mississippi to the San Joaquin Valley of California, they were looking for a better way of life for their children away from racially prejudiced Mississippi where they feared that a son or daughter would say or do something that might cost them their lives. She thought of her family as having middle-class values and expectations— they owned land in Mississippi and in California and were advocates of higher education. Six of their nine children continued into college. Her father's favorite joke was a boast about how long it had been since he had new shoes because his money went for school clothes, books, and college tuition. Her mother went back to college at age seventy for an associate's and bachelor's degrees and then began to work on a master's.

Johnson's parents found overall improved opportunities for African-Americans in California, but as a young girl Johnson learned that the Golden State was not completely free from racial restrictions. She saw signs, "Colored trade not solicited," and knew of an incident involving the proprietor of a skating rink who took the precaution to furnish police protection when a group from a black church booked a party. He was embarrassed when his anxiety about possible trouble proved unfounded.

The entire family took an active part in their Baptist church. Often at night Johnson heard her mother praying when she thought all the kids were asleep. In her prayers she would ask God over and over again, "Give me strength," to deal with the daily obstacles and dilemmas that come with raising nine children, and to make the right decisions.

Johnson chose nursing as a career when she was in the tenth grade. Her interest was kindled by her research for a school assignment into the training requirements for registered nurses. After high school she went to Fresno State University, and then transferred to the School of Nursing at Stanford and finished both the R.N. and B.S. degrees in 1952. She worked at Stanford for nine months and then enrolled in Columbia University for a master's in nursing. When she returned to California in 1958 she went to the Alameda County Department of Public Health as district nursing director. From 1977 until her retirement in 1990, she held the position of director of public health nursing and was responsible for maternal and child health and communicable disease control. Her responsibilities covered a broad spectrum that included tuberculosis, enteric diseases, and AIDS, especially in the maternal and child health area.

In June 1978 the voters of California reacted to the seemingly endless escalation of property tax rates by passing Proposition 13, which not only effectively lowered the rates but also significantly reduced the assets used to pay for hundreds of services that were funded by state, county, and city revenues. This started the drastic cut in the resources of the health department, which has rendered it inadequate. There has been not only a decline in county funding but also a decline in the outside funding and special grant monies that were used to hire nurses. Many hospitals closed or laid off personnel. In spite of the growth in home and community care, hospitals and agencies had to serve more people with less staff or with the same staff. Johnson did not totally disagree with the concept of home and community care, but she was not happy with the apparent rationing of health care in hospitals.

One main target group of Johnson's office was women who

do not seek prenatal care until late in their last trimester. Another big concern was with tuberculosis, which still remains a problem in Alameda County, and cyclic outbreaks of hepatitis, salmonella, and shigella, conditions that usually involve the handling of foods. There were even cases of malaria, meningitis, and some measles. Although the influx of immigrants—Southeast Asians, Central Americans, Mexicans, Cubans, Haitians, and Eritreans—had lessened, the county had to make sure that the health needs of the new arrivals were not a threat to the well-being of the total community. Additionally, the health facilities began testing for the HIV virus to relieve the pressure on the blood banks.

It is well known that the primary users of public health systems are poor people who fall into high risk groups. Many are welfare recipients who do not have the coverage of a health plan. They are unsophisticated in terms of proper health care and do not have the social connections with better-informed friends who will remind pregnant mothers that early prenatal care can prevent many complications or birth defects. They are not decision makers, nor are they newsworthy. Johnson saw herself as an advocate for such people. She was committed to seeing that as much of the population as possible had the benefit of public health services and that her staff produced a high quality of assistance.

During the war on poverty in the sixties, the county hired a large number of temporary health paraprofessionals whose positions expired with the funding for their project. When the financial support ended it meant a cutback in home health care services, which left a large cadre of women and some men unassigned. Johnson led the campaign to find alternatives for them other than layoffs or pitting one group of workers against another. Johnson's direction enabled her office to transfer those "project" employees into permanent positions with the same benefits as all other agency employees. She encouraged black and other minority staff members, who were less assertive than the white workers, to take promotional examinations even if they were not interested in the specific position; they should go through the testing experience and make themselves known to the administration. Johnson proudly pointed to this as a significant accomplishment during her years of work.

Johnson's primary involvement at Downs during Nichols's tenure was as chairman of the Commission on Social Concerns, the group that spearheaded the church into community and political action and sponsored educational programs. Once Dr. Wendell Lipscomb came to tell us about the alcoholism project he was heading for the state of California. Johnson walked precincts for Nichols when he ran for the Berkeley School Board, and for Wilmont Sweeney when he ran for the Berkeley City Council. Along with the community involvement at Downs, she received there the spiritual renewal that reinforced her religious faith and faith in herself as a person.

Wilma Johnson enjoys traveling to foreign countries. The trip that stood out in her memory was the visit to Kenya for a meeting of the International Nurses Association during the presidency of Madame Karenga, whose husband was in the cabinet of the president of the country. At the close of the meeting Madame Karenga invited the delegates to her home for lunch. The total event, the interaction with colleagues from other countries, the joint seminars, and the fact that it was her first time in Africa, made it a memorable event and an exhilarating adventure.

Before my conversations with Wilma Johnson I read an article in the *Oakland Tribune,* which was headed, "Public Nursing Threatened by Fund Cutbacks." The article was accompanied by a picture of Johnson and mentioned some of the challenges of the Alameda County Health Department, but it did not talk about her crusade to protect the jobs of the paraprofessionals and to see that they had seniority and equal benefits as professional workers. Nor did it say that her efforts forestalled an agencywide layoff that would have eliminated a large number of ethnics who had no status or benefits to protect them. Johnson was the first black public health nurse in Alameda County, but she would not be the last. The next article about Johnson in the *Oakland Tribune* told its readers, "County's First Black Public Health Nurse Retires." This announcement of her retirement in April 1990 paid tribute to her role in the upgrading of the quality of nursing in the Alameda County Department of Health.

Johnson is a woman who enjoyed her work and who loves her church life, family, and friends. She finds time to vary the tempo by traveling within and outside of this country, and she keeps up with the current theater productions. When you meet her for the first time you are struck by her self-assurance and her pleasant, contagious laughter that is hard to resist.

WESLEY JONES
Born 1931, Jacksonville, Texas

"I considered myself, and people referred to me, as the conscience of the welfare department."

The influence of Downs on young Wesley Jones began in 1950 when he was a young man of nineteen who had come to the church primarily in search of female companionship. Instead, he found Nichols, whose counsel was a motivating force in the evolution of his career in social services. Jones had a high level of participation at Downs, notably as youth director. His guidance had a positive effect upon the young people. Wesley Jones graduated from high school in San Diego in 1949 and came to Oakland to live with his sister and her husband while he studied at San Francisco State University. In 1952 while he was still in college, he married Dolores after she had finished high school. For many years they served as codirectors of the youth activities and were much loved by their younger charges as well as the older people of Downs.

Early in his career Jones decided that he was going to be the first African-American to head a county department of social welfare in California. He knew what the obstacles were and that he had to be well prepared, practically and academically. His plan was to get an advanced degree and become familiar with every phase of social welfare. He started as a social worker in the Alameda County offices of social welfare where he moved around, doing everything there was to do in that agency, so that no one could compete with him in any aspect of the work. By 1965 Jones's plan was well into operation. That year he earned his master of arts degree in public administration, which prepared him for his next step as deputy director of social services in Stanislaus County, California. From there Jones rose to director of the Public Welfare Department in Yuba County. Six years later he returned to Stanislaus County, this time as director, but left shortly thereafter to become the director of public welfare in the larger Santa Clara County where he had the responsibility of almost everything that involves human services, except medical care. Jones's office in Santa Clara County served an average of 230,000 people a month and reached a peak of 2,400 employees. Often Jones will remember the admonitions of Nichols who told him over and over again that the key to success was to outline his career strategy and work toward the goal by careful planning and preparation.

The next stage in Jones's plan was to take early retirement from Santa Clara County in 1983 to become a management consultant in Sacramento, involved with legislative services, health services, and social services. His office performed a management study for the organization of black social workers, made recommendations, and assisted in their implementation. He developed a training series for ethnics, which included instruction about job preparation, applications, resumes, examinations, and interviews. As a licensed lobbyist Jones represents the black social workers and the California Association of Adoption Agencies.

Proposition 13, by its mandate to restructure the property tax base, brought serious financial problems to the state's social welfare departments by severely reducing revenues. To deal with the resulting layoffs, Jones acted upon the board of supervisors' publicly articulated commitment to affirmative action and his personal desire to offer quality service to clients who need special attention because of language difficulties. In Santa Clara County where 12 percent of his caseload dealt with Southeast Asians and 10 percent Hispanic, Jones had to defend himself against lawsuits because of some of the employment procedures that he utilized to make the services most beneficial to those clients. He had to face the union's system of seniority with the last hired being the first fired, which would result in the loss of caseworkers who could speak the languages of the ethnics whose command of English was limited. He created new job designations with added compensation for people who were bilingual and who would work exclusively with the non-English-speaking caseload. This demonstrated that those workers were more valuable to the service objectives of the department, and that even though some of them were not of the same culture as their clients, they could communicate with them in a meaningful way. There were African-American and white workers who were fluent in Spanish and who fell into the new category. Jones was victorious in that he was able to maintain some, but not all, of the positions, and it was an achievement that reflected the caliber of service and not merely retaining the jobs of one group of workers.

One of Jones's foremost interests was the adoption of black children. Placement of them within their cultural environment was his foremost priority; interracial placement was a last resort. He felt strongly that a young child should be given the opportunity to grow up with people who share his heritage. Whether the child would choose a different life-style or not as an adult was his or her decision. He thinks that there are many African-American homes that would respond if special recruitment efforts for a specific child were made through churches, for example, instead of using general television advertisements. He does not contend that it is possible to place every black child, but he regrets that children are being "warehoused" in institutions and foster homes when many of them should never have been removed from their homes in the first place. Jones is convinced that his colleagues in social welfare agreed with him about this.

Jones has laid a lot of the groundwork for the passage of Bill 633, which mandates priority placement in the identical ethnic and cultural background. This bill would provide a task force to assist in implementation and an evaluation and reporting procedure for social workers. There are allies in the Jewish Family Service that feel Jewish children should grow up in Jewish homes, and the Catholic Social Services is also interested in the idea of religious preference. Jones will be relieved when the legislation is passed and signed by the governor because it will put teeth into the concept of placing children with families who care to teach them about their racial identity.

The philosophy of Wesley Jones is epitomized for me by two concerns that have been paramount to him. He has campaigned for adoption placement of black children with their own ethnic group to increase the likelihood of success in the adoptions and for their personal development as adults, and he has protected the quality of service to non-English-speaking clients by challenging the seniority system of last hired, first fired.

The battery of occupational tests that Jones took in college was correct when it indicated that he would do well in human services. He is very proud of his accomplishments in the social welfare arena of California. When he sat with his colleagues at the state level reviewing legislation that would affect human life, his vote was worth as much as any of the other fifty-seven county directors, and his ideas were respected because of the integrity that he brought to his position. The walls of his office in Santa Clara County were full of plaques, awards, and citations from scores of organizations and agencies that testify to the value of his work.

HAZEL KYLE
Born 1921, Pensacola, Florida

"Downs loves me; they think I can do no wrong because of the singing."

The greatest gift that Hazel Kyle brought to Downs church from the late fifties until she became quite ill in the latter part of the eighties was her beautiful singing voice. She loved to sing just as much as we loved to hear her. She and Birel Vaughn, the music director during the Nichols era, understood each other, and for years blended their talents for our enjoyment.

In the segregated society of Pensacola the swimming pools, the schools, everything was separate. There was little friction because the black people knew the rules of the city and did not risk challenging the way of life; challenges came later with the civil rights movement. People in all sections of Pensacola, Florida, knew Hazel Kyle's family. In addition to Hazel there were her three brothers, her father, a shoemaker who made all of the shoes that his children wore, and her mother, a petite lady who only stood five feet two inches tall and who, according to her daughter, could "jump up" to her sons and demand better behavior. There was also her father's sister, Aunt Gertrude, who treated Kyle and her brothers as if they were her own children. Aunt Gertrude taught in Pensacola for fifty-one years, and after she retired, she continued as a substitute teacher. On her ninety-seventh birthday people spoke of her as a teacher who would stay after school to help any one who needed special tutoring.

Hazel married Clarence in 1941 during the days when the nation was in an uproar over the Pearl Harbor attack. He had already joined the navy, and for the first couple of years they lived apart: she in college in Florida and he in the military. She completed her studies at Bethune-Cookman College in Daytona, Florida, and joined him in California in 1943 before he was discharged. In spite of her degree in elementary education Kyle's interests were not in teaching. Friends put pressure on her to teach in the Bay Area where the number of black children was increasing daily; employment agencies also tried to shame her into accepting a teaching job. She stuck by her decision not to go into education, however, and after a series of smaller jobs she took a temporary clerical position with the East Bay Municipal Utility District (EBMUD). She had responded to a newspaper advertisement, even though it was a well-known fact that the only black workers at EBMUD were a few unskilled male laborers. To her surprise she got the job.

This temporary position evolved into twenty-three years of uninterrupted service with EBMUD until she took early retirement in 1977. She became an engineering aide and was the first woman to work in the engineering section of Water Resources and Planning at EBMUD. Whenever Kyle described her work she said facetiously, "I count rain drops," which was not a very great exaggeration. She kept computerized records of data from the field that indicated rainfall, reservoir levels, and home and business consumption of water. Every morning her telephone rang constantly from contacts relaying water information in designated areas. Using these figures she made correlation analyses that were used to project the anticipated rainfall and to determine whether or not there should be restricted water usage in the area.

Kyle worked with a group of men who treated her with respect and good humor. She literally ran the office, and they would greet her with mock nervousness and fear, singing out in unison, "Here comes Hazel." She would chide them by saying that they were wasting their time; all of the numbers on their desks would do nothing to increase the number of raindrops that came down. If a newcomer had an inquiry that related to Kyle's sphere of responsibility but sought to bypass her and deal with a higher authority, her male colleagues informed the visitor that he would have to talk to Mrs. Kyle or to no one else. Such was their relationship.

The first reason Kyle came to Downs church was because she wanted to hear more of Nichols's teaching; she first knew of him from the South Berkeley Community Church. The second reason was to sing in the Chancel Choir, which was directed by Birel Vaughn. She liked the music that Vaughn selected; it was the music she had sung for years in schools and churches in Florida: hymns, Negro spirituals, and songs from the European masters. For more than thirty years Kyle was president of the Chancel Choir at Downs and frequently sang solos or took the leading parts. She sang often at weddings, funerals, recitals, and concerts, but she never accepted compensation; it was her way of returning the musical gift that she has been blessed with. Kyle said, "This is what I do for the Lord." Her preference was spirituals, Bach, Beethoven, and Brahms, and operatic music. She did very little pop, and no gospel music.

During Holy Week 1988 Kyle was soloist for a performance of "The Seven Last Words" at Oakland's Elmhurst United Methodist Church. On the morning of the final rehearsal her doctor told her the cancer that had been in remission had come back. Her energy and her spirits were at a low ebb. However, she got through the rehearsal and sang beautifully the next evening, the night of the program. Kyle thought of her singing as therapy, as a way of extending her life creatively in a manner that she enjoyed. When "The Seven Last Words " was over, her granddaughter said, "I hate to brag, but the lady should have been an opera singer."

When I wrote Hazel Kyle's profile, she was no longer singing because of the effects of her illness, but she still radiated the magnetism that endeared her to people. She is now dead, leaving a void for her family, for the community, and for the people of Downs church who loved her not only for the music but for her personality that reflected the beauty of her voice. Kyle's funeral, which was called "A Celebration of Thanksgiving and Praise for the Life of Hazel Kyle," had an appropriate emphasis on music. The combined choirs of the church and the instrumental musicians provided an abundance of music, songs that were her favorites and those that we associate with her.

During one part of the celebration, "Open Expressions," people were invited to share their special memories of Kyle. The sincerity of these spontaneous statements was epitomized by Nichols. He began by asking the members of the early Chancel Choir who sang with Kyle to stand in tribute as he spoke. After his brief expression of love he ended with a recitation of the poem by Henry Wadsworth Longfellow:

> I shot an arrow into the air,
> It fell to earth, I knew not where;
> For, so swiftly it flew the sight
> Could not follow it in its flight.
>
> I breathed a song into the air,
> It fell to earth, I knew not where;
> For who has sight so keen and strong,
> That it can follow the flight of song?
>
> Long, long afterward, in an oak
> I found the arrow, still unbroken;
> And the song, from beginning to end,
> I found again in the heart of a friend.

DOROTHY LEE
Born 1922, Oklahoma City, Oklahoma

**"I enjoyed working with kids who often get 'lopped off' on the end,
and I like trying to get teachers to do more individualized instruction,
even though they have a classroom full of kids."**

When Dorothy Lee's oldest child was quite young, his nursery school engaged Nichols to teach a six-week course for the parents. The session on religion motivated Lee to visit Downs, and from that time she has been an active participant, serving in such roles as superintendent of the Sunday school and organizer of the Mother's Fellowship for women who had children the same age as hers. During the construction of the sanctuary she was a dependable member of the kitchen corps and helped prepare meals for the volunteer workers.

From her early childhood Dorothy Lee's life has been church-centered. Her father believed that anytime the church door opened he and his family should be there. When she was a child in Oklahoma City the whole family went to the Church of God in Christ "day and night." The parents' discipline was centered upon the teachings of the Bible. Lee remembers her mother as a hard worker, a domestic and a caterer. Much of her work required her to spend hours on her feet, and she suffered frequent painful leg cramps. Many times Lee woke up in the night to hear her walking around and around the dining room table trying to shake off the cramps. Her father was employed as a janitor and assisted with the duties of the catering parties.

Lee did well in school because in her home it was understood that she and her brother would attend college. Lee went to the University of Kansas and completed a bachelor's degree in 1943. While she was in Kansas her parents separated, and her father came to San Francisco to work in the shipyards. When he died in 1946, Lee and her husband, Emanuel, whom she had married in 1944, came to California to settle her father's estate. They did not return to Oklahoma after that. Initially Lee took a series of civil service jobs in Oakland and San Francisco and worked at the University of California in the accounting department of the university library. The most rewarding part of her employment in California—in public education—began by luck. A friend informed her in 1968 that Richmond schools were hiring kindergarten teachers for an internship program. Lee was concerned about her possibilities for selection out of the three hundred applicants for a limited number of slots since she had been out of college for twenty-five years. She need not have worried. Three things gave her a preferred place among the candidates: her maturity at age forty-six, the two years of elementary school teaching in Oklahoma between graduation from college and the migration to California, and having already completed the requirements for a California teaching credential. She was hired immediately as a kindergarten teacher.

Through the first years in the schools of Richmond she taught kindergarten, worked as resource teacher, and coordinated the district's advisory committees as parent liaison. By this time she had gotten a master's degree and an administration credential from San Francisco State University. She was appointed principal of Broadway Elementary School where she remained until she retired in 1984. While Lee was an administrator in the Richmond schools, she became involved with the California Association of Compensatory Education (CACE). Through this agency she encouraged parents and school staff to use their energies to better the quality of education for disadvantaged students, and she disseminated information to parents about the available programs and facilities. This statewide organization held workshops to show teachers how to use team learning and individualized instruction to reach students who are often forgotten or overlooked by traditional teaching methods. Lee held the office of regional director in CACE, as did Dorene Walton and Ella Wiley.

Lee has been active in community affairs beyond the scope of her jobs throughout her life. Through her involvement with the Oakland Older Adult Center, she assisted in the production of a television program that was broadcast over the Oakland Public Schools television station, KDOL. Elizabeth Pettus hosted the show that featured live interviews with people who talked about current events and local services. At the Center for Employment Training, Lee was a part of a federally funded project that trained adults for employment as automated office workers, shipping clerks, and janitors. It also provided supplemental instruction in reading and mathematics to correct deficiencies in these areas. When the students finished the course, the job developer of the project found work for them. One of Lee's favorite projects was sponsored by the Delta Sigma Theta sorority: she established computer instruction centers in three Oakland churches and hooked them up to the computer center at Merritt Community College. The classes were designed for people age eight to eighty. In connection with this project the sorority worked with state assemblywomen Teresa Hughes and Gwen Moore for passage of a telecommunication bill to provide funds for learning centers to teach adults to read.

Dorothy Lee appears to be a quiet, soft-spoken woman, whose outward appearance does not give full evidence of her dynamism. She describes herself as "a very giving person who has to do something to help serve somebody somewhere." When she considers the present condition of black people—the power of the drug menace, and the continued existence of some families on welfare benefits without a change in their status—she becomes somewhat pessimistic, but it has never discouraged her efforts to better the quality of life in her community. She has been sustained in the past by the successes at the Center for Employment Training, particularly the participants' improved self-esteem and victory over drug addiction.

RUTH LOVE
Born 1938, Lawton, Oklahoma

"There was a great support system at Downs without you knowing you had a support system. When you went away and came back it was like coming back to your family."

Ruth Love described Nichols as a theologian who understood the real world, someone who could help people cope with whatever they had to cope with. When she came to Downs fresh out of undergraduate school in 1954, she was just starting her career and appreciated the comfort and support of the minister and the Downs family as a whole. The pastor was always accessible to discuss personal problems or ideas for church projects, and the congregation continually extended their love through their concern for her welfare.

There is no need for family reunions in the usual sense of that term for Ruth Love's family. At the slightest tinge of homesickness they arrange by telephone a weekend together. These frequent gatherings along with regular long-distance conversations keep alive the oneness of the family. Love's father was a contractor in Bakersfield where the family had lived since they left Oklahoma when she was two years old. Much of his time and money were used to help people get a start when they first reached California. In her younger years, Love's mother was active in the organization of the Negro Business and Professional Women.

Ruth Love's maternal grandfather, who lived into his nineties, had a profound impact upon her. He was an accomplished storyteller who entertained the children with stories about successful black people, always ending with a moral about the value of hard work. He was a scholarly man, the first person Love knew who read the *New York Times*. Despite being born into slavery, he became a professor at Langston University in Oklahoma. People in Oklahoma remember him as the founder of the Frederick Douglass School, which still exists in Lawton, Oklahoma. It stands as a tribute to his interest in the education of African-American children.

Love's first teaching job was in an elementary school in West Oakland. Although she had spent four years in college and was employed as a public school teacher, her father still exercised parental authority over her living arrangements. He did not want her to live alone in the heart of the city, but it was all right for her to move into the downtown YWCA's Blue Triangle Club near Lake Merritt where there were nice apartments for business and professional women. Before long someone mentioned the dynamic minister who was at Downs Methodist Church, and she was "sold on it the first time I went." She knew some of the people there, Dorothy Pitts, Walter Pitts, Audrey Jordan, who was her big sister in her first year of teaching, and Jordan's sister, Etta Hill. It seemed to Love that the total membership of Downs was interested in her well-being and in her progress in the field of education. The effect was a support system that was never obtrusive but strengthened her development. Hearing Edna and Milton Combs talk about their years in Burma as missionaries inspired Love to travel. When she first went to West Africa and learned that missionaries were not as welcome as they had been in the past, she abandoned her original intention to serve in that capacity, but her resolve to travel abroad remained strong.

Love's resolve to continue her education also remained strong: she earned a master's in guidance and counseling from San Francisco State University, and finally, in 1969, a doctorate in human behavior from United States International University, San Diego, California. After five years in the classroom in Oakland, Love went to England on a Fulbright Exchange Teacher fellowship during the 1960–1961 academic year. This first trip out of the country whetted her appetite for further foreign travel and for interaction with the people of other countries and their cultures. The next year Love spent the summer in Ghana, West Africa, as director of Crossroads Africa, where twelve American university students shared with African students projects to improve the living conditions of a village in the northern part of that country.

Before she entered school administration Love had extensive, all-encompassing experiences in education. She was an elementary, junior, and senior high school teacher in Oakland; taught in a school and a teacher training college in Britain; represented Oakland schools in the capacity of counselor/consultant in a Ford Foundation Great Cities Project; worked as project coordinator of a Girls Correctional Institution for the American Friends Service Committee in Albuquerque, New Mexico; and taught an adult education class in Oakland.

Love's initial venture into educational administration began with the California State Department of Education in Sacramento. Her first assignment was as a consultant to the Bureau of Pupil Personnel Services: she was responsible for the counseling and guidance services for ethnic students on a statewide basis. Two years later she became chief of the Bureau of Compensatory Education Program Development where she was involved in the establishment, operation, evaluation, and reporting of programs for disadvantaged youth. She gave testimony to Congress on related subjects and took part in the national dialogue about education as a member of the first Health Education and Welfare Commission, and as a consultant to the Office of Economic Opportunity and the Office of Education.

From Sacramento, Love went to Washington, D.C., in 1971 to direct the Department of Education's Right to Read project. Here she administered the national campaign to improve reading and reduce illiteracy. After her extensive experience at the state and national levels, Love reentered local public education as chief administrator of the schools in Oakland and Chicago. She was superintendent of schools in Oakland from 1975 to 1981, and general superintendent in Chicago from March 1981 to 1985. There was widespread student apathy when she returned to Oakland, but she was heartened when the scores on standardized tests reached the national norm. Love was pleased with the Artists and Scholars Program and brought distinguished visitors to Oakland, among them Alex Haley, Coretta King, James Baldwin, Jane Fonda, Mario Obledo, Mortimer Adler, and General "Chappie" James, so that the children of the district could interact with well-known and successful personalities. In preparation for each celebrity, students did extensive research and wrote reports about their achievements. Its companion project, the Scholars and Achievers Program, identified and recognized students who had shown scholastic or leadership potential and encouraged them to develop these abilities.

Ruth Love did not seek the superintendency in Chicago, but residents of Chicago sent her material about the city, and a delegation of community women came to Oakland to persuade her to come. Meanwhile, Jesse Jackson, who was promoting the candidacy of a man already in the school district, telephoned Love to discourage her. Jackson's first message was, "Do not come, please do not come." With subsequent calls his plea became more insistent: "You had better not come. We are not having any outsiders." In spite of Jackson's efforts to deter her,

Love accepted the Chicago job to meet its enormous challenge. "Experts" told her that it was impossible to make any difference in the schools because of the city's political tradition. Being told that she could not make any positive changes made her more determined. She said that pessimism "just goes against my grain."

Love came to Chicago in a time of controversy and showed that she *could* improve the quality of education. People no longer believed that it was possible to make the schools better; there were over half a million students in the system, and the obstacles seemed to be insurmountable. Among the challenges were the ties of the school system to the political structure of the city, continually increasing enrollments, student and parent indifference, and competition with the higher-paying jobs in the private sector for the service of well-qualified teachers. In spite of the problems in the schools, in 1982 Love demonstrated improved standardized test scores in reading and mathematics in 435 of the 600 schools. She credited this achievement to the hard work of the teachers, and to the implementation of an approach to teaching reading to all of the students who were below grade level, the Chicago Master Reading Learning Program, which was developed during her tenure.

When Love left public school administration she made the logical transition into the business world with the organization and management of Ruth Love Enterprises (RLE), which provides products and services for the overall improvement of education on an international basis. Her background as teacher, counselor, and administrator of local, state, and national educational agencies had thoroughly prepared her.

RLE has created video and computer software for educators to increase their effectiveness at the school sites. It has implemented the Effective Schools Program (ESP) that is based on research findings that say all children can learn regardless of their ethnic or economic background. ESP is a "media-based training program" that school districts can buy to use for inservice sessions to help teachers and administrators improve classroom instruction, general school climate, and parental support and involvement. RLE also recruits school district superintendents and directs national institutes that focus on approaches that have been shown to work successfully with high-risk students, teenage pregnancies, and drug abuse.

In her pursuit of improving educational opportunities for the economically and socially disadvantaged, Love has had an advantage that few educators have had: she has been able to ask assistance directly from highly placed figures, most notably former President Jimmy Carter and Sen. Edward Kennedy, because of her friendships with the families. In one instance she obtained, barely five minutes before he went onto the Senate floor, a commitment from Kennedy to speak in favor of literacy legislation. He did so, and furthermore, he used his influence to pass the bill, which had implications for a large portion of the population.

Love believes that public education will continue to have a hard time withstanding the idea that is consciously or unconsciously held by some people in powerful positions that education is not a basic right of all children. In many cases these decision makers are more sympathetic to and, thus, more inclined to give support to private and parochial education than to public education. She thinks the survival of public education will depend upon the advocacy of educators for their profession and a rebuilding of confidence in public schools; furthermore, she believes it is the obligation of educators everywhere to see that there is something special about every school in order to eliminate the second-rate schools that are now so commonplace.

I first met Ruth Love when she was a newly employed teacher in Oakland. She was an attractive young woman dedicated to her career and fun to be around. She was part of a group of friends who met monthly at each other's homes to listen to music and enjoy social times. Love and Audrey Jordan, who were coteachers, usually came together. When Love was superintendent of schools in Oakland, I worked in the personnel office and could observe her method of operation. This was a period of time when she was effectively overhauling the administration offices and classrooms. There was vocal criticism from staff members who did not want to change from their comfortable pace and who resented Love's impatience with people who were not willing to go the extra mile for their students. I knew that there was the wagging of tongues about her political orientation, although most of her adversaries realized that her contacts made it easier for money and other favors to flow into the district. I heard no one deny that the uppermost thought in her mind was the welfare of the students of Oakland.

RAMONA MAPLES
Born 1928, New Orleans, Louisiana

"I just wish that people would be more involved in what is happening in their lives, and watch the politicians, and try to keep everybody honest."

As she sat on the counter and watched the neighborhood pharmacist in New Orleans mix his medicines, preschooler Ramona Maples had her first encounter with someone who was addressed by the title *Doctor*. He wore a white coat, and people came to ask his advice. This was her "first grand experience," one that made a lasting impression on her.

Maples's parents tacitly accepted the racial situation, but even as a small girl she resented the prejudice and discrimination that she saw all about her. She had to walk past three schools to get to the one for black children. Her mother and aunt were domestic workers who cooked, cleaned, wet nursed the babies for white families, yet small children addressed them by their first names. Once she said to herself, "On a given day if every cook would throw some arsenic in the pot, we could wipe out the white people." To her young mind this would solve all of the racial problems. Maples believes that the social status of black domestic workers in the South was determined by the wealth of the people they worked for. If you had rich employers you learned "American culture," how to eat with seven pieces of silver, and how to use correct English. The employer of Maples's aunt, Miss Peterson of the Helman Mayonnaise firm, was an example of the type of people whom Maples knew it was better to work for. Peterson encouraged Maples to go to the University of California, which she classified as one of the finest universities in the world. When Maples was a senior in high school her family migrated to Oakland. She wanted to stay in New Orleans to attend Dillard University because she thought it unlikely for any college to surpass Dillard. Her father insisted that she come to California. Before long Maples had forgotten about Dillard and was admitted to the University of California–Berkeley.

After college it was not as easy as Maples expected to get her first teaching job. She taught as a student teacher in Albany, California, but the promised job there was not forthcoming because the black teacher who filled their quota of one did not resign. Berkeley would not hire her because they feared that people born in the South were too emotional. Even though Oakland did not offer a job, Richmond had a place for her. She began teaching in Richmond in 1950 in a school that was half African-American with the remainder whites, Hispanics, and Chinese.

When Maples started teaching in the Berkeley schools in 1957, she questioned the popular conclusion that poor academic performance was endemic among poor people because their children could not learn. She was outspoken about the professional responsibilities of teachers, and she wanted to improve test scores. With the late Larry Wells as principal and Maples as vice principal, Lincoln Elementary School began to see some changes for the better. The teaching staff was a fine group of black and white teachers who had chosen to work at that all-black school. The changes in student conduct and parental interest started to show as the children began to achieve.

But the coming of integration to Berkeley schools interrupted the progress, and Maples faced the conflict of having been a strong proponent of integration, yet seeing the definite shortcomings of its implementation. With the shift in teacher placement to achieve ethnic balance at school sites, Lincoln could not retain the staff that was making great strides, and it lost its exclusively African-American students for which the school's program was tailored. It also lost grades kindergarten through third and kept only grades fourth through sixth, and the students came from all over the city instead of from the nearby neighborhood. The parents who were formerly involved no longer felt secure with the new situation, and the new parents were more affluent white citizens whose approach to the education of their children reflected their own academic achievements and more comfortable financial status.

Maples was not happy to admit that the gains at the school were a casualty of integration. She had hoped that students who sat in an integrated classroom with a good teacher would have the benefit of better instruction, but she did not know that so little of that would really come about. On the positive side, she saw a reduction in racial incidents; there was a more honest relationship and more of a feeling of acceptance. In Maples's opinion the lack of scholastic progress for black students was due to several things: There was the misuse of the instructional aides, paraprofessionals who were not teachers trained to instruct. The "black, slow, unmanageable" kids worked with the aides, and since their parents did not come to the school and protest the lack of attention their children received, they stayed with the aides. Maples feels strongly that since desegregation did not solve the problems, it is even more important for parents to remain involved in the child's progress at school. The exodus of the black middle class from Berkeley also had an effect upon the quality of education. Those parents who would have spoken out against the negligence moved to the suburbs where comparable housing was more affordable, and the schools had fewer of the problems that are prevalent in inner city schools; or they sent their children to private schools where the chances of more desirable companions were greater.

At the end of twenty-five years at various school sites, Maples became director of Research and Evaluation. Since her retirement in 1987, she has donated time to the Department of Education, reading proposals to determine which colleges would be approved for grants for services to underprivileged children, and assisting senior citizens in preparing their income tax forms. In addition, Maples has taken on the responsibility of legislative director for the Retired Teachers' Association of Berkeley-Richmond.

Maples and Carl Mack, Sr., of Berkeley, have been precinct chairs for practically every African-American candidate in the East Bay: Roy Nichols, John Miller, Wilmont Sweeney, Warren Widener, Ron Dellums, Lionel Wilson, and for the fair housing legislation, which was sponsored by Byron Rumford. Her house was campaign headquarters for Warren Widener's race for mayor of Berkeley. She has been on the Democratic Central Committee and served on Berkeley's human relations and welfare commissions.

Not long after the establishment of Downs church in the forties, Ramona Maples identified it as a place with a cadre of hard workers who shared her convictions about spirituality and community welfare. She found her niche there right away, teaching in the Vacation Bible school, participating in retreats, and coordinating lunch for the volunteer workers every Saturday during the building project. Maples remained a vital part of Downs for just about twenty years until the upset of her divorce caused her to look for other ways to spend her Sundays and her leisure time.

In 1981, after an absence of at least ten years from religious involvement, Maples converted to Buddhism. Buddhists place great emphasis upon world peace. Unlike many other religions, Buddhists do not hold prayer sessions regularly in a church building. Their temples are reserved for special observances. The believers say their morning and evening prayers (chants) in their homes because they believe that the church is within the heart, and within the home. The chants are for "enlightenment and happiness, not to let the environment control you, but to try to control your environment through your life-style." When she converted, Maples had to deal with the curiosity of friends and relatives about her chanting before her altar, but they are no longer surprised by her change in religious practices. Her mother, sister, and niece join in the chants, and Maples's daughter, Karen, is an active Buddhist and was married in the temple.

My first conversation with Ramona Maples took place in her office in the old city hall of Berkeley, which is now the administration building of Berkeley schools. Her desk was covered with the papers of work in progress, and there were pictures of children all around. One was a large black-and-white reproduction of students in a classroom; another was a color photo of boys and girls on a playground. For our next talk I went to her home. A table in her living room was covered with pictures of her daughter, sons, nieces, nephews, and grandchildren, and there were toys for the young ones to play with when they come to visit.

I saw Maples's altar where she chants, and she told me the meaning of each item on the altar. It was my first opportunity to get a close look at this religion. Maples is now a blending of the African-American culture of the South with the Buddhist religion of the ancient East, having retained the best qualities of each.

WALTER MORRIS
Born 1921, Mobile, Alabama

"Anything that is done is helpful nowadays to deliver health care to those who do not have the income to do it themselves. That is a very pressing need."

The first trip that Walter Morris made to Downs was not the result of careful selection of a place to worship; it was a matter of expediency. When he came to Oakland in 1952, his work schedule as a medical doctor just starting his practice made it necessary for him to reduce his travel time as much as possible, and Downs was just a few blocks from his home. He stayed at Downs because he liked the philosophy of the minister and the warmth of his peers. Since his first visit, he has occupied many positions of responsibility and still maintains an active membership.

Walter Morris is proud that his father lived to be nearly one hundred years old, and his mother died when she was well into her nineties. His father was a devoutly religious man who was superintendent of the Sunday school of their Baptist church in Mobile, Alabama. One of the meeting rooms of the church has been named in his honor. His mother was also equally active. Mobile still remembers Morris's father's leadership in the establishment of the Mobile County Training School, the school that Morris attended until he was nine years old. Dean Moss (one of the founders of Phi Beta Sigma fraternity at Howard University), principal of the school, detected academic promise in one of Morris's sisters and urged their father to send her to school in Boston. The senior Morris sent his daughter and two of his sons to Massachusetts with their aunt (his sister) as chaperon. When the aunt suddenly returned to Mobile leaving the young people unsupervised, Morris's father insisted that their mother drop everything and hurriedly prepare herself and the three younger children to leave four days later to go to Boston.

They had no idea at the time that the move would be a permanent one for the whole family. During the thirties Mobile's waterfront was in economic chaos, leaving Morris's father among the hundreds who were without jobs. His stable employment as a longshoreman ceased to exist. He, too, went to Boston, thinking that he would return to Alabama when conditions returned to normal. After a period of taking whatever work he could find, Morris's father became the custodian for a large apartment complex where the duties included taking care of the huge coal furnaces to heat the units during the winter. On Saturdays his sons went with him to help with the cleaning, polishing the brass fixtures, and removing the trash. After a while he got a job in the service department of the post office where he remained until he retired.

Two incidents that occurred before Morris was fifteen years old helped him decide upon medicine as a career. A visiting minister fell down the stairs in his home, and Morris helped his parents take care of the man. Another time an elderly relative became very ill in their home, and Morris helped the doctor give an intravenous injection and handed the physician instruments as his assistant. He got a satisfying feeling both times and wanted to continue doing similar things; it was the only career he ever considered for himself. With his bachelor's in zoology from the University of Washington, he went into the school of medicine at Howard University in Washington, D.C., and received his medical degree in 1952. He and Lela were married in 1949 in Tacoma, Washington, after she had completed nursing training while he was in his second year of medical training.

After his internship and a residency appointment, Morris went to the University of Pennsylvania for a year of graduate work in his specialty, orthopedics. His first choice was to practice in the state of Washington, but his classmate Vertis Thompson, who had come to the Bay Area, assured him that there was ample work for him in California. Morris, Thompson, and Benjamin Covington, who had been at Freedmen's Hospital in Washington, D.C., at the same time, opened offices together on Shattuck Avenue in Oakland, under conditions that would have discouraged people who were less committed. The three operated the emergency room at Herrick Hospital in Berkeley around the clock. In addition to the emergency room schedule and his regular office hours, Morris also worked at the hospital at the Presidio of San Francisco. The Presidio, headquarters of the Sixth United States Army located on the scenic marine headlands just under the Golden Gate Bridge, was a beautiful place to spend the additional hours of his strenuous schedule. He kept this up until his practice was well established. Weekends were the only time he had to rest.

Morris has been involved in extensive community interests. Gov. Jerry Brown appointed him to the San Francisco Bay Area Water Quality Board for a two-year term. He was a boy scout leader and became one of the vice-presidents of the San Francisco Council of the Boy Scouts. The boys who were in his troop are men now; some went to Vietnam. Morris had the chance to talk with a few before and after the war and saw the effects that conflict had on them—effects that appeared in varying degrees, depending upon the individual.

Prior to the merger of Herrick and Alta Bates Hospitals in Berkeley, Morris was on the board of trustees of Herrick Hospital. He was chairman of the board of the Bay Area Black Consortium for Quality Health Care, which directs health care to the disadvantaged population. Along the same line he was an active member of the St. Luke's Society, a group of doctors and ministers that attempted to meet the health care needs of the underserved community. The ministers and doctors combined their skills to do what they could to improve the quality of life through health facilities. They coordinated a food program for needy people, advised church members about hospital and medical care, and sponsored programs to educate the community about AIDS. The latest of the numerous recognitions for his extensive public service came to Morris from the Bay Area Black United Fund in January 1990—the organization's Walter

Bremond Award for superior community involvement. This award recognized Morris's work in the medical field and his devotion to projects that benefit all of the citizens of his society, young people as well as old.

I met Morris and his wife, Lela, shortly after they first came to Downs. I have maintained contact with the family as their three children grew up. In past years Morris, Lela, and I have been part of a caravan of bicyclists who are guaranteed to attract attention on a Saturday morning as we ride in the streets of the town of Alameda across the estuary from Oakland, or on a bicycle path beside a highway in the Napa Valley. We form a column of more than a dozen black men and women, all much beyond fifty years old with varying degrees of skill in balance and maneuverability.

ROY C. NICHOLS
Born 1918, Hurlock, Maryland

"One of my professors said to me, 'Roy, are you going to waste your life as a minister?' Instead of discouraging me, that just made my determination to be even stronger."

The destiny of Downs Memorial United Methodist Church was determined in great part by the leadership and personality of Roy C. Nichols. From 1949, when as a young man of thirty-one he answered the call of the newly formed congregation, he guided our lives until he left California in 1964 to take over the spiritual reins of a much larger church in New York City. Under his guidance Downs responded to the religious, social, and political needs of its congregants and the community at large. In addition to leading the religious services of the church, Nichols stimulated us to take action on pertinent local issues. On the lighter side, we went to dinners at restaurants where we were pampered, and to plays, musical and dance presentations, picnics, and spent time together in a relaxed atmosphere simply to enjoy each other's company.

Roy Nichols was born on the eastern shore of Maryland but spent his childhood in north Philadelphia. His mother became ill with tuberculosis and died when he was five. Nichols's father was a chauffeur who worked seven days a week, but he devoted every available moment to his children until he died two weeks before his son graduated from high school. Although the father was a young man when he was widowed, he remained single and took care of his young son and two daughters. To the eight-year-old Nichols, his father's love was epitomized by his answer to the boy's question as to why he had not remarried. He replied that he had not been able to find a woman who would accept all three of the children; his was a firm resolve to maintain the unity of the family.

When Nichols reached the fifth grade his teacher, Natalie K. Wallace, sparked his interest in school work, and Dr. Schmidt, his high school advisor, demanded that he buckle down to serious study. Nichols had no aspirations for college and had been surprised when he qualified for entrance into Philadelphia's elite Central High School where admission was based upon the student's academic record. The scholarship demands at Central High and the incentives of Dr. Schmidt, coupled with the encouragement of Frank Morris, Nichols's best friend, began to improve his self-confidence. The friendship between Nichols and Morris flourished. Their conversations about the years to come after graduation from high school were enriched by Morris's advantage of having a mother who was a college graduate.

All through Nichols's life the church has been a dominant force. After his mother died he changed from the Methodist church to the First African Baptist Church in Philadelphia, a church where he saw in the same pews black people who ran the gamut of job classifications, professions, and educational achievement. They were all there—models for the young people to pattern their lives after. The Reverend William A. Harrod provided inspiration for the young people and the chance to sharpen their talents by participation in the affairs of the church. At home Nichols enjoyed the love and protection of his family, but his father and sisters were unable to give the kind of stimulation that he received at his school and church. In the First African Baptist Church the seeds were sown for him to begin to recognize his potential. He developed a commitment to the church and in the eleventh grade made the decision to go to college and then to seminary.

To prepare for college Nichols went to Atlantic City to spend the summer working as a waiter. From his wages and tips he saved one hundred dollars. This amount, his state scholarship, and the pay from his dishwashing job on campus, made it possible for him to enter Lincoln University in Pennsylvania, the oldest African-American college in the nation. It was at Lincoln that one of Nichols's professors said to him, "Roy, are you going to waste your life as a minister?" Instead of having a discouraging effect this statement strengthened Nichols's determination to follow his commitment. As a member of the student Christian movement, Nichols developed a relationship with the "dean" of African-American theologians, Dr. Howard Thurman, who was teaching in the theology department of Howard University and who made frequent visits to other black colleges. Dr. Thurman was a mentor to church-oriented college students and suggested that Nichols apply to the Pacific School of Religion (PSR) in Berkeley to test that institution's admissions policy for black students. The response was favorable and came with the guarantee of a job. He made plans to enroll in PSR in September 1941.

In addition to his studies at PSR, Nichols functioned as student minister in Oakland, first at Beth Eden Baptist Church, and then at First African Methodist Episcopal Church. He interrupted seminary to cofound with fellow seminarian, Robert K. Winters, the South Berkeley Community Church, one of the first interracial churches in the country. When he returned to PSR he worked nights at the Veteran's Hospital in Oakland. After graduation from PSR in 1947, he continued to work at the hospital and study until the call came to him from Downs.

At one of the informal Sunday Evening Hours that were sponsored by the North Oakland YWCA for young black men and women during the time that Nichols was a seminary student, he met his wife, Ruth, a podiatrist who had an office in the prestigious I. Magnin store in San Francisco. After an acquaintance of about two years, they were married in July 1944 in a ceremony conducted by two eminent and internationally known theologians: Dr. Buell G. Gallagher, a teacher at PSR and copastor with Nichols of South Berkeley Community Church, and Dr. Howard Thurman, the copastor of the Fellowship Church of All People in San Francisco.

Early in 1949 a neighbor approached Nichols at his home and asked him to assist with the work of the church two blocks away. That church was Downs, and it needed a minister without delay because its pastor, the Reverend John N. Doggett, had been appointed to a church in southern California. Within a short time Downs had a new leader, the Reverend Roy C. Nichols. Nichols remembered with fondness the erection of the present church structure with the leadership of B. L. Vaughn and Irvin Fuller, one an experienced builder, the other a professional mason. Men, women, boys, and girls nailed the roof, painted boards, and wielded hammers and shovels; women and girls climbed scaffolding and ladders along with the men and boys. The months of hard labor was a time of exhilaration and camaraderie, and Nichols led a great celebration when it was all over.

With the agreement and support of the administrative assembly of Downs, Nichols approached his political activities as an extension of the mission of the church. His first campaign for the city council of Berkeley in 1959 was not successful. A subsequent candidacy for the school board in 1961 won him a seat with that body. Nichols's election came when black people were just coming onto the political scene in Berkeley, boosted by the creation of a political coalition. The first coalition had been one of black preachers in south Berkeley, led by the Reverends Edward Stovall, P. C. Washington, James Stewart, and Herman Riley. It grew to include other black residents from the flat lands, white liberals from the hills, and university students. This was the beginning of black representation in the governance of Berkeley, and it served as an incentive to surrounding communities. From 1963 through 1964 Nichols was the first African-American school board president in California. As vice-president to Frankie Jones of the Berkeley NAACP and chairman of the committee on education, Nichols led the first protests about the inequalities in the city's public schools. His election to the board meant that he could play a substantial role in desegregating the schools and passing a bond for the construction of new schools. Actual desegregation was not inaugurated until after thorough, and sometimes acrimonious, hearings and exhaustive studies. Finally the board voted to begin with the junior and senior high school grades because it could be realized without bussing. Bussing for the elementary grades was the second stage, and Nichols had already left the Bay Area before the plan for the lower grades was put into action.

Nichols knew that desegregation had its disadvantages: bussing destroyed the concept of the neighborhood school and had a disruptive effect on schools that had well-organized faculties that were providing excellent educational environments for their all-black students. The NAACP looked upon such excellent situations as aberrations; the majority of African-American children were not being taught under these ideal conditions, even after desegregation. Schools with a majority of black children would still receive less than their fair share of the educational dollar and would not have the best-qualified staffs. A combination of an understanding of the NAACP's attitude, which fully supported desegregation and bussing as one way to achieve this goal, and doubts about the realities of the questionable benefits of integration presented a dilemma to some black people, including Nichols, who still could not endorse the status quo. The least objectional solution was to work for integration.

More than twenty years later Nichols saw evidence that bussing was not the consummate answer to the educational needs of ethnic students. The anticipated improvement in progress did not materialize for black or white students; there was still a sizable gap between the accomplishments of white and non-white pupils. For one thing, many white and middle-class black children transferred to private schools, and in Nichols's estimation, Berkeley schools made the mistake of emphasizing experimental projects that came at the cost of basic teaching. "Berkeley's school administrators were getting grant money for everything. What actually happened was that the school system never settled down to the job of educating. It was always experimenting with nuances," such as the schools of choice: the Hispanic schools, black schools, and Asian schools, which were meant to address the unique instructional needs of students of those ethnic groups.

From the East Bay the next stop in Roy Nichols's career was New York where he replaced the late Reverend Joshua Williams, minister of Salem United Methodist Church. Fellow clergymen and friends who knew Nichols well and who were familiar with Salem were not optimistic about the prospects for his success in that large church in the heart of Harlem. They thought that fifteen years at Downs would make it impossible for him to cope with that more folklike setting. They did not know that from age eight to seventeen Nichols had been intimately involved in a similar situation with a Baptist church in Philadelphia. He needed only to recall the memory of those times to make the transition into a different tempo of worship that was comfortable for the Salem family.

There were resemblances and contrasts between the two churches. Both had people who reacted in a warm and loving way to a minister who loved them and who worked on their behalf. Downs had a total membership of 773; Salem's membership was 3,000. Salemites expressed their emotions vocally. Some even left their seats and walked in the aisles to demonstrate their gratitude to God; members of Downs were usually quiet in their response to the services. The majority of the congregants at Downs were middle class, students, college graduates, or enrolled in graduate courses. At Salem the people were generally older and less educated. Many of the residents of the nearby low-income housing project attended Salem. Nichols credited the people of Salem for giving the lie to the stereotype of inhabitants of New York City as uncaring, hardened, and aloof. His years there left him with numerous lasting friendships.

In 1968, four years after his arrival at Salem, Nichols became a bishop of the United Methodist Church. He spent his first twelve years as a bishop in the Pittsburgh area, and in 1980 he went to the New York area, which included over half of that state, Manhattan, Long Island, the state of Vermont, and a large part of Connecticut. Although the latter assignment was predominantly white, the churches in Manhattan contributed a rich ethnic mix of blacks, Hispanics, Asians, Haitians, and others from the Caribbean.

As full retirement neared, Nichols returned to Oakland in 1984 and resettled here. He left area supervision and assumed a position with the General Council on Ministry of the United Methodist Church as a specialist in local church revitalization. In this role he visited churches nationally and internationally and conducted seminars on church operation—the spiritual aspect and the personal development of parishioners, the business concerns, and the community and global responsibility of the church. He preached on Sundays and during the week acted as a troubleshooter to advise and motivate local churches. Working intimately and directly with the clergy and laymen to solve problems brought Nichols the gratification that he associated with being a pastor, the part of his calling that he loved the most. He continued in this specialized position until he was ready for full retirement.

Nichols was aware that his ministerial career had been both typical and atypical for black churchmen. The Downs-Salem pastoral experiences were typical for a black pastor, but the bishopric posts were surely atypical for a black person of the cloth. He wonders whether he has used his skills for the best advantage of his own people. In the two churches, he served congregations that were predominantly nonwhite; however, as bishop of the Pittsburgh area he worked with only a small number of ethnics, and the New York area was almost all white. He hopes that his friends are right when they say that he has made a meaningful contribution to his race by the example of his standard of service, where people of all colors could observe him demonstrate that black people are capable of functioning and relating in the way that he did. This was a benefit to black people, both in a direct and an indirect way.

The image in Nichols's mind for progress for African-Americans is a three-legged stool, the components being church, school, and home. Each leg works in perfect synchronization with the other two, but the church gives the greatest support because of its uniqueness. The church can satisfy the spiritual hunger and at the same time nurture developing minds to grow until the full potential is reached. Parental guidance at home, stimulating instruction in the school, and the work of the church form the three-legged structure upon which positive movement can be based. Nichols agrees that students need to enroll in challenging subjects, such as the sciences, and to involve themselves in economics and politics. But he stressed that, "Black Americans might just as well recognize that the most significant propaganda and educational agency at the adult level that we possess, own and operate is the church. Therefore, we need to encourage the ablest young men and women to choose ministry as vocations. The black pulpit is such an extremely influential agency for training and nurturing."

I think of Roy Nichols as not only my pastor and spiritual leader from the fifties and sixties, but as a friend whose company I have enjoyed from then until now, in church settings and in social times. He is a serious, thoughtful man when that is the nature of the hour, but when fun is the order, he is a good person to have around; one who can tell a joke well and appreciate one told by another person. I knew that Downs could not hold Nichols and rejoiced in each new phase of his career and doubled my pride when he was appointed bishop of the United Methodist Church. It was the logical next step in his career, a deserved opportunity to continue his leadership with greater influence and responsibility.

RUBY OSBORNE
Born 1922, Grenada, Mississippi

"I probably was the first student to get permission to get married in the history of Hampton Institute and get permission to return."

In 1945 when Roy Nichols was a seminary student employed as a night orderly at the Veteran's Hospital in Oakland, he took time out to visit a young patient, Ruby Osborne, who was recovering from hepatitis. His visit made such an impression on Osborne that four years later when she and her serviceman husband, Julius, returned to Oakland, they sought out the young minister and joined his new church. The couple became its first youth counselors, and over the span of time Osborne acted as superintendent of the Vacation Bible school and was part of the Commission on Missions and the Commission on Education.

Ruby Osborne's father was one of the black pioneers of Denver, Colorado, having migrated from Mississippi in the early twenties with his brothers to escape the oppressive racial conditions in their home state. His wife and baby girl came later. The brothers, who had been landowners and had operated a saw mill, went to the Denver area in answer to an appeal for men to work in a creosote plant. Although Denver was much less restricted than Mississippi, it was not totally free from racial limitations. Black people sat in the balcony in the movie house. The high school taught students from all ethnic groups, but teachers gave little attention to the performance of black boys and girls, and there were separate baccalaureate services and senior proms for the African-American graduates.

Osborne's mother died when she was fifteen, and her father saw to her needs after that. Out of respect for his daughter's fears of the stereotypical mean stepmother, he did not take another wife until years later after she had married. Osborne had always wanted to go to college. When her minister and a friend of her father—a man from North Carolina who was a Hampton alumnus—told her about Hampton Institute in Virginia, she chose that school. Before she finished high school when she was seventeen, she met her future husband, Julius, who was twenty-five at the time. Her father discouraged the mutual attraction because of their age difference, but when she was a student in Hampton they met under different circumstances: World War II had begun and Julius was in Officer Candidate School in Virginia, seventy miles from the college.

In her junior year at Hampton, Julius made frequent trips to the campus to visit Osborne. It was not long before he proposed. When he formally asked for Osborne's father's permission, his first question was whether or not she was pregnant; during her adolescent years he had told her that having a baby was not a good reason to get married unless there was real love between the expectant parents. In the dual role of father and mother, he had taken care to protect her as she grew up and told her that he would help her with any problems, that they would find solutions together. When admirers of his attractive daughter came to call, he cooked dinner, washed the dishes, and cleaned the kitchen while the young people courted in the front room. This was more acceptable to him than having her stand on street corners talking to boys. Osborne and Julius were married in Baltimore, Maryland, in April 1943 in her third year during the intersession at Hampton.

Being in the unusual situation of a married student in the forties, the next step for Osborne was to obtain permission from the administration to continue at the college. She talked to the Dean of Women, Dr. Flemming P. Kittrell, who in turn consulted the president of the Institute. The president's ruling was that she could remain, but she could not live on campus. Dean Kittrell did not agree. She argued that since Osborne had been a model student during the preceding years, was not pregnant when she married, and was not expecting a child while Julius was overseas, she could live in a dormitory; so Osborne remained in a dormitory at Hampton while Julius was abroad to complete her course work.

Immediately after graduation from Hampton in 1944, Osborne went to the University of Iowa to study for a master's degree in Early Childhood Education but left after that summer to return to Hampton to work for a year as head teacher in the preschool of the college's Laboratory School. When the assignment at the Laboratory School ended Julius was still overseas, so Osborne came to Berkeley to enter a graduate program at the university. She became ill with hepatitis, a condition probably brought on by exhaustion from overwork at the nursery school and the demands of the university course work. Julius came home Christmas 1945 and took her back to Denver to recuperate for the flight to Germany where they would be together from the early part of 1946 until he was reassigned in 1949. When the first school was organized for the children of American servicemen in Germany, the military base welcomed Osborne as a college-trained kindergarten teacher.

From Germany Julius was assigned to California. In ten years of marriage they had not had a child. Finally they decided to adopt, but before the final papers came for them to receive their four-month-old son, Julius was sent overseas again. The Children's Home Society was helpful in expediting the adoption procedure, and mother and baby son, Keith, joined the father in the Far East in 1954. This was a highlight in their lives, receiving their son and being reunited as a family in Okinawa. When the three returned to the United States in 1957, Osborne accepted a teaching position in north Richmond in a school that was all-black but for one white child. She saw the black children reject the white child as she had seen white students spurn African-Americans. Osborne took firm action to combat the racism and was pleased to see that the child became well integrated into the classroom. She was extremely proud of her ability to correct the injustice.

After nine years in Richmond, Osborne took leave from teaching and reentered the University of California to resume the study that had been interrupted by illness. This time she received the master's degree. Instead of returning to Richmond schools, she took a job in El Cerrito's Castro School where there were no black teachers and very few black pupils. Working with parents and other teachers, including Dorothy Lee, she developed "Project 88," a three-year undertaking that involved three schools, Castro, which was predominantly white with a small Asian population, and Cortez and Stege schools, which had mostly black children and a limited number of Mexican-American students. The objective was to involve parents and students in a school setting where eighty-eight students in grades kindergarten through sixth, from different ethnic groups and diverse economic status, received a quality education in an environment of cooperation from all of the participants. This was a good opportunity for the children to recognize their own identity, respect the concerns of others, and work for solutions to issues that involved the group. The students had a lesson in socialization, and the parents had a chance to become more involved in the school's activities. For her work in Castro School Osborne was chosen "Teacher of the Year" in 1972 by the Junior Chamber of Commerce of El Cerrito.

As she approached retirement Osborne searched for a productive undertaking that she would enjoy. She began a project to recruit students from the Bay Area for her alma mater, Hampton University. The Bay Area Chapter of the Hampton Alumni Association accepted the proposal for her and fellow alumna Dorothy Henderson to take graduating high school seniors to Hampton for precollege visits during Homecoming. Starting in 1974 Osborne made trips three consecutive years. The groups included four students from families that were associated with Downs church. From Hampton recruiter, Osborne progressed to admissions counselor, assisting seniors with the application process for entrance into colleges all over the country. She did not limit herself to information about schools that have predominantly black enrollments but amassed a great store of information about hundreds of institutions of higher learning.

It is difficult to imagine Ruby Osborne's adult life without the influence of Downs church, the army, or Hampton. Downs was the center of her spiritual and civic activities in the East Bay Area, the military determined where and how she would develop her family, and Hampton Institute set the foundation for her attitudes toward work and community obligations. Hampton taught her that it is impossible to separate the caliber of the professional work of the individual from the quality of her personal life: how you live reflects how you teach. Teaching in military schools gave her a chance to enrich the lives of children who had not seen black people other than those in servitude.

NELL IRVIN PAINTER-SHAFER
Born 1942, Houston, Texas

"The most important thing that came out of the study was how many brothers and uncles and fathers and cousins, who I assume had the same intellectual capacity, became casualties of racism."

Nell Irvin Painter-Shafer was first introduced to Downs church when she was in elementary school by her parents and without any feeling of coercion. She liked the church, the Methodist Youth Fellowship, and Nichols, who she thought was very smart and whose sermons were interesting. At just about the time Painter-Shafer went away to college in 1959, she discontinued participation at Downs. She had begun to have intellectual difficulties with religion, and this led to a disinterest that was not at all concerned with the way she felt about the minister, the members as people, or Downs as a church. Painter-Shafer's alienation from traditional religious teachings has continued; she has not been a member of any church group since she left Downs.

Beginning in primary school Painter-Shafer was a serious student who did very well, but she was not happy about the quality of her education. She was convinced that the public school education that she got in Oakland, while probably just as good as in any public school system in the country, did not challenge her to the full extent of her abilities, partly because of her race but also because the teachers were not prepared to do a better job. However, her secondary school training was sufficient for her to be admitted to the Santa Barbara campus of the University of California right from Oakland Technical High School. After her freshman year she transferred to Berkeley to study for a bachelor's degree in anthropology. Before the degree was conferred in 1964, she had participated in Berkeley's initial Education Abroad Program and spent her junior year in Bordeaux, France. Her academic preparation includes a master's degree from the University of California, Los Angeles, granted in 1967, and a doctorate from Harvard, which she received in 1974.

Painter-Shafer thinks the most meaningful part of her education began when she left the United States and explored subjects and concepts that had been taboo in American schools during the Cold War. In Ghana, West Africa, she began to read and learn about the Third World, imperialism, the economic basis of politics, the class aspect of human history, and the United States' place in the world. Ghana was her first exposure to any sort of leftist views of history. She discovered new ways of looking at world events that were useful to her as a historian. In the United States she knew about the importance of race, but in Ghana she learned about the economic dimension of political issues.

After a less-than-satisfying year of teaching at San Jose Community College, which included being distracted by the Black Panthers and other groups who made demands upon her as an academician that she was unable or unwilling to meet, Painter-Shafer realized that she wanted to follow up on her interest in history. The reading and study in Bordeaux and Ghana had aroused a curiosity that called for further study about new and fascinating ideas. In France and in West Africa Painter-Shafer had enjoyed history, which directly contrasted against her experience with boring high school American history classes and their accent on the advantages of life in the United States. Her response had always been, "What about Alabama?"

Painter-Shafer went to Harvard in 1969 to work toward a doctorate in history. She gave credit to the practical advice and counsel of her dissertation advisor, Frank Freidel, who guided her through those years of study. She has passed the skills she learned from him to the graduate students she now advises. After completing her doctorate, Painter-Shafer taught history at the University of Pennsylvania, the University of North Carolina in Chapel Hill, and then at Princeton University. Even though she has reached her professional goals, she would like to make teaching secondary to writing. Her three books and other publications have been well received, and she is in demand as a speaker. *Standing at Armageddon*, which was published in 1987, has been greeted as a trendsetter in the writing of American history because it discusses the plight of black people, labor, and women along with the actions of the white male power structure.

During her senior year at Berkeley, Painter-Shafer worked as a research assistant for a study of "upwardly mobile Negro males," an experience that brought her firsthand knowledge of the appalling cost of racism. To her the most striking finding was not the data about the fear of failure, which is certainly an important consideration, but the secondary information that emerged about the unsuccessful male relatives who were equally as bright as the more fortunate brothers, but who, because of racism, did not reach their potential. Some had obtained doctorates but worked in the post office, gone insane, or committed suicide out of frustration. These findings were a devastating discovery for her, one that Painter-Shafer has not forgotten.

When Painter-Shafer thinks of positive changes for African-Americans, she gives political action top priority as a vehicle for improvement. She is encouraged by the effects of increased participation of black citizens in the political process for the election of Mayor Harold Washington in Chicago and the mayors of other cities, and by the emergence of Jesse Jackson as a symbol of the election possibilities for black candidates. Given the importance of politics in American life, and the fact that the black vote is generally liberal, Painter-Shafer thinks black people can bring about positive change if they vote in large numbers. Their liberal votes hold the key to changes that would benefit the country as a whole.

How can I speak objectively about a daughter who I think is just about perfect in almost every way? I can not do so, and I will not try. I can begin by recalling my feeling of absolute happiness at 8:00 A.M. Sunday, August 2, 1942, when the doctor in the delivery room of Houston Negro Hospital placed in my arms the most beautiful baby girl ever born. The sun was beaming into the window and all was right with the world. That baby grew into a gifted woman with a career that is continuing to reach new heights, one who loves her parents and demonstrates this affection by sharing her joys and challenges and by thoughtful gifts to tell us that she returns our love. Being a part of the Downs family where Painter-Shafer was in the company of her peers in the Methodist Youth Foundation, boys and girls who were headed in the same direction that she was, and who came from homes similar to her own, surely contributed to her growth and development

ELIZABETH PETTUS
Born 1923, Oakland, California

"My father was fifty years ahead of his time in terms of organizing people to fight against discrimination."

I was seated in the pews the Sunday when Elizabeth Pettus was welcomed into Downs. It was refreshing to see the enthusiasm she brought with her and the willingness to share her multiple talents. It was not long after she joined that she was involved in a variety of activities: coadvisor to the youth group with her husband, John, planner of special events, member of more than one committee. Downs had found a special member, and it was the perfect base for her spiritual and social nourishment.

Elizabeth Pettus's father was a minister in the Church of God in Christ and a bishop in the Triumph Church of God in Christ, the founder of the Triumph Church on Twelfth and Center streets in Oakland. He was an early-day Martin Luther King, Jr., president of the Oakland branch of Marcus Garvey's Universal Negro Improvement Association, and one who organized people to fight racial injustice. Pettus marched in her Sunday best with members of her father's church in parades with the Association, beside men in the familiar Garvey-type regalia and women in starched white dresses. Almost every Sunday afternoon they made their way down Eighth Street in west Oakland to the meeting hall.

Pettus had a total of twenty-three siblings; her father had ten children with his first wife and thirteen with Pettus's mother, his second wife. Her mother, a quiet, sweet person was twelve years younger than her husband and worshipped him as a "great spiritual father" as well as a husband. Pettus was raised by her sister, Corine, twenty-two years older than Pettus, an evangelist in her father's church who devoted her life to serving God. As in most large families where older children take on the care of a younger sibling, the relationship between Pettus and Corine was more like mother and daughter than sisters.

Pettus heard gossip which intimated that Corine was her mother, and she silently wondered whether it was true until she was twelve years old. In reality she knew who her mother was, but her young mind was disturbed by the neighbors' whispers. The doubts were definitely laid to rest one day when some friends of her mother came to their home for a quilting bee. As Pettus was helping serve gumbo and lemonade to the guests she overheard the visitors talking. One of the friends, an outspoken woman who used profanity for emphasis—always followed by an apology—said, "Now, I can put a stop to that damn shit right now. I was there when that little heifer was born." This declaration ended the speculation in Pettus's mind and in the thoughts of others.

With the family's move from Oakland to Wasco in the San Joaquin Valley of California (when she was five), her father's position as bishop of the church, owner of a grocery store, and political leader of the black section of town assured Pettus the status of a favored person. These advantages were of small comfort, however, because as she was growing up she had to respect the teachings of her father's religion. She envied the fun of her peers who could go to dances and movies, and who could walk in the streets engaged in girlish conversation.

In 1942 Pettus, who by that time had moved back to Oakland from Wasco, married John, who had also come to the Bay Area from the San Joaquin Valley. Neither of them had any idea that their childhood acquaintance would eventually lead to marriage. At Downs, Nichols told Pettus that she and John should resign from their social clubs and other activities; the church would take care of all of that. Downs did more for those needs than it did for the spiritual side of Pettus's life, which already had a firm foundation. She learned from one of Nichols's workshops titled, "Get Your God Out of the Box," that she had, in fact, put her God in a little box, and the world was outside awaiting her help. Nichols's political action on the Berkeley School Board and in the NAACP renewed her awareness of the world around her and motivated her to increase her involvement. She knew that she could be more effective if she returned to college.

Almost simultaneously, Dorothy Pitts had put an employment application into her hand and started her on the road to turning the hours of volunteer work in the recreation department into a paid position. She enrolled in the University of California–Berkeley and obtained a bachelor's and a master's degree in 1971 and 1972 respectively. Right after that she went to work at McClymonds High School and stayed with Oakland schools as teacher, counselor, and dean of students until she retired in 1982. Her first assignment at McClymonds was with the "Learn and Earn Program." The principal, Dr. Willie D. Harper, said to her, "I have eighty students, they're all yours. You either save them, or I am kicking them out of school." She went to government installations and found jobs for the boys and girls and followed them like a policeman, seeing that they got out of bed, taking them to work, and when necessary telling the boss a plausible story why they were not at work. It was a hard job, but it was successful. Some of the young people went into positions that they kept after graduation.

Before she returned to school, Pettus had worked for three years as head director of the Alexander Recreation Center in west Oakland. She became district girls' athletic trainer and taught classes for other athletic directors. She conducted seminars in the actual sports, in ways to motivate children to participate, and in the management of problem situations. Unlike public schools, recreation centers serve children who come of their free wills and not because of any legal requirements. The successful head director must know how to discipline and control her charges, and how to cultivate relations with the total community.

For twelve years Pettus and John, with the Reverend Whitney Lester, of the Independent Community Church in Oakland, and Lester's wife, Luella, served Christmas dinner to people in west Oakland. With a truck, Coleman stove, and a fold-up table, they made the rounds of street corners to fill the plates of anyone who came forth. Most of the people were needy, but some were wage earners who merely had no family base for the holiday. From the start Pettus and John supplied the funds for their share of the food, then Downs donated the money for the expenses.

Pettus likened the first day of retirement to the departure for a long-awaited trip—the planning had been so much fun that the actual day was anticlimactic. Suddenly, she had no job to go to. She thought, "I'm not going to have a reason for doing something every day; I am no longer useful." After grappling with these feelings for a while, she submerged herself in social activities until teaching became a part of the past. Since retirement Pettus has been active in Delta Sigma Theta sorority, serving as vice-president and president of her chapter, and president of the Northern California Coordinating Council, which is made up of all of the Delta chapters in northern California. Under her presidency the chapter held a regional conference in Oakland, the first in the Bay Area for nearly twenty years. A highlight of the conference was the Black Repertory Group's production of Abrem Hill's *Striver's Row*. Those were times of growth when the chapter expanded to include women from a broad span of ages—new college graduates and retirees. Out of her involvement with the Oakland Older Adult Center, Pettus became hostess of a series of television programs produced and televised by senior citizens. Before the show was discontinued because of a lack of funding, she had interviewed a variety of guests such as Mrs. Mary Wright, who serves meals at a downtown park; a builder on the Golden Gate Bridge and the Bay Bridge; Royal Townes, a pioneer black Oaklander; and a representative from the Japanese-American community.

One of Pettus's most exciting and satisfying responsibilities is as commissioner of the Consumer Affairs Commission of Alameda County where she helps people find solutions to consumer dilemmas. Equally as exciting and rewarding is her contribution as a member of the advisory committee of the California Department of Corrections' Committee of Correctional Education. In this capacity she visits the correctional facilities of the state, and after interviews with the wardens and observing the vocational and academic classes for the inmates, she prepares reports to the state director of prisons with recommendations that are considered in the development and evaluation of the prisons' educational programs.

The years have not dimmed my memory of when I first met Pettus at Downs. I was amazed by her willingness to invest so much of herself. I doubted that her interest would endure much beyond the initial enthusiasm. As I watched her I saw that she did not give up. On the contrary, her wealth of energy seems unlimited and has continued for over thirty-five years.

DOROTHY PITTS
Born 1913, Memphis, Tennessee

"I learned that we cannot solve the problems of blacks through social work; it will have to be through economics."

One of the aspects that Dorothy Pitts liked about Downs was that she could use her training in group work and social work in assignments at the church, which she participated in from the fifties until she terminated her membership in 1977. The planning and implementation of programs and the fund-raising projects in the church setting were not greatly different from the sort of things she did in her work. At Downs she had the additional satisfaction of working with people who shared her ambitions for the community. But the greatest thing about Downs was that it was where she was introduced to her husband, Walter, by friends, Downs members who could see that the two would make an ideal couple.

In the twenties, when Dorothy Pitts was a girl, north Memphis was an unincorporated area just outside of the city limits. Her father was knowledgeable in economics and city planning and knew that the Ford Motor Company would expand into south Memphis where he owned land, and that the street they lived on in north Memphis was going to be a state highway. He was certain that his investment in real estate would be productive. Ford built the plant in Memphis as he expected, but by that time it was too late for him to realize the profits he had expected; the land had been lost through a combination of racism and the economic condition of the country.

In a unique situation in Memphis, Pitts attended one school, Manassas High School, for the entire twelve years of her public education and got a well-rounded education from teachers who had been trained at Tennessee State College, Fisk, Atlanta, and Howard universities. Manassas High began as a one-room school. It grew and prospered under the direction of the principal, Cora P. Taylor, who added grades until the school offered a complete curriculum from kindergarten through grade twelve.

An aunt wanted Pitts to work in her grocery store instead of going to college, but she had no interest in business; she wanted a college degree. With her aunt's help, she entered LeMoyne-Owen College in Memphis and remained there until she graduated in 1935. Following graduation Pitts taught in Memphis and in Arkansas until she enrolled in Howard University for the next degree, a master's in French, which she received in 1940. Then for two years she taught at Paine College in Augusta, Georgia. From 1942 to 1945, Pitts worked in the Bureau of Census and the office of the Surgeon General in Washington, D.C., before going overseas to the Philippines and to Japan for the American Red Cross. The Red Cross work ended with a stint at Camp Stoneman, near Pittsburgh, California, where she was attracted by the beautiful, dry, warm weather, the lush fruits and vegetables, and the physical scenery of San Francisco, Oakland, and Berkeley. Rather than return to Tennessee to help black people there, she opted to use her skills for the benefit of the thousands of newly arrived black immigrants to the Bay Area.

Pitts started working for the recreation department in Oakland in 1947, first as resident director at deFremery Park and then as head director. From that position she was promoted to supervisor of recreation and consultant. The recreation department position was the start of thirty-one years of public service in the East Bay. Oakland was looking for "Negro" leadership for its increasing black population. There were hundreds of black youths who needed guidance to escape the traps of juvenile delinquency, and the city officials thought that recreational programs could be preventive measures. Pitts made a lasting impression on the youths who came to the deFremery Park in west Oakland through the teen clubs she set up on a structured basis, which included elected officers and parliamentary procedures. She wanted to develop the whole individual by teaching them to play sports for amusement and physical growth, and by teaching them social skills so that they could become responsible citizens and relate to their community in a constructive way.

When the recreation department wanted Pitts to deemphasize training in leadership and human relationships and return to pure recreation (which the department heads defined as handball and first aid), she resigned and went to Richmond as part of the War on Poverty. There she led the Richmond Community Development Demonstration Project whose goal was to demonstrate that poor black people are capable of holding jobs and taking charge of their community. As the supervisor of New Careerists, she trained twenty-five grass roots men and women to move into new careers in the schools, police department, probation department, and the University of California. These were people who had not been eligible for promotions in their previous employment before the training in the New Careers Program. One year later Pitts became director of Community Organizations, a black community project also in Richmond. She left after six months because of problems with the management of the program's government funds. She had inherited a debt that had resulted from prior mismanagement and incomplete reporting. She saw no solution to the intolerable position, one that was not of her making, and one that should have been cleared before she came aboard. It was impossible for her to remain under those circumstances. She left in June 1966 to work in Berkeley.

Initially, Pitts was a neighborhood consultant in Berkeley's Department of Social Planning. The position was designed to bring a black department head into the governance of the city. One of her projects was with the teenagers in the Neighborhood Youth Corps. She recruited Nora Vaughn to involve them in a dramatic production. The young people wrote and produced a play that they performed for an audience that included city officials. The last assignment Pitts had before retirement was chief of Berkeley's Division on Aging. Her first chore was to initiate a study of the needs of the aged in Berkeley and learned that the only facilities for that age group were in church basements. With this information and the results from visits to centers in other cities, she made the recommendations that resulted in the construction of three multipurpose centers. Mayor Widener secured the funds from the Jobs for Cities program.

Pitts has been intimately involved with the East Bay Area Club of the National Association of Negro Business and Professional Women's Club, which was organized primarily to help African-American women improve their positions as professional people. The women were especially interested in the development of black youth. As third vice-president, Pitts chaired the youth program and organized teenage conferences and coordinated career workshops with the public schools. Because of her interest in the elderly Pitts has worked in the community to improve their lot. Assemblyman Elihu Harris, now mayor of Oakland, appointed her to the California State House Commission on Aging, and she attended the White House Conference on Aging as a member of the national board of the Older Women's League.

In the late eighties and early nineties, Pitts's foremost interest (next to a book in progress about the deFremery Park alumni) was the LeMoyne-Owen College–Memphis Boosters Club's campaign for legislation to mandate that black history be included as an integral part of the history textbooks that are used in the public schools in California. Being involved with the Association of Negro Business and Professional Women in building Sojourner Truth Manor, a housing complex for seniors, Pitts learned that social work alone is not the answer for black people. Progress must come through economics. She recognized that since we live in a capitalistic society we will have to improve our ability to manage money. We will have to become socialists with the whole country sharing the wealth, as opposed to taking away from the poor and giving to the rich.

Dorothy Pitts has become less tolerant than she once was with people who are capable of taking meaningful action but are content to remain inactive. She now has no patience with ministers who are weak yet still hold on to their positions of leadership. Their churches do a disservice when they fail to meet the challenges, as do public schools with weak teachers and administrators. Pitts is not totally optimistic about the future for African-Americans in the social, economic, and political aspects, but she is hopeful that through the work of dedicated individuals, club groups, and churches, progress will continue.

Early in July 1988, Pitts left the Bay Area headed for Memphis, Tennessee, to occupy the home that was being built for her and Walter. This was a homecoming for Pitts, and she welcomed the move because Memphis has less air pollution, which would be better for her physically than the atmosphere in the Bay Area, and the city has good, low-priced housing. I greeted the news of the Pittses' move to Memphis with disbelief. It was difficult to think of this area without her in the forefront of any action for the concerns of African-Americans, whether it was for senior citizens, women, or young people. But I have now accepted the fact that her home is in Memphis, Tennessee, and not in El Cerrito, California.

Before she left I asked Pitts if she could give up the deFremery book project or the campaign to put black history in the public schools of California. She assured me that air travel back to Oakland will be no problem because of the senior citizen discount rates that make flying much cheaper than it would otherwise be, and because relatives and friends will welcome her as a houseguest whenever she returns. In typical Dorothy Pitts fashion she had planned for the continuation of both projects.

With the move complete, Dorothy Pitts is totally involved in the affairs of the Memphis area and happy with her renewed membership of Metropolitan Baptist Church, her family church home, and in the environment of her public school, Manassas High School, and her alma mater, LeMoyne-Owen College.

VERA PITTS
Born 1931, Wichita, Kansas

"To go back into the 'real world' and validate what I have taught for the past eighteen years is an unusual opportunity. The things we teach really work."

The Reverend Roy Nichols performed the marriage ceremony of Vera and Leonard Pitts in 1952, in the structure that is now Downs's social hall, when the church was still in its infancy. Pitts had known Nichols from his work with the Oakland Boys' Club, the YWCA, and South Berkeley Community Church, and she knew his reputation as a strong supporter of community affairs. From the start of their association with Downs, the newlyweds were very active and took on a variety of responsibilities. Most likely the most important one was as coadvisors of the youth activities.

The life that Vera Pitts lives reflects the atmosphere of the home where she and her two sisters grew up in west Oakland. The family had migrated to California from Kansas when she was five years old. Her father's employment as a pullman porter brought a steady income sufficient to assure them a privileged status in African-American society. Pitts spoke of her father, Wade Johnson, as "probably the original militant in Oakland." He organized the United Taxpayers and Voters Appeal Union in the fifties to help his fellow residents deal with the disruptions of Oakland's Urban Renewal Project. At the outset the city's intention was to demolish all of the homes in west Oakland, forcing involuntary relocation of families. The Union, with Johnson's leadership, initiated legal action that forced the city to begin a rehabilitation program that would enable some families to save their homes by remodelling with their personal funds or with loans from the city. The Wade Johnson Park in west Oakland was dedicated posthumously to Pitts's father in recognition of his service to that community.

The undergraduate years at the University of California–Berkeley were exciting times for Pitts when the approximately seventy-five black students on campus went on to distinguish themselves: Congresswoman Yvonne Braithwaite, California Supreme Court Justices Allen Broussard, and the late Wiley Manuel, Oakland school director Alfreda Abbot, and two civic-minded Bay Area physicians, Dale Tipton and Robert Burnes. It was a group of upwardly mobile young black people. In addition to the Berkeley degree, a bachelor's awarded in 1953, Pitts holds a master's from Sacramento State University, awarded in 1960, and a doctorate from Michigan State University, which she completed in 1967. After thirty-three years of marriage Leonard died in 1985, leaving Pitts with loving memories and the finances that made working an option. They had married before either had finished the first four years of college, and Pitts was proud of their perseverance to amass five academic degrees between them.

During her career Pitts has run the gamut of experiences in public education. She has been a teacher, a public school counselor, and an administrator in a county office of education and in the Department of Education in Washington, D.C. In academia she was a professor in the departments of education in

City College of New York and California State University at Hayward, where her involvement in both cases was heavily related to teacher and school administrator training. During the 1987–1988 school year, Pitts took a year's leave of absence from her position as chairman of the Department of Education Administration and professor on the staff at Hayward State to work as associate superintendent in charge of Instructional Resources for the Oakland public schools.

Oakland schools were not a strange environment for Pitts, who had had the majority of the teachers and managers in the district in her classrooms. Here was her chance to prove the validity of the things that she had been teaching in her university classes for eighteen years, see the correlation between theory and practice, and appreciate the actual proof that the theories work when they are put into practice. Foremost among the challenges Pitts faced in the Oakland schools was to upgrade the instructional skills of teachers who had been in the classroom for more than twenty years and had not made significant changes in their teaching methods. Her task was to introduce new instruction strategies to this group. Another problem was the difficulty that public schools have in attracting college graduates to teaching. From the fifties to the seventies, when there were declining enrollments and limited slots for new teachers, young people did not gravitate toward schools because of the job shortage. But with the emergence of increased enrollments that brought added opportunities for beginning teachers, urban districts found it hard to compete with the broadened career avenues and higher-paying positions in other professions that women and ethnics could enter. This resulted in a struggle to maintain a good balance between student enrollment, number of teachers, and the adequacy of their performance.

As associate superintendent in Oakland, Pitts reviewed the curriculum of the individual schools to see that students all over the city obtain a functional knowledge of the basic skills, so that they can earn a living after they graduate or satisfy college entrance requirements. Her main objective was to improve the students' test scores, which she termed "the report card" for the district. She knows that this depends upon the day-to-day achievement of the pupils, which in turn can be no greater than the ability of the teacher to transmit information to the students. Pitts is gratified to see that instructional monitoring had been put in place; management staff is working directly with teachers to assess their instructional skills and offer assistance in rectifying deficiencies. She recognizes that there are some school sites where a greater degree of improvement in the standard of instruction is needed, and she welcomes the work that is being done to decrease the difference.

Subsequently, Pitts consented to return to Oakland schools as its interim superintendent to guide the district in its fight for survival as it struggled with a seemingly unsolvable financial morass, low employee morale, criminal charges against a growing number of staff members, and the apparent inability of the school board to cope. She remained for several months until the permanent executive came aboard, again having made a timely contribution to education at the public school level.

I first saw newlyweds Vera and Leonard Pitts at Downs working in the church as a team, radiating love and good humor, but at the same time presenting the scholarly bearing of serious students who had their goals firmly fixed. They knew what their educational aspirations were, and they set their priorities and planned their lives to reach their goals. It is not by accident that Pitts has a successful career and is making a meaningful contribution to her community, or that she lives a comfortable life. Both are the result of the foundation of her early life with her caring parents and the thoughtful planning that she and Leonard did before either had reached their midtwenties.

PHILLIP RAYMOND
Born 1927, Itta Bena, Mississippi

"The challenge for the individual is to become the best kind of person that he or she can be to create the best kind of world for him or herself and everybody else."

One of the gains that Phillip Raymond got from his twenty years at Downs was "a lot of personal growth, and a development of confidence" from the intense involvement in his many assignments. As his two sons grew up, his interest in church activities shifted to reflect their changing stages. By the time the boys reached adolescence, he had left the organizations that center on parenting and the concerns of young children and was concentrating on the Sunday school, the Commission on Evangelism, the Pastoral Relations Committee, and the Young Adult Class.

Itta Bena, Mississippi, Phillip Raymond's birthplace, is a small town in the Mississippi Delta, about ninety miles from Jackson. This area is typical agricultural delta land with wooded areas and a few lakes. The small town had a population of two thousand when he was a boy. Raymond did not go to the public school in his hometown; he attended a small Baptist-supported school until the sixth grade in Itta Bena, and when it closed for the lack of funds he transferred to a public school in Greenwood, about thirteen miles away. For a while he rode to and from school with a family friend, but for the greater part of those years he stayed with relatives in Greenwood or with an elderly woman as a companion in her home. He rode his bicycle back to Itta Bena on Friday evenings and returned to Greenwood before sunset on Sundays. From high school, Raymond entered Tuskegee Institute in 1944 and graduated with a major in elementary education in 1948.

At the invitation of a friend Raymond came to California to work one summer during his student years at Tuskegee. He took a job at the Richmond shipyard during World War II and was there when the United States dropped the atomic bomb on Japan. At that time he joined in the rejoicing because of the implications that the war would soon be over, and he accepted the idea that this was what the country had to do to end the war. With the passage of time, however, he considered the action with greater maturity and was distressed by the awful effects on mankind and wondered why Japan was treated differently from Germany and Italy who were also the enemies of war.

When Raymond came to California for his first visit he was tempted to remain and finish college here, but his father persuaded him to return to Tuskegee where he had a scholarship and could maintain his job in the office of the Auto Mechanics

Department, running errands, answering the telephone, and doing general clerical duties. Raymond has often thought about the turn his life might have taken if he had not gone back to Tuskegee. Would he have continued in graduate study as he did, or would he have given up those plans in the way that his friend abandoned his intention to study law? Luckily he did not need an answer to that speculation.

Having received the degree from Tuskegee, Raymond began to court Jessie, who had been his classmate throughout the four years of college. They were married in Montgomery, Alabama, in 1952 and started their life together in California. Raymond and Jessie joined Downs in 1955. They were quickly integrated into the program of the church and remained so for twenty years. He regretted leaving but felt that he had outgrown the usefulness of his service. After Raymond left Downs he and Jessie served for seven years as coadvisors for the Youth Group of the El Cerrito NAACP. The young people held regular monthly meetings, had fund-raisers, voter registration drives, national conventions, and cooperative programs with groups in other areas. Raymond continued with this until his sons reached the age where they had to go into an adult chapter.

By accident in 1979, Raymond's seatmate on a plane trip to a conference gave him an affirmation card from the Church of Religious Science and encouraged him to visit the church. Raymond went one Sunday and found that it focused upon the creative power of one's thoughts, the responsibility that a person has for his own circumstances, and the central importance of love—God's love for man and man's love for God and for his fellow man. These ideas were not completely different from what he had been taught in the Baptist and Methodist churches, but Religious Science had a different type of organization and presented exercises to reinforce these beliefs; for example, readings in the Science of Mind Magazine, affirmation cards, a Dial-a-Prayer program, and classes in the tenets of the church. In 1984 Raymond became a member of the First Church of Religious Science, and upon completion of four years of study, Raymond has found a more concentrated and systematic approach to spiritual materials and has become more disciplined in his daily devotions. He took the church-administered examination and became a licensed practitioner. As a practitioner he can give pulpit assistance on Sundays, participate in the Dial-a-Prayer program, and counsel people through the special sort of prayer of the church, Spiritual Mind Treatment.

Raymond's career in health education and public health came about by accident—by the juxtaposition of his two original interests. His initial desire to become a dentist had been sidetracked because of his limited undergraduate background in science and, expecting to become a public school teacher, he had pursued a bachelor's degree in elementary education. When he was trying to plan the next step after a term in the army he read an article in his hometown newspaper about fellowships for ethnic students to study for master's degrees in public health that emphasized health education. He reasoned that a degree in public health, in addition to his training in education, would strengthen his application to dental school and compensate for his less-than-adequate science preparation. With this line of thought he spent the first year after military service at the University of California School of Public Health in Berkeley and received the master's degree in 1953.

The public health course included a colorful, realistic film on oral surgery, which was vivid enough to convince Raymond that he would not enjoy the realities of working as a dentist. His reaction to the pictures contributed to a change in his career objectives. At the end of the fellowship, Raymond accepted employment with the California State Department of Public Health where he has worked from 1953 to the present. Eighteen years later, in 1971, he completed a doctorate in adult education at the University of California–Berkeley. He had undertaken this additional degree to prepare for advancement in the department, and to give himself additional options if he decided to enter academia.

Raymond's assignments at the state department brought more administrative responsibility at each juncture. He started as a health educator but was promoted to a training officer, then chief of the training and development section, and finally section chief in the Child Health Disability Branch. In this last position, he has worked with the Crippled Children Services, set up workshops for physical therapists and occupational therapists, and started conferences on cerebral palsy in the schools for physicians who treat handicapped children. His responsibility is to plan, organize, and conduct courses for staff development, provide in-service training to improve the performance of employees (technical, administrative, and clerical), and encourage their advancement up the career ladder. He handles administrative support functions in the child health program, which is administered at the state level to children from lower-income families. Private physicians and hospitals provide vaccinations, vision and hearing tests, and physical examinations to detect physical problems or defects early enough to take action that gives the child a better start in life.

Raymond is a deeply religious man who takes his role seriously, whether it is as husband, father, employee, or community member. He has a well-defined set of principles, which includes the belief that God works through him and that he must be the best instrument through which God can work. Very often he remembers that he is from poor economic circumstances in the deep South, and he is grateful for the educational opportunities and the encouragement he had—encouragement that he has passed on to his sons.

My spiritual life paralleled Raymond's when I became interested in religious science. Seeing his involvement was an added attraction to the First Church of Religious Science; if Raymond was a part of it, surely it merited my consideration.

PHEBIA RICHARDSON
Born 1932, Clinton, Louisiana

"We need to have massive educational kinds of seminars [on substance abuse and AIDS] for ministers, for everybody in the church. It can be on some Sunday mornings, instead of having Sunday services."

In 1957, six years after Phebia Richardson had united with Downs Memorial Church, and just a few days after her son was born, Nichols came to her home for a visit. He blessed the house and then picked up the infant and blessed him. With the serious business of the call done, they all sat down and Richardson's husband started playing the guitar. Nichols said to him, "David, I want you to show me how to pick this guitar." This set the stage for the rest of the afternoon—playing and singing—the highlight of which was a blues song that David made up on the spot.

As a "circuit preacher" in the Methodist churches of rural Texas and Louisiana, Phebia Richardson's father was assigned to as many as three churches at a time. He traveled from one town to another on Sundays, usually by horse but sometimes by bus when this type of transportation was available, to serve the people of his congregations on a rotation basis. The majority of his small-town parishioners were farmers who did not have money to contribute to the pastor's salary, so they often brought canned foods, vegetables, hams, or chickens to pay their minister. Twice a year the regional office of the Methodist Church sent new clothing, shoes, and money to augment the compensation from the local church. Richardson's father was moved to different assignments every three years, making it necessary to relocate his family at frequent intervals.

Richardson's introduction to community service came when she was a high school student in Orange, Texas. In the forties organizing teams from other southern states came to Texas to lay the groundwork for NAACP chapters. Orange was one of the towns where the organization took root, and Richardson and her friends participated in the youth activities and in fund-raising programs where Richardson took part as a singer. They held conferences and heard reports about the progress of the NAACP.

When Richardson came to California in 1950 after high school, her intention was to enter a school of nursing. Instead, she completed Laney Community College's program for medical assistants. She worked as an assistant to two black physicians in the East Bay but left when she chose to make different use of her energies. She started as a volunteer in the Oakland schools, which evolved into part-time work and finally a full-time position. She decided to obtain a college degree in an area that had piqued her interest and completed a bachelor's in community relations. The degree was awarded at California State University, Hayward, long after all of her children had finished public school.

Given the chance to live her life over, Richardson would go to college immediately after high school, taking full advantage of the educational opportunities that were open to her. Instead she had married David when she was eighteen. Together they reared their five children, which delayed the completion of her education to the time when they were self-sufficient. From volunteer worker in her neighborhood school, to PTA officer, to noon yard supervisor, to community liaison for the district, and to membership on the District Advisory Council, Richardson has been involved in public schools in a variety of capacities. First, she merely monitored the progress of her children, but gradually her concern carried over to students citywide. She began to arrange workshops for parents, and it became obvious that the parental concerns included the effects of drugs, a subject that had been more and more on Richardson's mind in relationship to her responsibilities as a mother and as someone who cares about her community. Now Richardson is the community consultant for the Richard Allen Institute, a health educator giving workshops on substance abuse and AIDS. She speaks to penal institution inmates, church groups, and to any assemblage that wants such information. Richardson has appeared before the older boys in juvenile hall, adults in jail, and public school students. The presentations are primarily involved with substance abuse, but they include facts about AIDS.

Richardson said that all of the information and training that the Richard Allen Institute provides has been furnished by gay men and lesbians, groups that are more accepting of the dangers of substance abuse and AIDS than the general population. The homosexual community has been less guilty of denial than otherwise well-informed people in the African-American community, whom Richardson expected to have more understanding of the risks than they apparently have. Many black people think that their heterosexual orientation is sufficient protection, and that AIDS is something completely apart from their personal experiences. To Richardson, the success of the instruction to black or Hispanic audiences depends upon the ability of the presenter to "speak the language," to communicate in a way that does not hint of condescension or moral judgment. When she gives workshops at a black church, Richardson offers a portion of the time to the minister to talk about the church's position relating to drugs and AIDS. She feels that failure to include the church's point of view would undermine the cooperation of the church with the Institute's efforts to educate the public.

Richardson believes that a barrage of concentrated educational presentations through the churches and schools is needed to stop the threat of substance abuse and AIDS. If she could plan her own program, it would begin in kindergarten, teaching children the importance of making the appropriate decisions about drugs. She knows that small children can absorb information that is geared to their level of development and understanding. Richardson would train ministers and community people in the special kind of counseling that is effective in dealing with addicts and with those who are related to addicted persons. She would have seminars for ministers, lay people, and the entire church on Sundays in place of a regular service. Churches have not used their potential to its full extent, and with the large number of religious institutions in Oakland, the effect of their united efforts would make a significant difference in the reactions of local adults and young people.

Richardson is also active in the politics of the Democratic party in east Oakland, having managed Sylvester Hodges's campaigns for election and reelection to the Oakland School Board. She was involved as a grass-roots activist when Ronald Dellums first entered politics, and in the efforts of Oakland Vice-Mayor Carter Gilmore, former Berkeley Mayor Warren Widener, and other local candidates.

Phebia Richardson is a community-minded person who has demonstrated her commitment to human service through her career, church and political participation, and through the care of her family.

THELMA SCOTT-SKILLMAN
Born 1949, San Francisco, California

"I work very hard because I believe in myself. I believe that I have skills that I can apply and assist other people in developing."

The exposure that Thelma Scott-Skillman had to Downs took place from when she was a very young girl until she was well into high school. She liked the feeling of being part of the "big family affair" of religious and community-related programs. Throughout her years at Downs, she often played the piano for the choir and took part in activities for the young people. And she learned to take an interest in the black nationalism of the time through a peaceful approach that advocated making a place for herself in her society. Before she graduated from high school Scott-Skillman realized that Downs had been a useful experience and had filled a need at the time, but had since lost its appeal. She was attracted to the doctrine and worship style of the Catholic Church. After several years of study she converted to Catholicism.

Thelma Scott-Skillman lived most of her childhood in Parchester Village, an annex of Richmond, California, a town where African-American families who came to the East Bay Area during World War II bought homes. Her parents, both from Texas, had come to work in the shipyards in the forties. They moved with their three children from Richmond to Oakland in time for Scott-Skillman to enter Oakland Technical High School in the tenth grade and graduate from there in 1967. While they lived in Richmond, Scott-Skillman's mother was not satisfied with the churches in her area and had gone to another church in Oakland, but she was disturbed by the noise of the service. She readily accepted the suggestion of one of her children's teachers to try Downs, and it turned out to be just the atmosphere she wanted for her family.

In Scott-Skillman's father's family there were college-educated adults who were physicians and school teachers. Both of her parents taught their children that education was an important key to economic independence. As early as the primary grades she knew that she wanted to be a professional person; her first choice was a medical doctor. At home she learned that if she developed to her best capabilities, the quality of her preparation would minimize the impact of racism in terms of employment. Being academically prepared with a master's degree from California State University–Hayward, granted in 1973, and a doctorate from Nova University, which she earned in 1987, Scott-Skillman has had a successful career in the Community College system of California, which began in 1973 at Los Medanos Community College in Pittsburgh, California, as counselor and instructor. Most of her time was taken up by personal, academic, and career counseling. Her goal was to counsel "myself out of a job" by providing all of the skills that a student needed to function without having to return for further advice, and to see students moving upward with her assistance.

Meanwhile, Scott-Skillman still continued to explore opportunities where she could utilize her training and make advancement in her career. California's Proposition 13, passed in 1978 by the voters to ease the burden of oppressive property taxes, greatly curbed the revenues of publicly funded institutions and caused Los Medanos College to institute a freeze on promotions, which effectively cut off any avenues for Scott-Skillman to pursue her career on that campus. As vacancies appeared at other colleges she applied for five positions, got four interviews, and was offered each of the four jobs. From the four, she chose dean of Student Services at Cosumnes River Community College in Sacramento.

Cosumnes River College is in south Sacramento, which is a growing residential area where houses were first built in the seventies on what was formerly agricultural land. The school has seventy-five hundred lower- to middle-class students from diverse ethnic backgrounds: Hispanic, African-American, and Asian (mostly Vietnamese), with a few Native Americans. Scott-Skillman's responsibilities as dean of Student Services included counseling assessments, placement in classes, career placement, child care, disciplinary actions, and directing a learning disabilities program that served the handicapped and disabled students.

While she worked at Cosumnes, Scott-Skillman was introduced to Frank when she facilitated an interpersonal-relations group seminar to explore problems between black men and black women. Neither one of them had come with thoughts of beginning a relationship with anyone, but as a result of that first meeting, they were married in 1984.

During her tenure at Cosumnes River, Scott-Skillman's ambition for upward movement grew, and she knew that through her professional ability and willingness to devote unlimited time to hard work she would reach her goal of becoming president of a college. She was chosen to participate in a leadership conference designed to help high-potential candidates prepare for promotional possibilities. In 1989 she left Cosumnes River to go to Cypress Community College in southern California as vice-president of Student Affairs. Again she had students from the lower- to middle-class families, but in this Orange County section of the state, there was a smaller percentage of black and Hispanic students and an increased number of whites. Cypress College stresses its academic offerings in science, mathematics, fine arts, and a vocational program for nurses.

After about a year at Cypress College, in July 1990 Scott-Skillman took another step forward in her career. She became vice-chancellor for the State of California Community College System, which she described as the largest educational system in the world. Among her duties is the responsibility for the admission to the counseling and other supportive services for 1.5 million students. One of her aspirations is to see black students coming through in larger numbers, and better represented in the educational arena.

Scott-Skillman's interest in human services began at age fifteen when she started as a volunteer tutor, first in the Homework Help Program at Downs and later in her home, working with students from high schools and community colleges. At Los Medanos, she took part in organizing cultural and educational programs for African-American students and faculty. She was an officer and a hard-working member of the Council of Black American Affairs in a full range of concerns of community college educators and students. The council encouraged and monitored legislation that affected them on a state level.

In Sacramento, Scott-Skillman was identified with two community organizations: The Literacy Coalition, which was concerned
with improving the reading skills in the work place and in the
home throughout the five adjacent counties, and the Drug Bust-
ers, an organization that provided activities for young people
who were mostly ethnic teenagers.

Classical music has been a source of enjoyment for Scott-
Skillman since she was a child. From elementary school to high
school she studied piano and took additional musical training at
Mills College in Oakland. Now she goes to the piano when she
needs to release the tensions and strains of the day.

There is no doubt that Scott-Skillman has not reached the
peak of her career. I was delighted by her self-confidence and
commitment to hard work. She has all of the necessary ingre-
dients for continued growth: training through formal education, varied experience in the field of education, a well-defined
dedication to public education, and the willingness to give the
physical and mental energy that is required.

EUGENE TARRANT
Born 1919, Ennis, Texas

"My mother gave me the survivor's skills necessary to survive in those times."

Although Eugene Tarrant is still a member at Downs and
comes to church regularly, he has reduced greatly his former
high level of participation. Tarrant was one of the most active
men of the church, singing in the choir and cheerfully accepting any responsibility Nichols brought to him. If Nichols wanted
a job done quickly and well, Eugene Tarrant was one of the first
people he thought of.

Ennis, Texas, the place of Eugene Tarrant's birth, is a very
small rural town thirty-six miles west of Dallas. When Tarrant
was three his mother left his father and took her two sons to
Dallas. He does not remember seeing his father after that. His
mother tried to answer his youthful questions about his father
in a way that discouraged hard feelings. She would say, "Your

father was a good man, but he didn't take care of his family as he should. That's why I left him." It was difficult for young Tarrant to understand why a man would not visit his children; it seemed that he would want to see them if only to satisfy a curiosity about their growth and development.

Most of Tarrant's mother's work was as a domestic servant for well-to-do white people; for many years mother and son lived on the residential premises of her employers. Tarrant's playmates were the sons of the families who lived in the exclusively white areas. They played the games that boys play and went fishing and boating in the stream that ran beside the houses. Tarrant's family expected him to follow the examples of other men in his family who were Baptist ministers. He probably would have done so had it not been for the trauma of seeing men die aboard ship in the naval battles of World War II. The suffering and loss of life caused him to question his beliefs in God and undermined his intention to maintain the family tradition.

Directly after he graduated from high school in 1938, Tarrant went into the navy and remained there until 1945. He had a good academic record and was an athlete, but in the thirties financial aid was nonexistent. After he was rejected by several colleges Tarrant turned toward the military. Having filled their quota of black recruits, the army was open only to whites. The Marine Corps would not consider black men, but the navy accepted his application. Tarrant's examination and basic training was the same as for all new recruits. However, he found out later that because he was black he was restricted to the mess division, and his rank of apprentice seaman was interpreted broadly to relegate him to the position of a mess attendant, or a cook, or a steward, no matter what his aspirations were.

Tarrant hated messroom duty, especially because he had no input into the choice of his assignment. In addition to cooking, messmen took care of the personal needs of the officers, shined their shoes, made up their cabins, checked their laundry, and held the platters and serving trays while the officers served their plates. He thought of this as degrading work, and his bitterness earned him the reputation of being a troublemaker. Even though he knew that the military had the authority, and enlist-ees could not win such a fight, he tried to organize the men aboard ship to refuse to do the work. He served time in the brig as punishment. After the war started and he realized that he was not going to be discharged, Tarrant accepted the fact that he must reconcile himself to his conditions and began to make the best of a bad situation. For the last three or four years in the navy he was a captain's cook, an assignment that was given only to workers who had demonstrated top ability. But he never lost his resentment of the enforced aspect of his status in the navy.

At the height of World War II, in December 1942, Tarrant's cruiser, the U.S.S. *San Francisco,* having sustained severe dam-ages in a battle in the South Pacific, docked in Vallejo for re-pairs. During his fifteen-day leave he went to Kansas to visit his mother. At her church that Sunday he was smitten by Mary, a soloist in the Christmas program. Four days later he proposed marriage, and on February 6, 1943, they were married.

As the war continued Tarrant was injured and was released from the navy in 1945. What began as a four-year enlistment had stretched into six and a half years in the midst of war. Finally it was over and he was a civilian back in Oakland. Three days after Tarrant reached Oakland he began work as a ste-vedore on the San Francisco waterfront. Waterfront work was a welcome change; he preferred the physical labor—loading and unloading ships, rigging gears and booms—to the soft work in the navy, and he enjoyed the stimulation of the conversations with the men on the docks. The waterfront had two disadvan-tages: longshoremen made good wages when ships came into port, but they earned nothing if there was no cargo to move. There was also the ever present possibility of strikes and work stoppages to cut off the money. Within the three years that Tarrant worked on the waterfront there were two strikes: one for seventy-eight days, and another for fifty days.

When he thought about the unevenness of a stevedore's pay Tarrant decided he needed a career that would bring more reli-able pay and used his G.I. bill to prepare for a different kind of employment. He undertook the grueling schedule of classes at Merritt Community College in Oakland, while working at the waterfront and as a bartender at a nightclub. He traveled by bus, streetcar, the Key System train that carried passengers across the Bay Bridge into San Francisco, or by walking. At Merritt he learned typing, accounting, and business management.

Armed with his new office skills, Tarrant looked into the civil service preemployment examinations and signed up to take the test for mail clerk. With a score of 99.6 percent, he was hired without delay and began twenty-five years of civil service, from clerk to civil service examiner; he also became one of the first black supervisors. As civil service examiner his primary function was to conduct civil service tests for four hundred job classifications.

By a special order issued in 1972 the federal government tried to lessen its financial burden by reducing the number of higher paid employees through early retirement of longtime workers. Tarrant qualified for the benefits of this order by having six and a half years in the military and twenty-six years as a postal employee. With this thirty-two-year combination, he was able to retire in 1972 at age fifty-three. Retired, Tarrant could choose the way he spent his day. He became a volunteer case worker for the Red Cross, providing social services to veterans and their dependents. His background of military and federal experience made him an ideal person to guide them through the maze of regulations and forms.

Next Tarrant went to the Berkeley police department as a civilian volunteer. He worked in the records department for two years behind a bulletproof glass, making reports and answering inquiries. Since 1973 Tarrant has been the coordinator of the Edwards Street Neighborhood Association, the oldest neighborhood watch group in Berkeley. The association represents sixty-four families who live on Edwards Street in a well-functioning organization that knows who belongs where and what belongs to whom. If a member of the group sees something unusual at a residence, he or she will call the house to investigate. If there is no answer he or she will then call the police, who are very cooperative with the citizens' efforts to protect their neighborhood. The Association honored Tarrant's dedication with a testimonial dinner and a plaque.

People have said that Eugene Tarrant is a stern, no-nonsense person who seems to be serious at all times. Still they know that beneath the austere appearance there is a warm heart and a willingness to help people solve their problems. To Tarrant, the rewards for extending himself to people in distress come from the people themselves, such as a veteran's widow who acknowledged his assistance by taking his hands and saying, "If you hadn't come along, I wouldn't have known what to do." Tarrant is a man of quick action; he evaluates a situation, plans the strategy, and starts to work toward the desired results. It took less than two days for him to know that he wanted to marry Mary Williams. Their marriage of nearly fifty years proves that it was a good decision.

Thanks to Tarrant, Frank and I had no worry about the care of our Oakland house when we were in West Africa; he assumed that responsibility without compensation for the full two years. By this demonstration of his love, we were relieved of that concern and could enjoy the full benefits of living abroad.

PETE W. TAYLOR, JR.
Born 1928, Houston, Texas

**"I worked with Joshua Rose for five and a half years, and he taught me very well.
He let me take my bumps, but he was always there to lift me up.
I had grandiose ideas, and he would let me get to a certain point, then he would
slow me down and show me where I was running into problems."**

When Pete W. Taylor, Jr., was first attracted to Downs in 1956, his major concern was the welfare of his small children. He liked the fact that he could remain in the nursery with them and still see and hear what was going on in the sanctuary. As his family developed, Taylor became more than a "bench member." He was a lay leader, president of the United Methodist Men of the California/Nevada Conference, and secretary of the national organization of Methodist men.

Before Pete Taylor and his parents left Houston, Texas, to come to California, his grandparents, uncles, aunts, and cousins all lived in close proximity to one another. Being the only boy in the group meant that Taylor enjoyed a favoritism that was denied to the girls. If the day's dinner did not suit his appetite, he would say, "I don't want this," and his grandfather would tell his wife, "Leola, fix him something else that he wants," and she would prepare another dish that was more to his liking. But when his doting grandfather was at work, he had to comply to his grandmother's rules. Her and his parents' training gave him the foundation for the standards of conduct that he has maintained all his life.

Taylor's father was impressed by workers in offices who sat on comfortable chairs in front of desks, sheltered from the weather, typing official-looking documents. The typists were white and apparently well paid, and their working conditions were in direct contrast to those of people who earned their living by outdoor physical labor. Knowing how to type became a symbol of success to Taylor's father, and he wanted his son to learn to type to escape the rigors of outside work. In 1942 Taylor's father came to Oakland to work in the war industries and was able to start right away because there was work for everybody. In five months he made arrangements to be reunited in California with his wife and fourteen-year-old son. Taylor went to school through the eighth grade in Houston and then completed high school in Oakland. He interrupted his college studies for two years of military service during the Korean War but returned to San Francisco State College for a degree in recreation in 1954.

During summer vacations from college and after class during the semesters, Taylor worked at the North Oakland YMCA under the direction of Joshua Rose, the executive secretary. When he graduated Taylor was employed as program secretary and embarked on a period of training where Rose taught him how to deal with obstacles and how to evaluate a puzzling situation before wading into its muddy waters unprepared. When he had been there for five and a half years, Rose convinced Taylor to leave the Y to become the assistant district executive of the Boy Scouts, serving the same area in which he had been working.

Coincidently, in this new assignment Taylor was an assistant to Carl Mack, Sr., the man who had been his first YMCA camp director in Houston. Year after year Taylor had gone to the Houston YMCA for after-school activities, and the Y summer camps were the highlights of his year. Mack had a place in those fond childhood recollections, but at first Taylor had no interest in moving from the Y to the Boy Scouts until Rose convinced him that the future was brighter with the Boy Scouts than with the Y. His maturing continued until he again reached the magic number of five and a half years, and Mack left the Boy Scouts to go to another position. Taylor took his place as district executive, still serving the youth in the same parts of Oakland.

Each work experience had an effect on Taylor's development as an administrator and added to his capabilities, so he was ready when the opportunity came to replace Barney Hilburn who had resigned as housing manager for the west Oakland area. Taylor took over the management of the housing in west Oakland as the first former resident to return in the top position of authority to the housing development where he had lived. In Taylor's twenty-three years in Oakland housing he has ascended from manager of West Oakland Housing to his present position of director of community services. Community services is divided into three sections: First there is Social Services, whose primary responsibility is to make home visits to assist new residents, help tenants with personal problems, and direct families to available local services as their needs arise. The second section provides social and recreational activities for senior citizens and encourages them to let go of some of the needless physical and social restrictions that they have placed upon themselves. This section serves hot midday meals at two centers and gives added support services at mealtimes. The third section offers youth activities, such as lunch programs, Boy Scouts, and Girl Scouts.

The youth section has taken hundreds of boys and girls on annual trips to Disneyland, an invigorating adventure for youngsters who have never left the limits of their city. They had no concept of the distance between the Bay Area and southern California, or any idea of the hours it would take to travel the miles. When they were only half way there, some were sure that the destination must be just around the corner. It was ex-

citing to Taylor to see the kids run around filled with enthusiasm, electrically charged by the fun of being in new and strange
surroundings outside of their usual routine. Taylor was sure
that the positive effects of the trips will remain with them and
add a new dimension to their lives: "Perhaps something that we
can't measure may rub off on the them." For the first time the
boys and girls stayed in a hotel where they shared rooms with
other youths and ate in restaurants where food was served to
them by waiters and waitresses. Taylor also thought of these
trips as lessons in human relations.

After the dissolution of his first marriage, Taylor married
Veronica, a woman whom he had met at Downs. They joined
her four girls and his four boys into one family. Downs became
the center of the activities for the eight children and their parents. As the young people matured they took part in programs
that were designed for their age groups. As time passed, Taylor
and Veronica took more and more active roles in the total concerns of Downs in addition to those that were for the exclusive
benefit of very young people.

Pete Taylor is a man who gives all of his attention to any
assignments he takes on. He has the commitment and the energy to do the things outside of work that interest him. The
twenty-four-hour day and seven-day week hold enough time
for church business, participation with the Boy Scouts as a volunteer, and anything else he may decide to do. If Taylor were
fired from his job tomorrow, he would find another need for his
skills. He could not remain at home. Television, gardening, or a
sedentary hobby would hold no attraction for him.

VERTIS THOMPSON
Born 1925, Muskogee, Oklahoma

"'By and By When the Morning Comes' is not always just when I get to heaven."

It was the coincidence of living less than five blocks from
Downs that caused Vertis Thompson to visit the church in 1957.
He had just arrived in California and wanted to find a base

for continued spiritual support, one that he could easily reach within the restrictions of the long working hours of a young medical doctor, and the difficulty of transporting himself, his wife, and two small children. Downs proved to be a perfect choice in all respects. "It was right down my alley," both literally and figuratively, and Thompson took as active a part as his demanding schedule permitted.

Election day was a big event in Vertis Thompson's home when he was a boy in Muskogee, Oklahoma. The night before the election his father would talk about the issues that were on the ballot. On voting day he came home from work, took his bath, and went to the polls. Thompson looked forward to the chance to cast his ballot, but the circumstances of his induction into the armed forces and the years of study in Washington, D.C., delayed his first vote until he was more than thirty years old and had settled in California. It was not until 1964, long after he had left, that people who lived in the District of Columbia got the right to vote.

In Muskogee, Thompson lived in a segregated society. He learned a most dramatic lesson in the discrepancy between the advantages for black and white people when he visited the white high school through a YMCA exchange program. He saw that each student had for his individual use as much equipment as the chemistry laboratory in his school had for the whole class. He said to himself, "Boy, if I had that kind of equipment to work with, what couldn't I do?" He was envious, but not bitter, because he believed that conditions were bound to get better.

Thompson had considered a career as a minister, but two years as a hospital corpsman in the navy helped him make the choice to be a physician. He knew that Jesus Christ healed the bodies as well as the spirits of men, but without a healthy body it is impossible to give serious thought to religion. Following the example of Jesus, Thompson set about to do something for the body to make it easier for people to be receptive to spiritual things.

After high school in Muskogee, Thompson entered Howard University in 1943 for premedical study. After one year the draft board called him into the navy for a two-year term. At the end of military service he returned to Howard and went straight through until he received his medical degree in 1952. He remained in D.C. for five more years for an internship and specialty training in obstetrics and gynecology at Freedman's Hospital. Before the end of his medical studies at Howard, Thompson married Mary in 1948. They had first met at Langston University in Oklahoma as representatives of their high schools in interscholastic state meets. At the time he thought that "she was the cutest thing I had ever seen." After many years they renewed the acquaintance while he was still in medical school, and she was an undergraduate at Howard.

From his time in California as a serviceman, Thompson knew that he wanted to live in that state, so he returned to the Bay Area to begin his medical practice. For the first months he worked at Agnew State Hospital, which gave him time to arrange with his friends Walter Morris, an orthopedist, and Benjamin Covington, a surgeon, to join forces in a medical practice. Thompson and Morris were classmates at Howard, and Covington was a student at Meharry Medical School. The three were at Freedmen's Hospital together for the specialty training. While Thompson worked at Agnew State Hospital, Morris was at the Presidio Hospital, and Covington worked at Modesto State Hospital, all in California. After eighteen months they pooled their resources and built a medical center for physicians, dentists, and a pharmacist in Oakland on Shattuck Avenue, half a block from the Berkeley line. They opened the offices in 1959 and continue to see patients there. After maintaining a private practice for several years, Thompson went to the University of California and got a master's degree in public health in 1974.

Thompson is a firm believer that the only way to achieve success is through the expenditure of time and energy in preparation for one's chosen career. He has used his efforts in two ways to influence students to take seriously the educational opportunities that are open to them. First, he was a member of the Laney Community College Licensed Vocational Nursing Program Advisory Board. This body helps design the program's curriculum to see that the graduates are qualified to satisfy state requirements and enter the job market. Once they become vocational nurses, he tries to lead them to continue study for the bachelor's degree and to become registered nurses. Then, as a practicing physician Thompson very often talks to bright African-American young people who are approaching graduation from high school, or who are already in college, about the possibilities of a career in medicine. He helps them fill out applications, writes letters of recommendation, and gives general guidance. Most of all he counsels them about the demands of the many years of preparation and the needed discipline to complete them successfully.

In order to become involved in the political aspects of medicine, Thompson became a member of the boards of local hospitals. By working on committees that set hospital policy, he helped to ensure that every hospital in the East Bay has some black physicians on its staff. As chairman of the board of Herrick Hospital during its construction in the late seventies, he enforced the directors' mandate that a minimum of 25 percent of the contracts be awarded to minority businesses. He was happy to see that in actuality, 38 percent of the contract dollars went to ethnic firms.

At this point in the history of African-American physicians, they are all members of the American Medical Association (AMA) and belong to their specialty societies, but Thompson strongly supports the continued existence of the National Medical Association (NMA), which is the predominantly black organization that was established in 1895 when the AMA withheld membership to blacks. The NMA addresses the specific needs of black people and is actively involved in the recruitment and retention of African-Americans in medical schools, the funding of financial assistance for students, and encouraging practitioners in the field. Thompson was president of both the state chapter and the national organization of NMA. A highlight of his tenure in the national office was the opportunity to attend the inauguration of Dr. Maurice Clifford as president of the Medical College of Pennsylvania in Philadelphia and witness the installation of that black physician into a top position of leadership. Another of Thompson's treasured experiences with NMA is his trip to Africa in 1971; he and other doctors presented papers before the Liberian Medical Society in West Africa, and in the eastern part of the continent they were privileged to have an audience with Haile Selassie. Even though he has relinquished official duties, Thompson still remains a hard working member of the local division of NMA, the Sinkler-Miller Medical Association, named after a surgeon and a urologist who are well respected by the local medical community.

Sinkler-Miller became actively involved with the plight of black medical students at the University of California–Davis in the post-Baake era. Baake, an unsuccessful white applicant for admission to the university's medical school, had test scores that were not on par with other white students who were admitted. At the same time, the university had set a quota system to admit a number of black students whether they met the usual test standards or not. Baake sued the university, saying that this quota system denied him admission to medical school. The United States Supreme Court upheld his charge of reverse discrimination in 1978. Thompson was concerned about the fact that admission decisions were based upon tests that had been proven to be biased in favor of the majority culture, and did not take into consideration other pertinent factors of personal orientation that would add to the assessment of the candidate's potential to become a medical doctor.

The Baake case created a hostile atmosphere that impeded African-American students from getting the best medical education at Davis. Knowing this, many black students who had been accepted to that campus refused to go. Thompson was able to assist one female student, a "very bright kid, a good student who was passing in all of her courses," but she was harassed and belittled to the extent that near the time of graduation she was convinced that she was not capable of becoming a doctor. He referred her to a black radiologist in Sacramento, Dr. Sarah Payton, who took the younger woman under her wing and nurtured her until she had received her degree and had begun a practice in internal medicine.

Fortunately, Davis got a new dean of the School of Medicine who was committed to making a change in the conditions and convened a faculty committee to counteract some of the negative things that were taking place. With the help of the NMA, and the start of a dialogue with the black community, including Ruth Love, who was then superintendent of schools in Oakland, the Davis campus has reversed the downward trend in the enrollment of black students. While still far from ideal, there has been a significant improvement in the racial climate.

Thompson's value to the East Bay has been recognized with many awards. In March 1984 he was the recipient of the Annual Humanitarian Award of the "Cindy" Smallwood Medical Education Financial Assistance Foundation. The citation referred to his "outstanding contributions in health and welfare through untiring efforts, long hours, hard work, and loving service to the low income and disadvantaged community without thought of personal aggrandizement." Three months later the Innovators, an organization of African-American business and professional women, paid public tribute to a group of citizens who had served in fields of human service to improve the quality of life for black people in the Bay Area. Thompson was selected because of his medical services. Further recognition came in October 1987 when the Sinkler-Miller Medical Association of the NMA presented him with one of its two annual Distinguished Service Awards, a fitting acknowledgment of his dedication to the profession that he loves.

Thompson feels that he is more fortunate than many other black people because he is involved in a career that he likes, and he had the chance to go through college and prepare for that career. He knows that there are countless other ethnic young people who are equally as capable, but because of economic restrictions or limits in terms of numbers, they were not able to do so.

When a patient enters the office of Vertis R. Thompson, M.D., Gynecologist and Obstetrician, she can see two pictures on the walls of the waiting room. Both are of a black mother and child. The one that struck me most shows the mother lying on her back holding her baby high above her, looking at the child with love. Seeing this striking picture displayed in full view of the women who entered his office said to me that he really understands the special relationship between a mother and her child. There is a modesty about Vertis Thompson that corresponds with his statement, "I have been busy, but I don't know that I've been doing too much." I can point to the difference he has made in providing health care in his private practice and in the hospitals where he has been an important factor in monitoring the quality of care for all people of the community. And I mention the emphasis he has put on the benefits of preparedness for any career because he is most proud of his role in encouraging young people to choose medicine as he did, and hopes that they will achieve similar satisfaction.

NORA VAUGHN
Born 1914, Utica, Mississippi

"Dr. Carver came once a year, to every Farmer's Conference, and he sat out on the campus looking like a little tramp. He wore an old coat, and I can remember him with that cap pulled down over his head."

The Vaughn family has a special place in the hearts of all the members at Downs Memorial United Methodist Church. They were one of the five original families that came to Downs before Nichols when it was the Golden Gate Methodist Church: Mr. and Mrs. Shirley; Mr. and Mrs. Loftin and their daughters, Gloria Bayne and Linnie Roberts; Mrs. Delaney and her four children; and Mrs. Nelson and her daughter, Earlene. Nora directed dramatic productions to celebrate the holy days of the church, and the dream that grew out of this experience gave birth to the Black Repertory Group. Her husband, Birel, although deceased, is still alive in our memories for his music and his indispensable role in building the church sanctuary.

By the time she was six, Nora Vaughn had already displayed her flair for the dramatic. One Sunday when she went with her mother to a Methodist church, the child "tore up the church." Her mother did her best to restrain the little girl who insisted on testifying and joining the church. That Sunday she broke ranks with her parents and became the only one in the family who was not a Baptist. Vaughn describes her emotional outburst as partly religious and partly a desire to imitate her godmother

Aunt Nora, for whom she was named. Aunt Nora had an outgoing personality, and her shouting and testifying in church had
captured the admiration of her godchild.

As a young girl Vaughn had no interest in any household
chores, choosing instead to find a peaceful spot to enjoy her
books. She was constantly scolded by her mother, "You little
heifer, you just sit and read all day." Years later she discovered
that her mother was really very proud of her academic and
dramatic accomplishments. Until she was fifteen Vaughn lived
in Utica, Mississippi, an all-black hamlet near Jackson, the home
of Utica Institute, a boarding school from first grade through
the second year of college. It had been founded by Dr. Holtzclaw, one of the first graduates of Tuskegee, who modeled Utica
after his alma mater. The school emphasized teaching students
how to work with their hands. Dr. Holtzclaw made periodic
trips north to raise funds for the Institute and to recruit white
teachers who were committed to missionary work among the
black people of the South. He brought back barrels of clothing from which Vaughn's mother made beautiful things for her
children to wear. Vaughn's early introduction to Shakespeare
was balanced by intensive exposure to African-American culture through the works of black writers, and by seeing in person artists such as Paul Robeson.

Vaughn's father, one of the black members of the faculty,
taught agriculture at the Institute, and Dr. George Washington
Carver came each year for the Farmer's Conference and became part of the life of Utica. The children from the primary
grades enjoyed their visits to his laboratory. Vaughn remembered the old coat and the worn cap that he wore down over his
head. She and her playmates would run up behind him and put
their hands over his eyes, and he would say, "Oh yes, I see you."
Then he would chase them in a game of hide-and-go-seek. Carver was frequently a speaker during the Institute's chapel services. Vaughn has fond memories of him telling the assembly in
his high-pitched voice, "God moves in mysterious ways, his wonders to perform. He plants his footsteps on the sea, and rides
upon the storm."

During the depression it became increasingly difficult to secure funds for Utica's operation, and its doors closed. Vaughn's family left the tranquil setting of Utica when she was in the tenth grade and moved to Jackson. The pace of life there was different from the all-black Utica where every person was well acquainted with everyone else and where racial prejudice or discrimination was less pronounced. She enrolled in a public school in the big city and had to make the adjustment to a completely new way of life. The family moved in with relatives while her father looked for a job and carved a new niche for himself and his family.

Vaughn graduated from Jackson State College in 1934 and took a job as teacher in Cleveland, Mississippi. There she met Birel, a graduate of Tuskegee, who was on the same faculty. They were married about a year later. She continued to teach in Mississippi until they came to California in 1943 to escape the racial conditions in that state. In 1948 when Vaughn's husband, Birel, was busy building the house for his family on Boise Street in Berkeley, Reverend Mr. Doggett, the minister at the newly created Downs Memorial Methodist Church, came to the house to visit. The minister ignored Birel's statement that he was a staunch Baptist and said, "Well, I tell you, Mr. Vaughn. I'm having some trouble getting the place cleaned up, and I need some work done. I'm new in the neighborhood here. I wonder if you would come over and help me with some carpentry work." Birel agreed to go to look at the building but became interested in more than the repair to the old building, and he and their two daughters joined the church before the end of that year. Vaughn was not with them because she was sick at that time. When she got well, she too became part of Downs in 1949.

October 11, 1987, was a day of fulfillment for Vaughn. On that date the Black Repertory Group Community Cultural Arts Center and the Birel L. Vaughn Theater on Adeline Street in Berkeley was dedicated after a long, exhaustive financial struggle. From its roots in the tiny social hall of Downs church to more than ten years in an equally small storefront, the Downs-born theatrical group now has a professional home. The first official production of the Black Repertory Group (BRG) was in 1964, but its start came long before when Vaughn began to produce dramatic presentations at Downs. Her casts were people from the church; they took the roles, made the costumes, and staged the events, all under her direction. She brought to the undertaking the training of four years in the drama department at college, and the spark of the creative personality that appeared when she was five years old and stood before the worshippers at the Methodist church in Mississippi and testified. Encouraged by the success at Downs, somebody said, "Why don't we keep this going rather than just working only on these particular holidays?" They chose Ossie Davis's *Purlie Victorious* for their debut performance at the San Pablo Center in Berkeley.

Vaughn realized that young people need to know who they are, where they came from, and understand that it is all right to succeed. This was foremost in her decision to develop the BRG as "Keeper of the Culture" and produce five major plays a year by African-American authors. In the early sixties BRG was speaking out through the works of black playwrights, but it was not completely accepted by the community because it was not a vehicle for the "fist shaking stuff, and the revolutionary type of things." In Vaughn's opinion black people were trying to get away from playwrights like Langston Hughes and James Weldon Johnson. In the late sixties and seventies, as the University of California turned toward the more revolutionary works, BRG continued its preference for the "classics" and added some more modern plays that bring inspiration from knowing that somebody accomplished something in spite of racism. Along with its theatrical productions, BRG has workshops for young people and outreach programs for the community and schools.

The first presentation in the new playhouse was Marc Connelly's *The Green Pastures,* chosen for beautiful music of Hall Johnson and the black dialect because both are examples of the historical background that BRG thinks of in its role as "Keeper of the Culture." To bring the work into perspective the program contained this note from the director, Danny Duncan: "Let us all remember that *Green Pastures* was written in the thirties, long before the civil rights movement. As long as we remember from a historical viewpoint, the show is still relevant today."

Accolades have come to Vaughn from schools, churches, and community organizations. In 1983 she received the Paine Knickerbocker Award from the Bay Area Critics Circle, an organization of dramatic critics whose reviews appear in local newspapers. The recognition was in tribute to the quality of her work as director of BRG. In the same year, the National Council of Black Studies presented its Distinguished Community Service Award to her "in recognition of your historic role in developing the creative arts in the black community, and your continuing efforts to assist and teach young artists." This honor was especially welcome to Vaughn because of her involvement in the makings of the black studies department at the University of California "during the turbulent sixties" and in the Berkeley community during that time. She had served as a guest lecturer at the university but never expected public honors to come from that. Since Birel's death, Vaughn has given herself to BRG and the pleasure that comes from contributing to the lives of young people. She admits that she is "truly committed, a very stubborn worker," who is determined to stay with whatever she starts out to do until there is a successful conclusion.

Nora Vaughn has seen her dream come true. The reality of the Black Repertory Group Community Cultural Arts Center and Birel L. Vaughn Theater came after more than twenty years of hard work, which was kept alive by her belief in BRG and her hope to reach a larger audience. The hard-working board of directors, made up primarily of members of Downs church, has a commitment to the philosophy of BRG as great as Vaughn's. They convinced the city of Berkeley to lease a vacant lot on the corner of Adeline and Fairview streets to the group for fifty-five years at one dollar a year, and to construct the theater with the costs shared by the city, the Department of Housing and Urban Development, and an ambitious fund-raising drive by BRG. BRG has use of the building with an option to purchase the facility in ten years.

DORENE WALTON
Born 1914, San Bernardino, California

"I was sent to Lincoln University in Missouri because in San Bernardino, California, there were very few blacks, and my exposure to black life had not been very extensive. My parents thought that an experience in a black institution would be helpful for me."

Without interruption from 1952 to the present, Dorene Walton has been intimately involved with the affairs of Downs church. She was an usher for many years, a member of the women's organizations, and a dependable supporter of all of its activities. Her son grew up attending Sunday school and the Methodist Youth Fellowship.

From the time of her parents' divorce, when she was nine years old, until she went to college Dorene Walton lived with her mother and father separately, and with her aunts. They were all church-oriented, devoted participants in religious activities, and they exposed Walton to that kind of training. The family attended Baptist and African Methodist Episcopal churches, and Walton went to Sunday services and took part in the Sunday school and youth activities of both denominations. Even though she did not live with her mother and father together, their influence was equal.

Walton's father and mother settled in San Bernardino, California, long before she was born; he had come from Georgia, and she from Texas. The largest ethnic group in San Bernardino when Walton was in public school was Mexican-American; they exceeded by far the number of black people in the city. Walton's early training centered around doing her best in school and growing up into a good citizen. Because of the smallness of the black population, the social and community activities for that segment of San Bernardino were limited and, for the most part, were connected with the church. To increase her interaction with African-American people and her knowledge of black culture, Walton's parents chose the all-black Lincoln University in Missouri for her to attend after high school.

Teaching and working with children had always been an aspiration for Walton, but she did not begin that career directly after college. For the first years she worked as an accountant in a cocktail lounge and then as a clerk for the Veterans Administration before she went to San Francisco State University and studied for her elementary teaching credential, school administration credential, and master's degree in education—all of which she received in 1951. It was not long before she began teaching in the elementary schools of Richmond, California. She progressed from classroom teacher to supervisor of the district's preschool program to her last assignment before she retired, principal of Kerry Hills Elementary School.

Throughout Walton's career in education she was much less interested in the arts than in the skills subjects; she thought that children should have a background in music and fine arts, and she instructed her pupils in those areas as she had been taught to do in teacher training classes. However, she was sure that proficiency in reading, grammar, mathematics, and the ability to relate to other people were the most important criteria for success as adults. Walton used her energies to transmit these skills to students, both as a teacher and as a principal. She wanted her charges to fit properly into the mainstream because this would be where they would have to make a living. To Walton, black English was a comfortable, intimate, cultural tool for use in informal, friendly surroundings, but it should be matched by a facility in communicating in the formal, sometimes hostile, business world. She was also convinced that there should be an accompanying knowledge of what constitutes acceptable dress in the competitive atmosphere of the work place, a setting where we spend a major part of our lives and which is not controlled by black people.

In her role as supervisor of the preschool program, Walton was involved largely with pupils from welfare families. There were times when she was greatly distressed by the disinterest of parents and second and third generations of mothers in the welfare system. She saw the effects that this had upon the likelihood that the children would receive proper care. She knew that she could not become disheartened, but it was nonetheless a real concern that she had to reckon with. Her response was to intensify her efforts and to make the best possible impact within her individual sphere of operation. For six years Walton was an officer of the California Association of Compensatory Education (CACE), which was involved with the quality of education for children from lower-income families, and which encouraged parents on a statewide basis to take political action on behalf of the schools that serve those students. She, like Ella Wiley and Dorothy Lee, served as regional director for CACE.

Before Downs came into being, Walton went to South Berkeley Community Church where Nichols was copastor. After he left to go to Downs she remained at South Berkeley until she became unhappy with the church's internal problems. These problems interfered with the spiritual satisfaction that she formerly attained, so she consulted Nichols in order to gain some guidance in coping with that situation. He offered spiritual counsel that brought her strength to weather the storm. It was sometime later in 1952 that she joined Downs.

Walton thinks of Downs as her family and as her greatest source of support. She spoke of the time when she lost in close succession her husband, mother, and father, and the consolation that the love of the people at the church brought to her. Now Walton is a widow, a retiree since 1977, who seldom misses a Sunday worship service at Downs, and who enjoys her favorite recreational activities, mainly bridge games.

My primary frame of reference for Walton is Downs church, but because of an unexpected meeting that took place about ten years ago, many miles from Downs, and in a totally unrelated situation, I have another lasting association with her. I did not know that Walton enjoys gambling in the Reno, Nevada, casinos as I do. In the predawn hours of one winter morning Walton and her husband, Grant (whom I had not met), and I were in the same casino. We had not seen each other until Grant called her attention to the amusing sight of a woman who was walking up and down a row of six slot machines seriously feeding coins into each of them instead of sitting on a stool playing a maximum of two machines at one time. Walton was surprised to see that the strange-acting woman was Dona Irvin, whom she knew very well from Downs. I was embarrassed at first but recovered my composure quickly enough to enjoy the humor of the spectacle.

Now whenever I go to Reno and succumb to the temptation to increase my luck by spreading my coins over a greater area, I think of seeing Walton there and my first introduction to Grant.

ZEPHYR WARD
Born 1922, Pine Bluff, Arkansas

"I have been singing since I was three. I felt that God had given me something that I could use and give to somebody else. It certainly was no good bottled up in me."

The music program at Downs has been enriched by the talent of Zephyr Ward and her gospel music. At first, she was the soloist for the newly initiated early morning Sunday services. Then she organized the beloved Gospel Choir, which brings beautiful music into the sanctuary and gives members the chance to participate in its performances. Ward has trained a children's choir and presented them in concert to raise funds for scholarships that were earmarked for children. In sum, Ward is a very vital element of Downs church.

Singing has been a part of Zephyr Ward's existence from when she turned three and sang her first solo from a tabletop. It was natural for her to join her family in their quartets, choirs, and combinations of all sorts to sing spirituals, hymns, and gospel songs. Her mother and fifteen children sang around the home, in every church, and all over the vicinity of Pine Bluff. One of the brothers traveled with the Piney Woods Singers from Piney Woods College in Mississippi, presenting concerts of spirituals and hymns in fund-raising tours.

A fond memory of Ward's childhood is of the trips to take lunch to her father in the cotton belt shop in Pine Bluff. He worked in a place where huge machines hummed and whirled away as they compressed cotton into bales. She was fascinated by the motion of the gears and wheels and by the clatter of the equipment. But best of all, there was the delightful aroma of the cottonseed oil that permeated the area. She would walk into the plant, through the sounds and smells of the building, to the place where he was working to give him freshly prepared food for his midday meal. These were very special experiences.

Because she had fifteen children to take care of, Ward's mother was always busy with household chores. She sewed for the girls, visited the children's schools, and attended PTA meetings. Nonetheless, she found time to sing in the church choir, chair the Mission Circle, and take part in other church organizations. The whole family was involved in their Baptist church. Ward's father taught his children that the way to get the white man's foot off their necks was to get an education. He wanted them, especially the boys, to be better prepared than he was. His philosophy was that if you have an education and the Lord on your side, you will be successful. At one time Ward's family had eight children in college concurrently.

The major portion of Ward's working years in Oakland has been at the Naval Supply Center, a military installation, where she went up the career ladder from entry-level records keeper to retail buyer in a preferred section of the center. Ward retired from that position in 1983. Not long after Ward came to the Naval Supply Center people discovered that she was a gospel singer, and she began to receive requests to sing at functions that the agency sponsored. She sang for black history celebrations, for programs in honor of Martin Luther King, Jr., and for hundreds of other occasions. She accepted all of the invitations with pleasure and thought of them as extensions of what she had been doing all of her life—using her musical talent for the enjoyment of others.

Nichols learned from Ward's brother, a minister, that his sister was a gospel singer at just about the time that Downs added an 8:30 A.M. Sunday morning service to the well-established one that started at 11:00 A.M.. There was no choir for the early hour service, so Nichols asked Ward to appear as soloist. She consented. Ward's music, which included a departure from the Methodist hymns, spirituals, and selections from Handel and Bach that the parishioners of Downs were accustomed to, developed its own group of admirers. Some people told her that they came to church with the hope that she would sing that particular Sunday, and others spoke of the soothing effect of her singing.

After Nichols left Downs, the Reverend Amos Cambric, his

successor, asked Ward to form a Gospel Choir. Ward had appre-
hensions about the success of such a venture, but Cambric encouraged her to "just try it" and put an announcement in the
church bulletin to attract singers. Ward did not require previous singing experience or a knowledge of music—only a desire to participate in that type of creativity. She soon brought
together a group of people who loved gospel music. On the other
hand, Ward heard comments to the effect that she should return to the Baptist church if she wanted to sing that kind of
music; it had no place in the Downs sanctuary. Despite the dis-
cordant reaction of some congregants, the Gospel Choir thrived
and grew into an accepted part of the worship services. It is
now on equal footing with the other musical groups at Downs.

In November 1986 Ward was honored in an evening of tribute
to her gifts of music to churches, schools, and civil and social
functions for more than four decades. The program was filled
with speeches of recognition and gratitude from her ministers
and friends. Zephyr Ward thought of singing for the public as
chances to fulfill her destiny—to bring pleasure and spiritual
support to her listeners. She does not limit her appearances to
church audiences; she has sung where she works, at social and
civic occasions, and at political rallies. There was seldom a community-oriented program at Oakland Naval Supply Center during Ward's thirty-year tenure that she did not participate in.
Ward has used her voice on the steps of the Berkeley city hall to
aid the campaigns of candidates Roy Nichols for city council
and school board, and Warren Widener for mayor of Berkeley.

WARREN WIDENER
Born 1938, Oroville, California

**"We clearly demonstrated at a time when white America was abandoning the cities
for the suburbs that cities could be viable."**

As a newly married young man and a student at the University of California–Berkeley, Warren Widener with his wife, Mary,
was codirector of Downs's Methodist Youth Fellowship. Together

they guided and trained the teenagers of the church within the framework of Christian principles. Their goals were to instill a sense of responsibility into the young people and to encourage them to plan meaningful programs that would be conducted in accord with regular parliamentary procedures.

Widener showed his concern and love for Downs and its welfare by sending monthly financial gifts to the church and carrying on a regular communication with the minister when he was stationed in Oklahoma, as an officer of the United States Army. At another stage of his life, Downs provided an effective launching pad for Widener's political career and a contingent of enthusiastic followers who formed a working support group.

The formal high school structure in Oroville, California, did little to encourage black students to enter college unless they showed athletic ability. Since Warren Widener played football and was a good academic student as well, he attracted the interest of his science teacher, an alumnus of the University of California–Berkeley who became his mentor and guided his study to make sure that he qualified for admission to Berkeley. He worked out Widener's schedule for the four years there and continued to watch over him until he was on a sure path to graduate. From the sixth grade through high school in Oroville, Widener had been in love with his childhood sweetheart, Mary. They were married in 1959 when he was a junior at Berkeley. They have continued their lives together in the East Bay, raising their three sons and both working in housing for the people of their community.

Two years after he completed law school at the University of California, Widener entered his first political campaign as a successful candidate for the Berkeley City Council in 1969. Then he won a mayoral race and was later reelected to a second term. During the second four-year term, he ran unsuccessfully for the state assembly and continued as mayor. His mayoral terms spanned the years from 1971 to 1979. Widener's incentive to become mayor came from his desire to bring about progress in areas that were usually overlooked. He saw efforts to keep the sewers clean, the streets swept, and the garbage removed, but he saw little concern about child care, recreation and open space, and housing for people who could not afford the available bank loans.

Through hard work Mayor Widener was able to prove that urban areas could remain desirable places to live, and that black people could reverse the tide of decline in the cities when the affluent white residents were moving into the suburbs. He pointed with pride to the difference between San Pablo Avenue in Oakland and in Berkeley. After a major fight to get funds from the state and county, he converted San Pablo Avenue in Berkeley from a six-lane highway to a four-lane street with trees and a decorative planter in the center. The wheelchair ramps made it easier for handicapped people to travel, and the center divider provided a resting place for slower walkers who could not cross the total distance during the time of one traffic signal.

Widener is proud of having developed Berkeley's housing loan program that made money accessible to poor people for home repairs; it kept the neighborhoods from deteriorating into slums. Two of his favorite accomplishments are the construction of the three senior centers and the James Kenney Park on Virginia Street, which is primarily for the youth of the city. Kenney Park made a statement with its quality equipment to the young people that theirs was a first-class facility for first-class individuals. Dorothy Pitts, in Berkeley's Department of Social Planning and in the Division on Aging, contributed to the accomplishments of Widener's administration in the areas of public services.

While Widener's sons were completing high school, he gave priority to their development and did not seek elected office, so he could have the flexibility of time to attend to their needs. He wanted to be able to take the time to visit their soccer practice field, attend their school or social functions, supervise their growth, and most of all, engage in thoughtful man-to-man discussions with them. After all three were well on the way to adulthood, he was ready to return to the political arena.

On the last day of January 1989, the Alameda County Board of Supervisors appointed Widener to fill the seat that was left vacant by the death of twelve-year veteran John George. From the beginning it was certain that reelection time would bring a battle for the votes. The lines were drawn early by a statement of fellow supervisors that Widener, a "political moderate," will not be popular as a replacement for the "left-leaning" George. However, when the election came in June 1990, Widener survived a challenge from his opponent, an aide to the popular Congressman Ronald Dellums. Widener's election was not officially confirmed until weeks later after the loser had demanded a recount of the votes. Widener's success was due in great part to his championing of the causes of the west Oakland residents, whose homes had been damaged in the October 1989 earthquake, and his waging of a vigorous protest to the replacing of the quake-damaged freeway in its old form. He has been outspoken against that unattractive concrete construction down the center of one of the busiest streets in the flat lands of Oakland. He understands the people's wish to be rid of that unsightly elevated blight through the heart of west Oakland.

From 1973 to 1977, Widener gave full time to his office as mayor of Berkeley, but he was not paid at a full-time rate. To supplement his earnings he went on a lecture circuit to speak to black students at universities about Black Power in the urban environment and to broader audiences about general urban affairs and his experiences as mayor. He had often told young black people that standing outside shouting and picketing, although an important tactic, was not the only way to bring about progress. He wanted them to know that another strategy was available to them—to get into a position of power, such as the mayor's seat, and use that as leverage to force change. Once, at the University of Utah, he debated William H. Kunstler, a white defense lawyer who is known nationally for the Chicago Seven case. The subject was whether one could be more effective inside or outside "the system."

As the debate proceeded, Kunstler listed a number of things that needed to be done, such as improved housing, health care, and education, but were not done even when there were well-meaning politicians at the local level, in Congress, and in the Executive Office. Kunstler ended with mention of the trial of the Chicago Seven. Widener's response was, "Well, I think that adequately proves my point. You are in the system. You are a lawyer, nothing is more in the system than a lawyer and the law, and if you did not really believe that you could be effective inside the system, you would not be going to court trying to defend these people who have taken whatever position they have taken." Widener was struck by the reaction of the almost entirely white audience whom he thought of as being on the conservative side. They were listening to a young black radical debating with an older white radical, and until that moment they had not been able to totally relate to either one. But with that response Widener saw an indication that they had heard something that rang a bell in their minds, and they were saying to themselves, "Oh, yes. We can stay in the system. We don't have to be a radical and be arrested and do all of those terrible things in order to be effective and be something worthwhile."

Since the early seventies Widener and Mary have been involved in public housing. Long before that, however, he had recognized that housing was one of the basic needs, but his interest was intensified when some of his white friends said that they had observed that white people bought nice houses, but black people spent their money on big cars. As he began to understand social conditions, he learned that the system prevented blacks from buying in the neighborhoods where the big houses were, and the sections where they lived never got their share of services. He wanted to do his part to see that sewers all over the city were fixed and not just those where the wealthy people had their homes. Residents of the depressed areas needed to be told to stop accepting substandard conditions, pool their political resources, and present their demands to the city government. As a united force, they could get loans to paint the house or add the needed bedroom, and then perhaps, buy a smaller car.

In 1977 Widener formed the California Neighborhood Housing Services Foundation. The foundation raises money and distributes grants for Neighborhood Housing Services (NHS) programs in California. NHS is community oriented in that it forms a partnership of residents and business enterprises in a nonprofit corporation to upgrade and maintain neighborhoods. Widener's role with NHS is to provide political support for them with local and national administrations and to raise the funds. In a dual role, he is president of the Urban Housing Institute, which assists in the development of low- and moderate-income housing, and manages the projects from the acquisition of the sites and construction of the houses until they are sold.

Widener maintains that in order for African-Americans to survive they must have power, know how to access power, and how to use it; power in the positive sense, the sort of influence that elected officials use for the good of their constituents. As an attorney for Safeway Stores, he saw the way the corporate system operates; as mayor of Berkeley he learned about the political system. These valuable lessons are not taught in schools. Middle-class white young people get the training from their fathers who are employed in large corporations. Widener's sons have each worked in his office doing all sorts of jobs to become familiar with that kind of environment. He felt that it was important for them to observe the hard work that comes with it, and learn that they must set their sights early in the right direction. Widener believes that it is not sufficient to have the desire to help fellow black people without the knowledge of how to access and use power.

Mary often teases him by saying that he is the only black person alive who has a superiority complex instead of an inferiority complex. Competing in the traditional white world never bothered him; he never lacked self-confidence, and he always knew that he could do whatever he wanted to do. The stage was set when he was elected mayor of his school in Oroville when he was in the eighth grade. He would like to teach other people that confidence can be 40 percent of accomplishment, that victory often comes not from physical or mental ability, but from the aura of self-confidence that intimidates opponents. Scores of African-American elected officials have more innate ability and are brighter than Jesse Jackson, but they lack the self-confidence to mount two national campaigns for the presidency.

In an effort to effectively balance his time between the demands of a career and being a husband and the father of three sons, Widener had gradually discontinued his attendance at

Downs. However, with his reentry into the political arena he returned to Downs after an absence of nearly twenty years. One Sunday he heard the minister, Rev. Douglass Fitch, make a reference to the need to undergo a metamorphosis to ensure success before approaching a new venture. This was not long after Widener took the supervisor's seat, and it seemed that the words were directed personally to him. That sermon and the reports that had come to him about the rejuvenation of Downs were his signal to rejoin his former church.

ELLA WILEY
Born 1920, Shreveport, Louisiana

"You had the water fountains for coloreds and for whites. I always got my water at home. The bathrooms naturally were separate, and I did that, too, at home."

Very often Ella Wiley sang the soprano solo part for the Chancel Choir's anthem, hymn, or spiritual on a Sunday morning at Downs. We felt her presence through her voice in the choir, her management of the Sunday school for more than five years, and her direction of the youth group.

Because Ella Wiley was an only child, and her parents separated before she reached school age, her mother has been her companion and best friend most of her life. Her religious foundation and encouragement for study came from her mother. She did not see her father after she was four years old. Her mother sheltered her as much as possible from the trauma of segregation in Louisiana and tried to counteract its effect by instilling in Wiley a strong feeling of self-respect. She taught Wiley to satisfy her thirst for water at home instead of depending upon the substandard "colored" drinking facilities in town, and to make full use of the bathroom before she left home.

The major portion of Wiley's work years has been in education. It began right after she finished the eleventh grade curriculum of her high school in Louisiana and went immediately into a year of teacher training. Soon after her eighteenth birthday she started sharing with another teacher the instruction of all of the students in a rural one-room school. The second teacher was reassigned midyear, leaving Wiley with the full responsibility for the whole school. After two years her supervisor convinced Wiley's mother that her daughter should go to college for a degree in education, which would give her a firmer foundation in public school teaching. By the time she came to California in 1945, she had completed a major in secondary education at Southern University and had taught at that university for a year.

Not long after Wiley settled in California she was employed as a teacher in Richmond. Meanwhile, she took courses at San Francisco State College for a master's degree. Initially she was not sure that she wanted to move into administration because of the added obligations and increased hours, but certification for administration assignment and continued encouragement by her principal prepared her for that next step. Wiley worked as vice principal and principal in elementary schools for twenty-one years until she retired from Richmond schools in 1986. Her last assignment was as principal of Martin Luther King, Jr., School, a nontraditional year-round site.

As a school principal, Wiley provided workshops to keep her staff from becoming lethargic and to avoid letting improved methods pass by unnoticed. Her students were predominantly black from low-income families, children who were in danger of not getting the concentrated attention that they needed. Wiley thought that some of this oversight was due, in large measure, to the teachers' ignorance (African-American as well as white) about what to do for the youngsters. Wiley encouraged teachers who were not comfortable with minority students to transfer to other sites, and she informed the personnel office not to send any teacher to her school who did not want to work, and work hard.

The Richmond school district's approach to integration was to move its teachers, thinking that the quality of education would be improved by balancing the ethnic composition of teaching staffs. The district sent black teachers, often the best instructors, to white schools, and white teachers to schools that had large numbers of nonwhite students. Sometimes the ethnic children suffered because they lost their teachers who had a demonstrated commitment to working with them. In many instances black teachers who had been reassigned took the first possible opportunity to return to their former locations and to their former pupils.

Two years before Wiley retired, King school went to a plan of year-round operation as opposed to only nine months. Students attended classes for six consecutive weeks and then were out for the next three. This schedule repeated itself throughout the whole year. Wiley thought that this concept would be the way of the future. The rationale for taking children out of school for the summer no longer exists. There is no need for boys and girls to use that time for work in the family fields, and it has been shown that students lose a portion of the nine months' learning during the summer vacation. Fiscally, it means that the district can use the site more effectively—the building does not stand idle for the three months of the summer.

The success of the year-round school depends upon having a staff who will agree to work the unaccustomed schedule, and parents who can arrange their work and vacation schedules around the children's school days. Wiley found much less resistance than she anticipated from both staff and parents. Most of the teachers agreed to remain under the new system, and parents from all over the district took advantage of the open enrollment plan and brought their children to King for the twelve-month instruction.

During Wiley's years as a principal in Richmond, she was active in the California Association of Compensatory Education (CACE), an organization comprised of parents, teachers, and administrators of schools where state funds were allotted to augment the programs for staff and students. There were local, regional, and state meetings of CACE to discuss pending legislation that would be to the advantage of the pupils. CACE kept its members informed about the status of the schools and encouraged parents to continue their involvement with the education of their children. Wiley acted as regional director of CACE for two years, as did Dorothy Lee and Dorene Walton. The three followed each other as regional director in succession.

Since 1982 Wiley has been intimately involved with Nora Vaughn in the Black Repertory Group (BRG). She began as a singer in productions and then was elected to the board of directors. She is committed to BRG's goals of being a viable community vehicle to train young people to use their talents of speaking, acting, and dance in an environment that will add to their knowledge of black culture and lead to increased self-esteem. Wiley is happy with the newly constructed theater, its greater space and added amenities, but she knows that realization of all of BRG's goals and objectives depends upon adequate staffing, which in turn is possible only with sufficient funding.

Wiley described herself as people-oriented, not a "thing person." She was always impatient with the paper work in teaching and school administration; she would rather be outside in the schoolyard with the children than making reports. I recall Wiley as superintendent of the Sunday school at Downs in the fifties and sixties, walking from one class to the other, checking on their progress, much as she did in the administration of her public school. Recently I saw her at a fund-raiser for BRG with apron and cap, serving salads at the crab feast. It made no difference that she was president of the board; she was working side by side with the other directors.

CLEOPHAS WILLIAMS
Born 1923, Velie, Arkansas

"We lobbied social bills and labor bills. It was very difficult to separate what was good for seniors, for education, for health, for labor from what was good for blacks and minorities."

Hearing Nichols's sermons at Downs and seeing people there doing things to bring about social change motivated Cleophas Williams to join in the action. Prior to that he had thought of himself as being on the sidelines, merely an observer. He began to take part in church projects in connection with the activities of his labor union, a combination that he found completely compatible. Williams has been a forceful, supportive presence at Downs, responding graciously to any request for his skills and his time, and serving the community beyond Downs as secretary of the East Bay Methodist Men.

It was not until long after Cleophas Williams came to California in 1942 that he realized his father would have been classified as handicapped today because he had lost his right arm in a hunting accident as a teenager. He had tripped over a bush, and in doing so, had caused the gun to fire into his arm. However, the loss of his arm did not restrict the actions of the proud, strong man who was a schoolteacher, a minister, and a counselor to people in his community.

Williams's mother died when he was three and a half years old. His parents had worked together as teachers in the rural schools of Arkansas. After his mother's death his father remarried, and Williams was "gifted with a very concerned second mother." The teachings of his father and stepmother were responsible for the quality of his development into an adult. The love of his father and his status in the community as an educated man who assisted townspeople through the bureaucratic labyrinth of the political and social systems was a great stabilizing force. He taught in the WPA school during the depression and dispensed advice to men and women, young and old. In his youth, Williams learned from his father that the circumstance of race need not be a devastating encumbrance.

Williams finished high school in Texarkana, Arkansas, in 1942 and went directly to Arkansas Mechanical and Normal College. He left after a few months because he heard that it was possible to avoid the interruption of his college education by the draft board if he went to California and got a defense job while he continued to take classes. Once here he went to work in the shipyard as an electrician's helper.

With the end of hostilities and the reduction of personnel in the shipyards, Williams was not certain what to do to make a living. As he sat awaiting his turn in Sid Scott's Barber Shop on Thirty-sixth and San Pablo streets in Oakland, he overheard a discussion about work for longshoremen on the San Francisco waterfront. Someone said, "Oh, yes, that's a good job. They always have security, even after the war is over. It's a good job if you can get it." This assurance prompted him to apply, and he was employed by the Pacific Maritime Association. He stayed there in different capacities for thirty-eight years.

Starting at the bottom, Williams loaded and unloaded ships as they left port or returned from overseas and eventually grew into an official of the union and one of its more influential members. The nature of the longshoreman's work was such that there were often extended lulls between spurts of activity. Williams joined the political discussions that were common on the San Francisco waterfront. They talked about employment, the status of workers all over the world, the need for unions to represent working people, and the atomic bombing of Japan. They proudly marched in the May Day parades. The union wanted to change the world and was sure that it could make a difference.

Williams's development of social understanding came from several directions, beginning with his reading of Richard Wright's *Native Son*, Karl Marx's *The Communist Manifesto*, and some of the works by Hewlett Johnson, the English ecclesiastic who was known as the "Red Dean" of Canterbury. From these literary works and the dockside discussions, his level of consciousness rose about social concepts and the rights of workers. He attended classes at the California Labor School in San Francisco to learn more about the haves and have-nots of the world.

One day Judge Horace Wheatley's father asked Williams to support him at a union meeting, the International Longshoremen's and Warehousemen's Union, Local 10 (ILWU). The senior Wheatley was campaigning to be the black brother who would go with a white brother to represent the union in the 1959 march for integrated schools in Washington, D.C., which was being organized by A. Phillip Randolph of the Brotherhood of Sleeping Car Porters, with Tom Mboya of the government of Kenya and Harry Belafonte among the participants. Right away Williams thought of his work in the community that made himself a good candidate: he had been a top solicitor of memberships for the NAACP and had worked with Mrs. Frankie Jones, Arthur Goodrich, and Joshua Rose in that organization. The idea of such a trip was attractive, in spite of the fact that in fifteen years he had never spoken at a union meeting and was an unknown with no possibilities to marshall the required votes. That night he took the microphone and recounted his experiences as a dock worker. He told the men that he had attained his manhood on the waterfront and had earned money to educate his children and to buy automobiles and homes. Along the way he had seen men lose their hands, their lives, and one man whose leg was so entangled in the cables that he had to be cut loose and have a tourniquet applied on the spot. He had been "down in the dust inhaling the rust of the ships, smelling the urine, and coming out into the fresh air whenever I could."

When the time came to nominate the delegates one member said, "I nominate Williams who made the speech a few minutes ago." The entire group stood up and elected him by acclamation. He went to Washington, but many of the old-timers resented the audacity of the young man "stealing" the trip. After this initial appearance, Williams continued in the union as a member and an official and worked to "show that labor unions are not corrupt, this union is not corrupt, and labor leaders don't have to be corrupt."

For the last four years before he retired, Williams served as legislative representative for ILWU in Sacramento. Williams's efforts were aimed toward the welfare of ordinary people—laborers, seniors, children, and minorities. In concert with other like-minded groups, he attended legislative sessions and hearings, testified, and met with elected officials to lobby for social and labor bills. The issues ranged from school lunches and class size to the monitoring of health facilities and rest and convalescent homes for senior citizens. He joined Jessica Mitford in the campaign against the high cost of dying, and the strong labor lobby helped defeat a Right to Work amendment on the state ballot.

Williams is saddened by the portrayal of labor unions as being on the defensive now. Since this depiction is propagated by the media, there is widespread doubts about the value of union representation, and people believe that any individual has the opportunity to emerge from the pack and get career advancement and additional benefits with the bosses' blessings. But he still thinks that the best interests of labor can be served by the organization of workers and by entering into bargaining procedures on a collective basis. Just as manufacturers, doctors, and teachers have organizations, parents have the PTA and students have student unions, so must the trade union movement have the interaction that strengthens the cause for each person as a unit.

I had not visited with Williams and his wife, Sadie, for many years when Frank and I went with them for their early morning brisk walk around Lake Merritt in downtown Oakland. We met on a crisp morning. As the four of us walked Williams and Sadie pointed out the well-kept condition of the parklike areas along our route, the absence of debris, and the clear, clean water of the lake that had recently been dredged to remove the algae. Sadie told us about the efforts of the city council to maintain the lake as a place for people to enjoy, just as we were doing. When the walk was over, the four of us had a leisurely breakfast in a small restaurant beside the water where we could continue to admire the scenic view and see the ducks and sea gulls that passed our window. This was a relaxing way to begin the day.

FOUR

Reflections upon Downs Church and Its People

The origin of Downs Memorial United Methodist Church co-incided with the arrival of hosts of black people in the East Bay during the boom of World War II, which also marked the beginning of African-Americans participating in the social and political activities of the Bay Area. As the demographics of north Oakland changed to almost totally black, the abandoned Golden Gate Methodist Church was rededicated and named Downs Memorial Methodist Church to address the spiritual needs of the new residents. Knowing the legacy of the Reverend Karl Downs as an activist in the religious and social world, we set about to follow our leader, Roy Nichols, whose commitment was akin to Karl Downs's. Those who were new to the state brought with them the aspirations that they shared with the native Californians, namely improved financial and social conditions. The financial gains came more easily than the social. In California they found abundant employment but not a perfect release from racial and social problems. One area that needed constant monitoring was the public schools; parents had to make sure that students were motivated to take full advantage of the learning opportunities.

An advantage of a small church is that its members can become well acquainted with the pastor and one another to function as a family. I did not know all of the people who belonged to Downs during my years there, their overall goals, or the pre-

215

cise measure of their contributions to the East Bay community, but I was close enough to a sufficient number to think of them as representative of the dominant philosophy, personality, and soul of the church. It was not difficult for me to choose the forty individuals to designate the "Downs people"; it was more of a chore to set a limit since I could not include all of those in the congregation who epitomize that spirit.

The Downs people came with spiritual foundations that had been set by their families and their former churches. The task for Downs was to build upon and strengthen that training. As a group, the Downs people did not depend in entirety upon literal acceptance of biblical teachings. The majority lived by Christian principles that affirm the importance of living a respectable personal life with concern for the welfare of all humanity. The Downs people agreed with the concept of Nichols's answer to the problems of black people in the United States: a three-legged stool, with the legs personifying substantial support from three principal elements—church, school, and home, each operating in its sphere of influence. At Downs Nichols encouraged us to read about, talk about, and listen to other people discuss political issues and political campaigns. His weekly sermons referred to things that were happening outside of the church, and public officials, candidates, and social activists came to stimulate our thoughts, increase our knowledge, and motivate us to take action for ourselves. We put our energies into the campaigns of Nichols for the Berkeley City Council and School Board.

The phenomenon of Downs, a black church and its people, is not unique to Oakland, California. There are other instances all over the country where young people, under the guidance of loving elders, can sharpen their skills in program planning and public speaking in an environment of spiritual growth and concern for the quality of life in their community. In churches like Downs, they are exposed to conditions that are conducive to the development of their full potential by associating with people who are socially and financially successful: doctors, dentists, teachers, lawyers, mail carriers, railway mail clerks, and Pullman porters.

Politically, the Downs people were allied with issues that addressed the needs of black people; they supported candidates and elected officials whose philosophies and actions were aimed toward these ends. They gloried in the unexpected success of Harold Washington's candidacy for mayor of Chicago. On the national scene, the Downs people were unanimously proud of Jesse Jackson's emergence in the race for the presidency. To one man, Jackson's self-confidence to run amounted to a total victory, regardless of the ultimate vote count, because his participation injected serious issues into the race that would have otherwise been ignored by the other candidates. A woman chose not to hang her master's degree in her office because it had been signed by Ronald Reagan as governor of California and a member of the board of regents of the state's university system.

One Sunday in mid-July 1988 I spent the morning worship hours at Downs, and I compared the music of that day with the offerings on a typical Sunday in the fifties and sixties. In the previous years the Chancel Choir, the only choir at Downs, wore unadorned black robes, like those seen at college graduations. At the appropriate times the Chancel Choir sang an anthem, a hymn, and usually a Negro spiritual, all under the direction of Birel Vaughn.

That Sunday in 1988 there were two choirs that took part in the service. The Chancel Choir, wearing maroon robes topped by broad white collars with embroidered bright red decorations, led the procession. They entered alongside of singers of the Gospel Choir, who wore black robes with wide white collars. There were four musical selections during the service, two sung by each choir. The Chancel Choir's selections were a song from a Johann Sebastian Bach cantata, and a contemporary gospel song by a member of the Hawkins family. First the Gospel Choir performed "Lord, Help Me to Hold Out," a standard gospel song. Its second number was another gospel song, "It's Real," a solo sung by a member of the Gospel Choir. I saw the effects of the passage of years that had brought the universal acceptance of different types of music in religious settings, including Downs. Our church had caught up with the musical evolution. It was a lovely blending of the classical and the modern, with equal appreciation for each.

With the pleasure of the music that Sunday, the pieces of the puzzle began to fit together, and I understood the difference between now and a Sunday in the earlier decades. At that time, we had not accepted the benefits of the civil rights and the black power movements with the freedom to release the self-imposed restrictions that prohibited us from giving gospel music its rightful place in our churches. In 1950 we thought it was our duty as better-educated, upwardly mobile black people to maintain a dignity that did not permit us to enjoy the more expressive, more "down home" music in our hallowed places. We loved to hear selections from the oratorios of Handel and Bach and the old hymns and spirituals that our parents sang on Sunday mornings, but we did not want to include gospel rhythms in the order of service for the Sabbath.

Thirty years later I realized that we were no longer restricted to that narrow concept of what was appropriate for us in the pews at Downs. Thanks to our increased confidence as an ethnic group, we are now able to accept this part of black culture and have given ourselves the license to publicly embrace the kind of music that we formerly kept in the closet. We have rewarded ourselves with the flexibility of choosing from a much wider range of orientations, from Beethoven and Bach, the stately Methodist or Baptist hymns, and the more contemporary gospel songs. Our lives are richer for the change. Seventeen of the Downs people were there that Sunday. They seemed as comfortable as I was with the music of that day.

A major attraction of Downs Memorial United Methodist Church for me was its dedication to the integrity of the family unit. We worked in husband-and-wife teams and shared the responsibility of such offices as superintendent of the Sunday school, sponsor of the youth groups, and chair of commissions and committees. We had an active couples' club and put on annual sweetheart banquets, weekly family potluck dinners, and regular family picnics. The young people had activities that catered to their interests, as did the adults, but I thought of Downs primarily as a place where the family came together for worship, for social times, and for community-related projects.

I remember the Downs people in a family situation, so it came as a surprise to learn that the incidence of divorce among the forty was consistent with the national average of approximately 50 percent. The fact is that sixteen, 40 percent, are no longer with their original spouses, one marriage having been dissolved after thirty-two years. I was even more surprised to find instances of the Downs people having terminated more than one marriage. It is not yet clear how the Second Generation will compare, but so far they too have been part of the national trend toward divorce. It appears that young people who are exposed to a consistent religious environment and whose parents have long-lasting marriages are not automatically guaranteed the same for themselves. Church and parental background alone do not seem to be sufficient; there must be freedom from the stresses of other areas of life to maintain a whole family structure.

In my ideal situation, all of the Second Generation would be as devoted to a church as their parents were. Those who have any involvement participate to varying degrees, but as a group they have not been nearly as active as their parents were thirty years ago. In reality the children of ten of the Downs people have no church affiliation; however, one young man is a theologian, a professor in the School of Religion at Howard University, and another has expressed an intention to enter the ministry.

Despite the support of family, church, and friends, there have been incidents of drug abuse among the young people who are related to the Downs people. I am aware of the viciousness of the drug and alcohol scene in the United States and have seen the related criminal atrocities in the Bay Area, and it all seems to indicate that there is no easy, quick solution. This is painful to me, and I am distressed that it has affected the Downs people. One case involves a college student of the Second Generation. He had gotten his associate of arts degree but soon allowed a promising career to be impeded by drug experimentation. Happily, he is now on the way to rehabilitation, employed, and saving money for expenses when he returns to college. There is another instance of a young man of the Second Generation who was exposed to the counterculture's permissive use of drugs when he was in college during the seventies and was unable to resist the trend. This was the beginning of trying times when his parents, siblings, minister, and loving friends gave support that had little effect. The curative benefits of rehabilitation agencies, although of a more lasting duration, did not result in permanent relief. However, this son has the commitment to continue his work as a public servant where he puts monetary gain in a place of secondary importance. There is not yet a successful end to his trials, but he is continuing to work toward complete rehabilitation so that his gifts of love for humanity will not be wasted. The support of his family has not wavered.

One of the insidious aspects of the drug culture is the temptation to acquire immediate rewards without the usual physical labor or personal sacrifice. The financial gains from drug sales are greater than the salaries of workers in a forty-hour work week under less than desirable conditions. A son of one of the Second Generation, who can be spoken of as belonging to the Third Generation, has fallen prey to the enticement of easy money. His parents were divorced before he was school age, and his life from that point on took a different turn. The boy and his brother lived with their father, an excellent parent, but still he was lured to make money by selling drugs to his schoolmates. During this time he was apprehended by the authorities, but because of his father's intercession and demonstrated determination to support his son, the youngster was not incarcerated. This Third Generation son missed the love of his mother, and the real tragedy of his young life is that she was a drug abuser. He had tried, unsuccessfully, to help her to kick the habit, but she died of an overdose in his presence when he was fifteen. The young man did not finish high school; instead he chose to leave his father's home when he was seventeen and is now making huge sums of money from drug sales and living the opulent yet fragile life of people in that trade. The parents and grandparents have not lost the confidence that their son, who once responded to their love when he was a very small boy, will return to the family and fulfill the promise that he showed then.

Although the reality of the personal lives of the Downs people and the Second Generation is not the complete paragon that existed in my mind, they continue to prove to be a unique group of African-Americans who encourage their children with their love and support and often professional assistance throughout these painful experiences of substance abuse. And their concern reaches far beyond their immediate family into political and social arenas that are committed to eliminating the problems that beset the black community, such as the rise in the numbers of youth-at-risk students and school dropouts, drug and alcohol abuse, and the high infant mortality rate.

In the face of frustrations and disappointments, the Downs people have not lost their sense of hope. They are sustained by the accomplishments of their own concerted efforts, and by their shared belief in the coming of better times—professionally, politically, and socially. This attitude is typified by Vertis Thompson's statement of conviction that improvement is bound to come: " 'By and By When the Morning Comes' is not always just when I get to heaven."

Very often I reminisce about Downs and its motivational role in the development of its young people. I remember Ruth Love when she came to Downs at the beginning of her first classroom teaching assignment in a small elementary school in west Oakland. I recall Warren Widener, a young serviceman not long out of college, who had yet to announce his interest in being a Berkeley city councilman, mayor of Berkeley, or a supervisor of Alameda County. My thoughts continue to pre-teenage Gordon Baranco, hurrying into the sanctuary with his parents and sister and brother so that they would not miss the beginning of the worship service. I did not foresee that he would ultimately sit on the superior court of California. Nor did I know that Wesley Jones, whom I first met when he was a newly registered undergraduate at San Francisco State University, would be the first black director of a social service department of a California county.

Twenty-three of the Downs people are still part of the church. Of the seventeen who did not stay at Downs, twelve are affiliated with other churches or other denominations. Five of the seventeen do not attend any church on a regular basis. Within this latter group there is one who described herself as an atheist, having wrestled with philosophical and religious questions that she has not been able to resolve. The seventeen do not harbor any ill will toward Downs. No one in the group of forty Downs people expressed an overall disapproval of the experience of being at Downs during the Nichols years—of its pastor, the fellow members, or the church as a whole. Their feelings about Downs are very much like mine: they cherish the memories of that era and periodically return to enjoy the aura of that earlier time.

The saga of Downs Memorial United Methodist Church and the role of its people in the development of the community did not end in 1964 when Nichols left. The Reverend Amos Cambric, who succeeded Nichols, stayed until 1967 when he decided to use his talents primarily in special assignments within the War on Poverty, and at the same time took on interim appointments at various Methodist churches in the East Bay. The next minister, Rev. Charles Belcher, brought youthful enthusiasm to Downs, his first official commission after graduation from seminary. Having remained at Downs from 1967 to 1971, Belcher left active religious involvement to enter another phase of public service; he became administrative assistant to California Assemblyman John Miller. Subsequently, he reentered the ministry in southern California.

In 1971, the Reverend Charles H. Lee, Sr., answered the call to Downs from San Francisco public schools where he was a community coordinator. After sixteen years at Downs, Lee became district superintendent in the Golden Gate District of the California-Nevada Conference of the United Methodist Church. His place was taken in 1987 by the Reverend Douglass E. Fitch, who had experience in church administration, in academia, and at the pastoral level. He had been assistant to the bishop of southern California, administrator of the $8 million endowment of the General Board of Higher Education and Ministry of the United Methodist Church, and had taught at Boston University and Duke University. But with the experience of fourteen years as a pastor in Georgia still on his mind, he was eager to return to duty in a local church. Fitch has the commitment to work for the betterment of life for the people of the East Bay and the willingness to lead present-day Downs in activities toward that goal.

The Downs people share my conviction that our lives have been enhanced by our participation at Downs church, and that our value to society has been increased by the blending of the Downs teaching and training with that of our parents and dedicated school personnel. To complete the cycle, Nichols, now retired Bishop Nichols, has returned to the East Bay and has allied himself with the Downs of today; this time as a worshipper, and when needed, as an assistant to Fitch. He cherishes the memories of the fifties and sixties while he enjoys the warmth and the spiritual nourishment of Downs in the final decade of the century.

Epilogue
OCTOBER 1991

The notes that I mailed to the Downs people were invitations to come and bring their spouses to a Reunion at their church to renew friendships and share recent experiences with those who have been away from Downs for a while—in some cases more than two decades. This Reunion would be a time to recall the years when we were all there together and to talk with men and women whom we knew as teenagers in the Methodist Youth Fellowship and see how they matured as adults who were pursuing careers that are representative of the Downs people as a group. We could have lunch, and those who were returning after an extended absence could get to know present-day Downs and its minister, the Reverend Douglass Fitch. In addition, the setting was perfect to take pictures of the Downs people in situations similar to the fifties and sixties.

Some of the most poignant moments of the day came early, just after the first arrivals had entered the building. As soon as Wesley Jones (whom we remember as youth director) and Herman Bosset (a spirited, almost rambunctious adolescent member of the youth group under Jones's leadership) recognized each other, they warmly clasped hands and began to laugh. For what seemed to be at least sixty seconds they held hands tightly and continued laughing without speaking any words. Everyone who saw this exchange recognized it as an eloquent, emotionally charged dialogue. A stream of memories that did not depend upon vocalization for appreciation were returning to both and, at the same time, were stirring similar recollections for the on-lookers. This exchanged proved to be a preview of the mood of the hours that the Downs people spent together: it was an afternoon of happiness in the opportunity to greet one another and to reminiscence about times past, both in our personal lives and our participation at Downs.

The Downs connection was very much in evidence in the technical aspect of the Reunion. The extensive sound system that Downs now uses, which was available to us that day, was a gift from Phebia Richardson and her family in memory of her youngest son, Phillip, who had died in 1989. Taking the pictures was Jonathan Eubanks, a professional photographer, and also a former Downs member.

During the mid-1900s, thirty-three of the forty Downs people were adults and had careers and families of their own well on the way. Now, many of that number have retired or are nearing that stage. Those who have left full-time employment do not lead inactive lives, as can be seen by their full schedule of activities. In the Nichols era, seven of the Downs people were in high school, or just entering college. In 1991 they are all past forty, engaged in fulfilling public service jobs.

Two of the Downs people are no longer living. Hazel Kyle died in April 1989, and Etta Hill passed away in July 1991. Kyle's husband, daughter, and son-in-law came to the Reunion, as did a daughter and granddaughter of Hill. Four people came from long distances: Dorothy Pitts flew in from Memphis, Tennessee; James Howard traveled more than five hundred miles from Julian, in Southern California, near San Diego; and Wesley Jones and Thelma Scott-Skillman drove the nearly one hundred miles to Oakland from Sacramento.

Prior to the luncheon and the picture-taking, we gathered in the church sanctuary for a program that opened with a statement by the Reverend Mr. Fitch. From the viewpoint of a minister he saw the Reunion—the coming together of the Downs people bringing love for each other and for their church, and the evidence of their impact in the community—as an indication that Downs has produced a group of people who consider the teachings of the church to be a serious part of their lives beyond hearing sermons in the Sunday morning services. For inspiration and musical pleasure we heard two of our favorite songs sung by Zephyr Ward: "I Love to Tell the Story" and "One Day at a Time." Any of the Downs people who wished to do so were encouraged to express their reactions to the Reunion.

Nichols came to the podium first and recalled his arrival in the Bay Area to enter seminary and his eventual appointment as the pastor of Downs. Along with fond tributes to individual people and specific events at Downs, he spoke of the happy circumstance of his beginning as pastor there in 1949, and returning forty-two years later to worship at the same site with beloved friends; this time instead of being the giver, he is ministered to by Fitch.

Herman Bosset was the next person to address the congregation. He recalled that he was a "pretty wild" young boy whose future may have taken a much different turn had it not been for the influence of B. L. Vaughn, who knew exactly how and when to apply the right degree of discipline that was tempered by an appropriate mixture of love and care. Wesley Jones added the necessary motivation to keep him involved in the youth program. As a probation officer, Bosset is in constant contact with disturbed young people whose futures appear to be in jeopardy. He believes that an environment of love and support such as he had from Vaughn, Jones, and the total Downs experience would eliminate the problems of many of the boys who are under his supervision.

In her remarks, Ruby Osborne began by speaking of having been a young bride living in the college dormitory at Hampton Institute when her husband, Julius, returned to duty overseas during World War II. Her subsequent move to Berkeley introduced her to Nichols and began her involvement with Downs, whose members she referred to as her "family." She recalled that she and Julius were the first youth counselors at Downs. Now that Julius has a life-threatening illness, she depends upon her "family" for support during this stressful period in the same way she has relied upon them in the past.

With a display of the oratorical ability that the Downs people associate with him, Laurence Bolling quoted a passage from Kahlil Gibran's *The Prophet* to emphasize the importance of the roles of parents, pastor, youth leaders, and the church as a whole in the development of young people. The success of the younger members of the Downs people and others of that generation who have had the benefits of church, school, and family motivation confirm his belief. Bolling spoke of the employment opportunities in the newly constructed office buildings in Oakland's Civic Center, and the need for African-American students to prepare for those jobs. He was happy to say that at Castlemont High School in East Oakland, the black students have demonstrated an increased seriousness in study and have begun to match the Asians at that school in scholastic achievement. To build upon this developing response, he called upon the black church to double its determination to reach young people and guide them to prepare for the changing economic conditions.

Gordon Baranco came to the microphone to "co-sign and amen" the things that Bolling had said and to add his call to the church to extend its program to include all people rather than exclude a portion of its neighborhoods. He is convinced that we must prepare people to deal with the present by a show of unconditional love to everyone—our children, our friends, and to our enemies. Baranco gave thanks to Wesley Jones and other people at Downs for the motivation they gave him in his formative years.

When Wesley Jones spoke he made it clear that the memory is still very keen of himself as a young man, a freshman in college, sitting on the ground in the sun outside of the original building that housed the church, talking with Nichols. Those conversations helped to direct his career to the area of public service and led to a desire to share with others in similar situations the motivation that his mentors have given to him. Jones agreed with the preceding speakers, Bosset, Bolling, and Baranco, that there are thousands of young people whose lives are not touched by a church program, and that organized religion must rededicate its charge to reach that segment of our youth.

The next speaker, Thelma Scott-Skillman, drew the analogy

between standing at the podium at that instant to the incident of giving her first speech from the same location when she was fourteen. Having been forced by the counselors of her Methodist Youth Fellowship group, Mary and Warren Widener, to accept the assignment, she had talked about her aspirations for the future. Relying on a combination of support from the Wideners and the training from her mother and grandmother, she had assured her audience that the incident of her racial identity should not determine her desire to achieve or limit her success. In the position as vice-chancellor for the State of California Community College System, she is saddened to see that the educational opportunities are not reaching large numbers of black students; too many under the age of twenty-four are in prison, on probation, or on drugs. She is committed to gathering and guiding as many as she can.

Cleophas Williams, the speaker who followed, told of having come to Downs after being long disassociated from religious involvement. At Downs he was motivated to take part in the affairs of his union after sitting quietly in the background for fifteen years, and to participate in the political and social action programs of the church. Williams and Dorothy Pitts were the leaders in Downs's NAACP membership drives, which set records in the East Bay.

The last of the Downs people to share reminiscences was Dorothy Pitts, who had just suffered the loss of her husband, Walter, whom we all knew and loved, in the previous month. She welcomed the chance to come to the Reunion because it would be comforting to return to the place where she had first met Walter and enjoy the presence of the friends whose support she had received from Downs. Pitts has worked in the East Bay Area in a variety of situations, serving youth groups as well as senior citizens. She endorsed Scott-Skillman's intention to reach out, especially to the youth, to include those who do not usually receive the benefits that are available to the total citizenship.

Since Eugene Tarrant was unable to be part of the official Reunion, he and I agreed to re-create a smaller one of our own. We met in the sanctuary, and I told him about the people who came, the outpouring of good memories, and the camaraderie. Tarrant had just returned from a four-day sail into the Pacific Ocean aboard the *Wichita,* a navy vessel, as a guest of the United States Navy. In World War II when he was an enlisted man in that arm of the military, he had no choice in his assignment as a messman; the placement had been made purely on the basis of race. But now, with new policies and attitudes, his position was completely different.

Tarrant recounted the events of the tour: being escorted with full honors, sitting at the captain's table, sleeping in officers' quarters, participating in the awarding of citations to enlisted men who had given outstanding service, and being served by messmen (no longer restricted to black sailors) in the way he had catered to the desires of his superiors. He was overwhelmed by a feeling of vindication for himself and others who had been denied the dignity of having a say in their appointments, and who carried the stigma of being limited to menial positions. Tarrant recalled the unsuccessful protests that he and his shipmates initiated and the resulting disciplinary actions. Experiencing the acceptance and recognition aboard ship during this four-day tour was an unexpected and welcome opportunity for him to take pleasure in the positive changes that had come about since World War II.

The Reunion of the Downs people was a time of fun and joy, singing and speaking, eating and visiting, and catching up with the latest news of family, career, social, and political interests. By way of their talks from the podium and the personal chats I had with the Downs people, I saw that my original impression of them as a group who had certain goals and aspirations in common was still valid. There had been no decrease in their commitment to make a difference in their worlds, and here was proof that they had maintained affection and loving memories of midcentury at Downs Memorial United Methodist Church. They congratulated each other and reflected upon their ambitions and accomplishments. It was a family affair—a great celebration.

The Downs people, with friends, in the pews of the church.

Downs people who addressed the assemblage.

Gordon Baranco

Epilogue

Laurence Bolling

The Unsung Heart of Black America

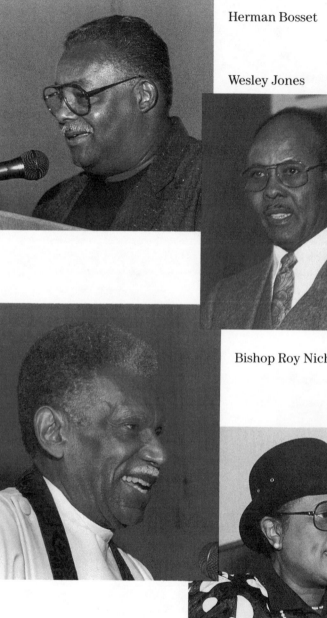

Herman Bosset

Wesley Jones

Bishop Roy Nichols

Ruby Osborne

Epilogue

Dorothy Pitts

Thelma Scott-Skillman

Cleophas Williams

Zephyr Ward singing for the
enjoyment of her fellow
Downs people.

Bishop Roy Nichols and the Reverend Milton Combs, Sr., assistant minister to Nichols at Downs.

Frank Irvin, host of the Reunion, welcoming the ministers: Roy Nichols, Milton Combs, Sr., and the present pastor of Downs, Douglass E. Fitch.

Left to right: Dorothy Pitts, Gertrude Hines, and Phebia Richardson.

Left to right: Ella Wiley, Nora Vaughn, and Zephyr Ward.

Left to right: Charles Aikens, Dorene Walton, Walter Morris, and Warren Widener.

Left to right: Cleophas Williams, Charles Furlow, Jack Costa, and Calvin Jackson.

Left to right: Curtis Bowers, Dorothy Lee, Ramona Maples, Ruth Love, Ike Buchanan, Ruby Osborne, and Vera Pitts.

Left to right: Wilma Johnson, Pete W. Taylor, Jr., and Elizabeth Pettus.

Left to right: Phillip Raymond, Katherine Drake, and Vertis Thompson.

The Downs people who were members of the Methodist Youth Fellowship three decades ago recall that time. *Left to right:* Gordon Baranco, Wesley Jones (former youth director), James Howard, Mary Ellen Rose Butler, Herman Bosset, and Thelma Scott-Skillman.

Epilogue

Dona Irvin and Eugene Tarrant.

The Unsung Heart of Black America

Etta Hill died in July 1991.

Hazel Kyle died in April 1989.

Nell Irvin Painter-Shafer.

Not present at the Reunion.

Appendix

PASTORS OF DOWNS MEMORIAL UNITED METHODIST CHURCH

John N. Doggett, Jr.   *1948 to 1949*

David Thomas and H. T. S. Johnson   *1949*

Roy C. Nichols   *1949 to 1964*

Amos Cambric   *1964 to 1967*

Charles Belcher   *1967 to 1971*

Charles H. Lee, Sr.   *1971 to 1987*

Douglass E. Fitch, Sr.   *1987–*